CAPITAL
AND RATES OF RETURN
IN MANUFACTURING INDUSTRIES

NATIONAL BUREAU OF ECONOMIC RESEARCH

NUMBER 78, GENERAL SERIES

Capital and Rates of Return in Manufacturing Industries

GEORGE J. STIGLER
UNIVERSITY OF CHICAGO

A STUDY BY THE
NATIONAL BUREAU OF ECONOMIC RESEARCH, NEW YORK

PUBLISHED BY
PRINCETON UNIVERSITY PRESS
PRINCETON, NEW JERSEY
1963

L.C. Card No. 62-21109

Printed in the United States of America

NATIONAL BUREAU OF ECONOMIC RESEARCH

1963

RELATION OF THE DIRECTORS TO THE WORK AND PUBLICATIONS OF THE NATIONAL BUREAU OF ECONOMIC RESEARCH

1. The object of the National Bureau of Economic Research is to ascertain and to present to the public important economic facts and their interpretation in a scientific and impartial manner. The Board of Directors is charged with the responsibility of ensuring that the work of the National Bureau is carried on in strict conformity with this object.

2. To this end the Board of Directors shall appoint one or more Directors of Research.

3. The Director or Directors of Research shall submit to the members of the Board, or to its Executive Committee, for their formal adoption, all specific proposals concerning researches to be instituted.

4. No report shall be published until the Director or Directors of Research shall have submitted to the Board a summary drawing attention to the character of the data and their utilization in the report, the nature and treatment of the problems involved, the main conclusions, and such other information as in their opinion would serve to determine the suitability of the report for publication in accordance with the principles of the National Bureau.

5. A copy of any manuscript proposed for publication shall also be submitted to each member of the Board. For each manuscript to be so submitted a special committee shall be appointed by the President, or at his designation by the Executive Director, consisting of three Directors selected as nearly as may be one from each general division of the Board. The names of the special manuscript committee shall be stated to each Director when the summary and report described in paragraph (4) are sent to him. It shall be the duty of each member of the committee to read the manuscript. If each member of the special committee signifies his approval within thirty days, the manuscript may be published. If each member of the special committee has not signified his approval within thirty days of the transmittal of the report and manuscript, the Director of Research shall then notify each member of the Board, requesting approval or disapproval of publication, and thirty additional days shall be granted for this purpose. The manuscript shall then not be published unless at least a majority of the entire Board and a two-thirds majority of those members of the Board who shall have voted on the proposal within the time fixed for the receipt of votes on the publication proposed shall have approved.

6. No manuscript may be published, though approved by each member of the special committee, until forty-five days have elapsed from the transmittal of the summary and report. The interval is allowed for the receipt of any memorandum of dissent or reservation, together with a brief statement of his reasons, that any member may wish to express; and such memorandum of dissent or reservation shall be published with the manuscript if he so desires. Publication does not, however, imply that each member of the Board has read the manuscript, or that either members of the Board in general, or of the special committee, have passed upon its validity in every detail.

7. A copy of this resolution shall, unless otherwise determined by the Board, be printed in each copy of every National Bureau book.

(*Resolution adopted October 25, 1926,*
as revised February 6, 1933, and February 24, 1941)

Contents

TABLES

CHARTS

Preface

CONSIDERING how often our economic system is described as "capitalistic" or "the profit system," it is paradoxical that we have had relatively little information on the stock of capital or the rate of profits it yields in various industries. Ralph C. Epstein's book of nearly thirty years ago, *Industrial Profits in the United States* (New York, National Bureau of Economic Research, 1934), was for long the only tolerably comprehensive source, and even now the Federal Trade Commission–Securities and Exchange Commission quarterly reports have important limitations.

I am confident, therefore, that economists will welcome the comprehensive and fairly detailed data on capital and rates of return in all manufacturing industries here presented. Their debt (and mine) is primarily to my two associates who conducted this laborious and difficult work. Mary O. Conlon and Claire Friedland have successively undertaken this responsibility and discharged it with skill and conscientiousness. At various times Nestor Terleckyj, Murray Brown, Arthur D'Antonio, George Fricdman, Ann Novick, and Robert V. Goldstein also assisted in this work.

The analytical essays which comprise the larger part of the text apply the data, with varying success, to three traditional problems of economics: the tendency of rates of return to equality, determinants of the rate of investment, and relationships between capital and labor. My debt to Miss Friedland is equally heavy in this work.

Various readers of the manuscript have offered helpful suggestions, and particular acknowledgement is due to Gary S. Becker, Ralph L. Nelson, and Victor Fuchs. I am also indebted to the Directors who reviewed the manuscript, Melvin G. de Chazeau, Murray Shields, and Boris Shishkin.

Thanks are due also to Margaret T. Edgar for a careful and thoughtful editing of the manuscript, and to H. Irving Forman for an excellent job of drawing the charts.

GEORGE J. STIGLER

CAPITAL
AND RATES OF RETURN
IN MANUFACTURING INDUSTRIES

CHAPTER 1

Introduction

Economists of the classical period divided the factors of production into land, labor, and capital. By the end of World War I, land had lost its autonomy, partly because the progress of economic analysis had enveloped it in a broader conception of capital, but probably even more because land had lost its quantitative importance in the developing industrial economy. We were left with labor and capital.

It would be difficult for the most uninformed person to say that the study of either labor or capital has been neglected by economists, however much one might quarrel with the directions of study. But it is possible, and correct, to say that the empirical analysis of capital has begun only recently, and is today far less well developed than that of labor. The difference in treatment does not represent a policy of neglect of capital, but simply the fact that until recently comprehensive information on the quantity of capital possessed by American industries was lacking and indeed, outside the areas predominantly corporate in organization, is still lacking.

We have sought in this study to construct a basic set of data, comprehensive over the universe of manufacturing and comparable over a period of almost two decades. Our capital concept is almost all-inclusive: it equals total assets, excluding investments in other companies; and our rate of return concept correspondingly includes returns to both lenders and equity holders. Our concepts and procedures, and the very serious limitations of the underlying data, are described briefly in section 2 of this chapter, and in detail in Appendix A. Selective summaries of the structure and trend of investment and rates of return are given in Chapter 2.

1. *The Problem*

In the period of our study there was an almost unbroken growth of capital in manufacturing, from $48.8 billion in 1938 to $203.3 billion in 1956, or by 8.2 per cent a year. Even in 1947 dollars the growth was from $94.2 billion to $175.9 billion, or by 3.5 per cent a year. The varying pace of that growth is examined in Chapter 2, where the wide impact of World War II and the subsequent demobilization and the investment boom of the 1950's are observed.

No industry is wholly sheltered from the impact of a major war or even a moderate depression, but these fortunately infrequent events are almost the least of the forces for change with which an industry has to cope. The market for its goods is in constant flux—growing with consumer incomes, gaining or losing from its shifting competition with foreign producers or with new kinds of goods designed to satisfy the same consumer desires. Its organization of production must continually adapt to changes in prices of inputs, the westward migration of population, the discovery of new resources or production techniques.

All these impacts and the adjustments made to them are portrayed in two basic data of each industry: its capital stock, and the rate of return on this capital. In a world of perfect anticipation of the future, there would be hardly any dispersion of industry rates of return (with qualifications that need not be noted here), for every opportunity for gain would be seized and every threat of loss evaded. The entire impact of the changes would be registered in the shifting rates of investment of the various industries.

And in the opposite world, where no change would ever be expected, the first impact of every change would be on rates of return: every surge of demand would find the industry unprepared, and its prices and profit rates would rise; every cessation of demand would find the industry overexpanded and its output selling at distress prices. Even in this case there would be large differences among industries in rates of investment, but they would lag behind the signals provided by the rates of return.

The facts suggest, on the whole, that the former assumption contains the larger fraction of truth. The industry rates of return are indeed far from identical—in a typical year (say 1955) a range of from −2 to +14 per cent is observed. But there is a strong central tendency in these rates: in that same year, half the industries earned between 4.8 and 8.8 per cent on capital. The rates of investment, on the other hand, were immensely more varied: from 1954 to 1955 the stock of capital fell 13 per cent in one industry, and rose 28 per cent in another. In that period one-fourth of the industries increased their capital by more than 15 per cent, another quarter had decreases or increases of less than 4.7 per cent.

These differences in rates of investment are of course the fundamental mechanism by which the capital of the economy is moved from where it is less needed to where it is more needed. There is some movement of specific capital resources: even in a prosperous postwar year an average of 10 out of 98 industries had actual decreases of capital, and in the postwar depression years fully half the industries suffered declines. But the main method of adapting the growing stock of capital to the changing distribution of needs has been by differential growth. Table 1 gives the average annual rates of growth of capital over the last nine years of our period, and these persistent differences are very large. Industries that grew at one standard deviation less than the average rate fell in a decade to half their initial size relative to industries that grew at a rate one standard deviation above the mean.

TABLE 1

AVERAGE ANNUAL PERCENTAGE CHANGE IN CAPITAL IN MANUFACTURING INDUSTRIES, 1947–56

Average Annual Percentage Change	Number of Industries
−3 to −1	2
−1 to +1	7
1 to 3	11
3 to 5	20
5 to 7	14
7 to 9	20
9 to 11	17
11 to 13	4
13 to 15	3
Total	98
Mean	6.14 %
Standard Deviation	3.67 %

SOURCE: Tables A-36 to A-59.

The belief that a large part of the ever-shifting pattern of industry demands for capital is anticipated with tolerable accuracy is not proved by this simple comparison of dispersion of rates of return and rates of investment.[1] There are two other lines of investigation, elaborated in Chapters 3 and 4, which give more cogent evidence.

On the one hand, the rates of return have no persistent tendency to remain in a fixed industrial pattern. It is true that, if we know the rates of return in a given year, we can predict the hierarchy of rates of return with considerable confidence the next year; the coefficients of correlation of successive annual rates of return are usually .7 to .9. But within a period of about six years the correlation has vanished: knowing which industries are prosperous or unprosperous in year T is of no assistance in predicting what they will be (say) seven years later. The positive correlation coefficients suggest that anticipations are not perfect; their decline

[1] If we visualize the supply curve of capital to each industry as being horizontal at a rate of return appropriate to the industry's risk, accounting practices, etc., the correct comparison is indeed between relative changes in capital (rates of investment) and relative *changes* in rates of return, not their absolute level. As we shall notice shortly, the short-run changes in relative rates of return are very small.

over time suggests that over a period of years the differences among industries in the (marginal) demand for capital are eliminated. This finding, it may be added, is of course wholly in keeping with the classical economic theorem that under competition the rates of return tend to equality. (This theorem receives reinforcement, indirectly, from the fact that in industries where a few large firms are dominant the correlations of rates of return between distant years remain fairly high.)

On the other hand, direct study of investment rates reveals a close, consistent relationship between these rates and the contemporaneous shifts of demand (measured by receipts). In the postwar period, the correlation coefficient between changes in receipts and investment rates averages about .7, even on an annual basis. Profit rates in the preceding year are also usually significantly related to investment rates. And when the period is lengthened to a decade, almost all the differences among industries in rates of investment are accounted for by the combination of changing receipts (sales) and profit rates.

We have no historical criteria by which to judge the efficiency with which investment responds to the shifting demands of our manufacturing industries. If we accept—or better, define—the dispersion of industry rates of return as the measure of the disequilibrium in any year, we can at least make several comparative statements. Dispersion is relatively greater in years of depression: industries cannot adapt to sudden decreases in demand as well as they can to expansions—in part, perhaps, because fixed capital is easier to increase than to decrease in the short run.[2] Dispersion is larger (as well as more stable) in concentrated industries: whether because of monopoly power (of which we find no reflection in average rates of return) or because of lesser flexibility of response to changing conditions, the industries dominated by relatively few firms are somewhat less efficient in adjusting their capital stocks.

The relationship between capital and labor, and between their rates of remuneration, are in the center of scientific and public policy interests. We find that in 1954 labor received approximately four-fifths of the income of manufacturing industries, and capital the remainder. The share of income going to capital decreased substantially in most industry categories between 1939 and 1954. The share of wages in the total income varies among industries chiefly with the greater variation in capital per laborer (which ranged from $3,200, for the least capital-

[2] It may be noted, however, that a test of Marshall's theory that the rate at which an industry approaches long-run equilibrium depends upon the amount of its fixed plant yielded no confirmation.

intensive tenth to $27,800 for the most capital-intensive tenth of industries in 1954).

Various procedures have been contrived by economists to measure the extent to which entrepreneurs can substitute capital for labor when the cost of labor rises relative to that of capital. One procedure compares trends in the relative use of capital and labor with trends in their costs, although independent changes in technology seriously becloud these findings. Our industry data, which are of course subject to this same ambiguity, show that industries experiencing relatively large wage increases increase capital per worker by larger amounts. Another type of comparison—that of small and large firms in the same industry—seems more appropriate to measure long-run substitution possibilities, because the differences in wage rates (and perhaps also the cost of capital, which we could not measure) among small and large firms are persistent. Our exploration of this approach leads to the tentative conclusion that capital per worker is highly responsive to wage rates.

This sketch of the problem of allocating capital among industries may serve to orient the reader to the analyses which follow. He will find elaborations and extensions of many points, but mostly he will also find large gaps in our discussion. Some are due to a lack of data, although on the whole the scientific investigator is hampered much more by lack of imagination than by lack of data. But the limitations of the data will be common to all economists, and they are sufficiently important to merit a brief discussion here.

2. *The Data*

A lengthy description of the method by which the basic data were constructed is given in Appendix A, but most readers will find this material unenticing. Yet no one should read our interpretations of the capital and rates of return material, let alone make independent use of it, without some appreciation of the very substantial limitations to which the data are subject. These limitations are of at least four sorts.

COMPREHENSIVENESS OF THE DATA

The basic data upon which everything else is erected are the compilations of corporation income-tax reports of the Internal Revenue Service. Aside from presumably minor problems of nonreporting and postaudit revisions, this material is comprehensive in scope, if not always in detail.

The tax reports, however, do not include the noncorporate enterprises, which in some industries are relatively large—so large in one case (furs) that nearly half the industry's output is noncorporate. This deficiency should not be exaggerated: in more than half the industries the noncorporate share of value of output is less than 4 per cent, and in four-fifths it is less than 12 per cent.

The estimate of the noncorporate sector is based upon the ratio of capital to receipts in small corporations (which resemble noncorporate enterprises more closely than they resemble all corporations). The main bench marks are provided by the *1939*, *1947*, and *1954 Census of Manuactures*, but the interpolation of intercensal years is modified by partnership and single proprietorship tax returns.

The rates of return are based upon corporate returns; no estimate for the noncorporate sector seemed feasible.

THE INDUSTRIAL CLASSIFICATION

The basic IRS data are classified into so-called three-digit industries. These classes were considerably revised in 1948, and a fair amount of estimation is required to construct 1947 figures on the 1948 industry classification.

The more important problem, however, is that, broad as the three-digit industries are, many companies operate in several such industries. In the first census of companies, in 1954, it was found that almost one-fourth of the establishments in manufacturing belonged to companies operating in two or more three-digit industries. Since a company is necessarily allocated to one industry, our data have an intrinsic element of heterogeneity.

Some quantitative notion of the fuzziness of industry boundaries at the three-digit level is given by Table 2. Ownership specialization is the term

TABLE 2

DISTRIBUTION OF INDUSTRIES, BY OWNERSHIP SPECIALIZATION AND INDUSTRY SPECIALIZATION OF COMPANIES IN MANUFACTURING, MEASURED BY PAYROLL, 1954

Industry Specialization (per cent)	*Ownership Specialization* (per cent)					
	90–100	80–90	70–80	60–70	50–60	40–50
90–100	20	12	1			
80–90	8	7	11	1	2	
70–80	3	2	2		2	1
60–70	1	2	1	1	1	1
50–60		1				

SOURCE: *Company Statistics, 1954 Censuses of Business, Manufactures, and Mineral Industries*, Bull. CS-1, Washington, 1958, Table 2.

used to describe the percentage of payroll expenditures of an industry made by companies classified in that industry. For example, 91.1 per cent of the payroll of plants making soap was paid by companies classified in the soap industry. Industry specialization refers to the percentage of payroll of companies classified in an industry that was paid by plants operating in that industry: in the example of the soap industry, 80.6 per cent of the payroll of soap companies was paid in plants making soap.[3] The mean ownership specialization ratio was 83.6 per cent, and the mean industry specialization ratio was 85.8 per cent. These ratios imply appreciable margins of fuzziness in the industry boundaries. What is even more troublesome, the companies often shift among industries, and an erratic element is introduced into the annual changes in assets. Our endeavors to cope with this problem at best eliminate the most extreme fluctuations.

ACCOUNTING CONCEPTS

The concepts permissible in income tax accounting are not always appropriate to the measurement of income. Accelerated depreciation, especially during World War II, sometimes represented the realistic recognition that a capital good had only wartime usefulness, but sometimes it ignored large postwar usefulness. Ordinary depreciation, especially before the statutory liberalization of 1954, generally wrote down asset values too slowly. Research expenditures (and for that matter, advertising expenditures) have capital values which are ignored when these items are charged against current income. Capital adjustments are frequently belated recognition of changed market situations.

On closer scrutiny one could no doubt find a hundred other differences in concept between tax accounting and economic income concepts,[4] and we have no basis for asserting their importance or unimportance. In this respect, all we can say is that our data are no less or no more vulnerable than other uses of business accounting records, such as the national income accounts.

THE UNIT OF VALUE

The dollar figures for assets and income are book values. Many represent current prices; if a firm sells its output at a uniform rate during the year, the unit of value is the mean price for the year. But many prices of the

[3] Since plants in turn are classified according to the value of their most important product, there is a second level of overlap of industries.

[4] One, excessive withdrawal of salaries by officers of small corporations, is discussed at length in Appendix A.

past are involved in book values—ranging from costs of durable assets purchased many years ago to inventory acquisitions of the recent past.

It cannot be doubted that book value data have a substantial ambiguity, not only in comparisons over time but also in comparisons among industries. Yet it seems impossible to make adjustments of the three-digit industry data which would be defensible: a set of quite extreme assumptions would be necessary with the available price information. We have deflated the broader two-digit industry data in order to get some estimate of the effects of deflation, and the results are analyzed in Chapter 2. Our general conclusion is that the pattern of investment and rates of return among industries is probably tolerably accurate, at least when large differences or changes are involved, but that the temporal pattern of investment is much distorted by price changes.

The reader will observe some variation in the periods covered by the various analytical studies. The chief reason is that this study has taken regrettably long to bring to completion, so considerable additional data accumulated while it was in preparation. Continuous recomputation on the basis of a longer period was not feasible, but it seemed unwise to omit from late analyses data not available for those carried out earlier.

Our basic tables (given in Appendix A) end in 1957. In 1958 the industry classification was substantially changed, so direct comparisons with earlier years are not possible. A reconstruction of 1957 data on the 1958 classificatory basis is given, with the 1958 data, in Appendix E.

CHAPTER 2

The Flow of Investment and the Pattern of Rates of Return

THE assets and rates of return of manufacturing industries have hitherto been available only for selected years or selected companies. It is only because of the statistical by-products of the collection of a corporate income tax that we now possess annual estimates of the stock of capital, and the rates of return thereon, for numerous manufacturing industries (rising from 96 in 1938 to 109 in later years of our study), for a period of twenty years. We begin by surveying the broad trends of the behavior of investment and returns. It is usually convenient for statistical as well as economic reasons to treat the period dominated by World War II (1938 to 1947) separately from the later period.[1]

We shall be compelled to deal chiefly with the dollar volume of assets and rates of return as they are reported in the balance sheets and income statements of businesses. It would be disingenuous to evade acknowledgement that our inability to adjust these data for price changes is a very serious limitation on their usefulness. In the final section of this chapter we examine so far as possible the relationship between assets and rates of return in book values and the corresponding quantities in stable (1947) prices. The correspondence appears to be sufficiently good for the broad industry categories, so that the larger differences (especially among industries at a given time) probably reflect differences in "real" capital and even more in rates of return.

Before we turn to the behavior of investment and rates of return—the two main subjects of this chapter—over the period of our study, it may be well to glance at a somewhat longer time span for which data for all manufacturing industries can be roughly pieced together.[2] The stock of capital in manufacturing and the rates of return after taxes are presented in Chart 1; the data are reported in book values.

The war and postwar years which constitute our special period form a striking contrast to the decade which preceded it. The stock of capital in manufacturing corporations had reached $64 billion in 1929; thereafter, it fell by almost $20 billion in the next six years and did not regain the

[1] The main statistical reason for the division is that extensive changes in industry classification were made in 1948—and, we may add, 1958.

[2] Before 1938 there was much less detail compiled or published on the manufacturing industries. The basic data for 1926 to 1938 underlying Chart 1 are described in Appendix B.

CHART 1

Corporate Capital and Rates of Return in Manufacturing Industries, 1926–58

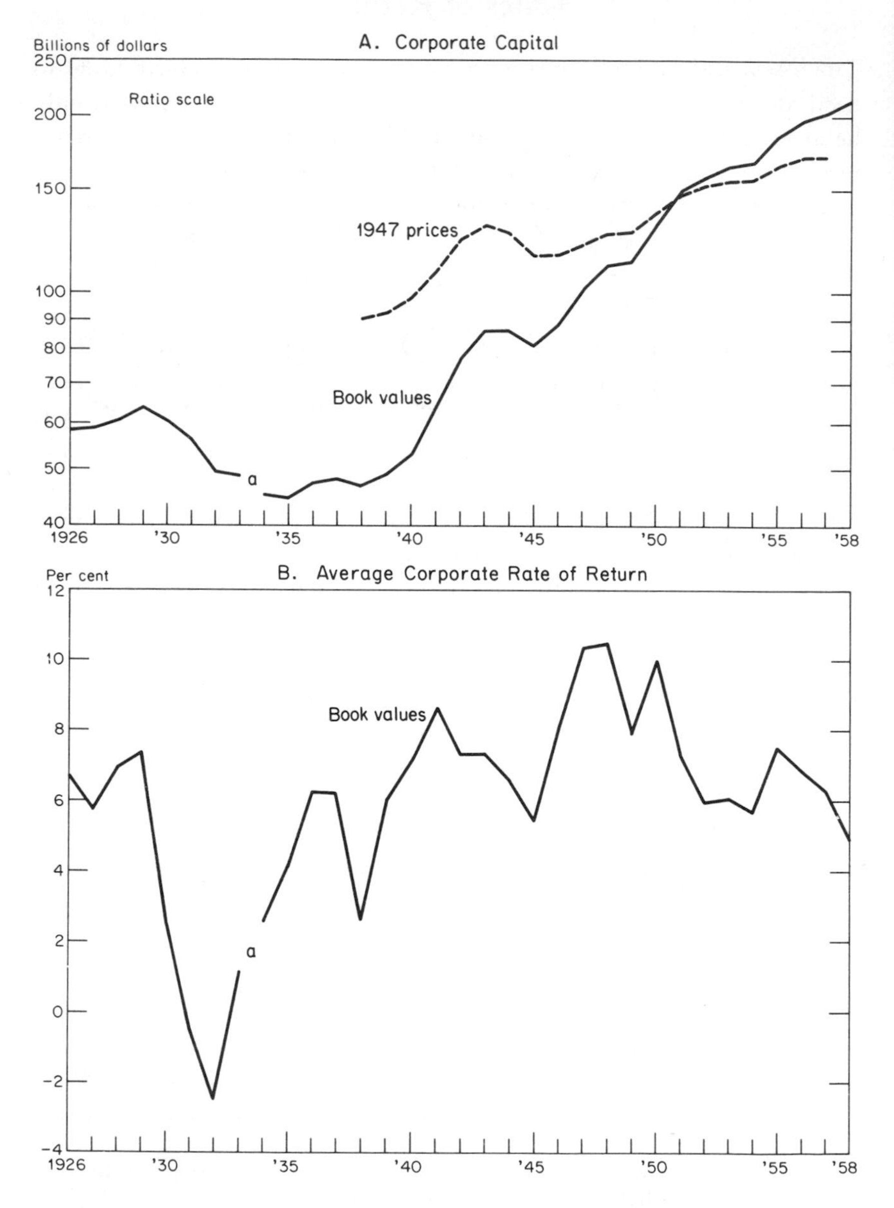

[a] Data for 1926 to 1933 are not strictly comparable to those for the later period. See Appendix B.

Source: The data on which the chart is based are to be found in Table B-1.

1929 level until 1941. A continuous and often spectacular growth began with the outbreak of World War II, interrupted only once by a moderate decline in 1945. It is doubtful that so sustained a rise in book values (reflecting, of course, price rises as well as real investment) had previously occurred in this country.

The contrast in the behavior of the rates of return in the two periods was less marked. In the late 1920's the rate averaged about 6.7 per cent. It fell to —2.5 per cent in 1932 and then began a rise which brought it back nearly to the level of the late twenties. The great contrast is between the 1930's when the rate never exceeded 6.2 per cent and the 1940's when it fell below this level in only one year (1945). The trend was steadily downward in the 1950's. Our period was characterized by persistent expansion (and inflation) and the absence of widespread business losses, which exclude a range of problems—such as "sick" industries and the mobility of capital in severe depression—which a longer time span would have presented.

1. *The Flow of Investment*

The aggregate assets in manufacturing rose by $161.0 billion, or slightly more than 325 per cent, between 1938 and 1957 (Table 3).[3] A considerable part of this immense increase took place in two great waves of investment: the first dominated by World War II, when $39.5 billion was added in five years; the second and more sustained wave running from 1945 to the end of our period, when another $123.4 billion was added.

If we turn to assets measured in 1947 prices, however, the picture changes radically. The total increase in capital is reduced to $81.8 billion, and the average annual rate of growth for the eighteen years falls from 8.0 to 3.3 per cent. The almost unbroken record of growth of capital in book values—only a 4.5 per cent fall in 1945 breaks the record—becomes wholly transformed: total capital reached a peak in 1943, declined by a tenth in 1946, and it was not until sometime in 1950 that the 1943 level was again reached.

The finding that aggregate capital did not surpass the 1943 peak until 1950 is in substantial disagreement with the Department of Commerce estimates. These estimates (which exclude working capital other than

[3] Unless otherwise qualified, "assets" or "capital" excludes investments in other companies, includes noncorporate business, and is reported in book values. Balance sheets for a given year usually refer to December 31 of that year, but a portion of corporations report on fiscal years falling within six months on either side; see W. L. Crum, *Fiscal-Year Reporting for Corporate Income Tax*, Technical Paper 11, New York, National Bureau of Economic Research, 1956.

TABLE 3

ASSETS IN MANUFACTURING INDUSTRIES, 1938–57
(dollar amounts in millions)

Year (Dec. 31)	Total Assets[a] Book Values	1947 Prices	Increase of Assets[b] Number of Industries	Amount (book values)	Decrease of Assets[b] Number of Industries	Amount (book values)
1938	48,846	94,189	—	—	—	—
1939	50,955	96,195	57	2,491	25	615
1940	55,049	101,817	70	2,690	12	207
1941	65,892	113,466	78	8,238	4	42
1942	80,303	128,549	62	9,298	20	623
1943	89,675	135,282	58	4,913	24	587
1944	90,511	132,623	63	3,333	19	527
1945	86,445	122,714	48	1,791	34	2,381
1946	93,156	122,186	78	11,048	4	661
1947	106,339	125,911	76	11,982	6	143
1947[c]	106,580	126,498	—	—	—	—
1948	116,160	131,118	81	10,237	18	508
1949	118,088	132,060	45	3,625	54	1,710
1950	135,142	142,056	95	16,800	4	141
1951	153,948	151,878	90	18,764	9	226
1952	162,853	157,327	—	—	—	—
1953	169,695	160,345	69	17,009[d]	30	1,369[d]
1954	173,111	161,229	57	7,005	42	2,787
1955	190,670	171,445	88	18,075	11	496
1956	203,107	175,710	70	13,714	29	1,380
1957	209,892	175,999	65	9,595	34	2,356

[a] Based upon 2-digit industrial categories.
[b] Based upon 3-digit industries; restricted to "basic" set of industries, described on p. 111.
[c] On 1948 industrial classification.
[d] For two-year period, 1951–53.
SOURCE: Tables A-14 to A-59.

inventories) suggest that a wartime peak (reached in 1942) was considerably exceeded by 1946.[4] So far as fixed assets are concerned, a major source of difference is that we accept, and the Commerce study implicitly rejects, the accelerated depreciation allowances permitted on facilities constructed during the war. Some comments on this question are offered in Appendix A; suffice it to say that *some* of the accelerated depreciation undoubtedly represented a correct recognition of the fact that plants constructed to produce munitions had a much reduced peacetime usefulness.[5] The true amount of depreciation that should have been

[4] Donald G. Wooden and Robert C. Wasson, "Manufacturing Investment since 1929," *Survey of Current Business*, Nov. 1956, p. 14.

[5] We also have higher deflated figures for durable capital in the earlier period because of the use of a different set of deflators. Possibly, Commerce's method of finding capital by accumulating previous investment (which requires knowledge of the share of investment goods purchased by manufacturing industries) is less reliable in the early years.

charged against the defense facilities cannot be known, and one is left with the ambiguous conclusion that it lies somewhere between the accelerated and the normal rates of depreciation.

If we cannot judge conclusively the popular view that the war left the American economy with a rich legacy of modern capital equipment suitable to ordinary peacetime purposes, we can at least shed some doubt on it. For our capital stock grew at the rate of about 5 per cent annually from 1939 to 1944 if most accelerated depreciation properly represented small postwar usefulness. This is not an especially large rate of growth from a depression to a period of high prosperity and, indeed, from 1946 to 1953 the annual rate was 3.9 per cent. It is often—and erroneously—said that, if a warring nation borrows (domestically), it is shifting the burden to future generations; we can at least suggest that World War II offers no support for the view that waging war confers an economic boon on these generations.

The capital movements from 1938 to 1946 were dominated by the mobilization and demobilization of the American economy. Most of the industries that make finished munitions were too small to be reported separately before 1942, but those that were segregated doubled their capital in 1940, again in 1941, and in 1942 quadrupled their capital. In 1939, assets in these industries were $0.6 billion; in 1943 they amounted to $13.4 billion, or one-seventh of all manufacturing capital. The subsequent decline was even more abrupt: within three years the capital of the munitions industries (by then chiefly aircraft and ships) had fallen to $2.4 billion.

Those vast movements of capital into and out of munitions did not occasion comparable movements of capital in the industries supplying material and equipment (see Table 4). In large part, the mobilization consisted simply of redirection of the output of producer goods industries—steel went into tanks instead of into automobiles.

Even in the capital reported in the munitions industries, however, we find a large amount of the capital which in earlier years was reported by other industries. The larger automobile companies disappeared from the automobile industry during the war,[6] because their major receipts then came from aircraft and tanks. The shift of an entire company to a new industry, when its sales may have shifted moderately in composition

[6] The number of companies making motor vehicles (including trucks and industrial trailers) with assets over $100 million varied as follows:

1942	3	1944	1	1946	0
1943	0	1945	1	1947	5
				1948	9

TABLE 4

Annual Percentage Increase of Capital in Munitions and Other Industries, Book Values, 1938–47

		Type of Industry		
Year	Munitions[a]	Suppliers to Munitions[b]	Other Producer Goods	Consumer Goods
1938–39	35.0	6.8	6.4	2.6
1939–40	96.3	20.9	7.4	6.5
1940–41	115.8	34.0	19.6	15.9
1941–42	355.8	39.2	9.5	7.2
1942–43	103.7	20.7	3.5	4.1
1943–44	−14.3	−1.3	−0.5	5.8
1944–45	−24.9	−12.3	−2.1	3.4
1945–46	−77.6	7.2	12.1	33.9
1946–47	−24.6	15.7	22.0	13.1

[a] Ships, aircraft, firearms, ammunition, tanks, sighting and firing equipment, and munitions n.e.c.

[b] Industrial chemicals, blast furnaces, structural steel, miscellaneous iron and steel, basic nonferrous metals, miscellaneous nonferrous metals, communications, engines and turbines, general industrial machinery, metalworking machinery.

Source: Tables A-14 to A-35.

(although of course the shift was complete for automobiles), is an undesirable statistical source of instability in the capital data, discussed below.

The opposite side of this picture was the much slower rate of growth of capital in the consumer goods industries. But even here there was no reduction of capital, even if capital is measured in 1947 prices: only two industries (furniture and motor vehicles) declined from 1940 to 1945; and the group of industries as a whole showed an increase of 12.6 per cent.

Two main developments dominated the growth of capital from 1947 to 1956. The first was the immense program of construction of housing, plant, and equipment. Between those dates the total assets in manufacturing rose 90.8 per cent, but the construction goods industries much surpassed that growth (Table 5)—indeed, of the larger industries only structural clay failed to exceed the rate of increase of all manufacturing. The expansion of construction was paralleled by a large increase in agricultural supplies (agricultural machinery and fertilizers).

The second development was the retardation of investment in the consumer goods industries. None of the four beverage industries, nor eight food industries (all except cereals), nor the two tobacco industries, nor the thirteen textile and apparel industries, nor footwear, had so large a rate of increase of assets as all manufacturing. The only large consumer goods industry whose capital grew rapidly was motor vehicles (and with it, petroleum refining), and of course it started from a somewhat fictitious

TABLE 5

PERCENTAGE INCREASE OF CAPITAL IN CONSTRUCTION GOODS INDUSTRIES, BOOK VALUES, 1947–56

Industry	Percentage Increase (total manufacturing = 90.8)
Concrete products	188.1
Fabricated structural products	158.1
Cement	187.3
Glass	137.2
Structural clay	89.1
Miscellaneous lumber	99.1
Machinery	
Office and store	152.1
General industry	128.5
Construction	149.2
Metalworking	112.9
Total manufacturing	90.8

SOURCE: Tables A-36 to A-59.

1947 base. The shift of consumers' expenditures toward services presumably was one cause of the slow growth of capital.[7]

THE DISPERSION OF RELATIVE RATES OF INVESTMENT

The great differences in the rates of increase of capital in munitions and nonmunitions industries has already been noted (Table 5); similar though smaller dispersion is common even among nonmunitions industries, and in peacetime. But before this characteristic is looked at more closely, some cautions with respect to the data are in order.

The annual rates of increase of capital are unfortunately much influenced by deficiencies of data. The reclassification of a single large firm—even among our fairly broad industries—can lead to a fictitiously large increase in one industry and a fictitiously small increase in another. Beginning with 1942 (when the asset-size classes were first given in tha *Source Book*), the behavior of large firms was examined in those industries where an annual rate of change of assets fell outside two standard deviations of the rates of increase for that year. When shifting of large firms appeared to be the source of the large rate of change, it was sometimes possible to adjust the data, and in others at least to detect the incomparabilities. But the reclassification of large firms cannot always be detected

[7] Too small a share of service enterprises is incorporated to place much confidence in the asset figures for this category, but it is worth noting that assets of corporations in retail trade and services rose by only 94 per cent over the 1947–56 period—slightly more than the figure for all manufacturing.

and that of smaller firms is even more elusive, accounting for a portion of the observed dispersion. Where the reclassification of firms was detected but adjustments were not feasible, the industry was excluded from the "basic" set of industries, described on p. 111.

In only five years of the entire period was the average rate of increase of assets as large as the standard deviation of the rates (Table 6), despite the

TABLE 6

PERCENTAGE INCREASE IN TOTAL ASSETS IN MANUFACTURING INDUSTRIES, 1938–57

PERIOD	Number of Industries	PERCENTAGE INCREASE OF ASSETS Average	Standard Deviation	Quartile Q_1	Q_3
1938–39	82	3.72	9.42	−1.73	7.92
1939–40	82	7.93	10.37	1.77	13.39
1940–41	82	17.38	12.81	8.27	25.36
1941–42	82	11.10	14.53	1.94	20.75
1942–43	82	5.85	10.79	−1.25	11.94
1943–44	82	4.63	7.53	0.09	9.83
1944–45	82	2.01	9.58	−3.21	7.36
1945–46	82	19.94	16.27	10.58	27.19
1946–47	82	15.06	10.43	8.83	20.28
1947–48	99	7.60	8.44	2.42	12.85
1948–49	99	1.04	7.08	−3.66	4.60
1949–50	99	15.78	10.47	9.61	21.02
1950–51	99	12.45	12.68	4.38	18.83
1951–53[a]	99	3.06	6.19	−1.14	6.74
1953–54	99	1.34	7.78	−3.45	5.10
1954–55	99	9.77	8.30	4.67	15.00
1955–56	99	3.86	8.05	−1.11	9.00
1956–57[b]	99	1.89	8.62	−2.19	6.80

[a] Annual rate for two-year period.
[b] For percentage increase in corporate assets only.
SOURCE: Tables A-14 to A-59.

fact that ordnance industries and other industries with obvious incomparabilities were excluded. In five years, more than a fourth of the industries increased their assets by 20 per cent or more and, despite the almost continuous rise of price levels, in eight of the nineteen years more than one-fourth of the industries had decreases of assets. Rather systematically, the dispersion of rates is larger, the larger the average rate of increase, but the dispersion of rates varies less than the average rate, so the dispersion of rates is smaller relative to the average rate in years of large investment. The distributions of rates of increase are presented in the various panels of Chart 2.

One might conjecture that the largest and smallest rates of increase are found in the smallest industries, where smaller absolute increments or decrements of investment will suffice for large relative movements of capital.[8] There is scarcely any relationship, however, between the standard deviations of the rates of increase of capital of individual industries from 1947 to 1954 and the size of the industry (measured by 1950 assets).[9]

The mobility of capital among industries can be defined in such a way that it is measured by the dispersion of rates of increase of capital. Mobility must be measured from a base representing immobility, and one base would be provided by the assumption that the assets of all industries grow at the same rate: then capital could be considered to be moving from slowly growing to rapidly growing industries. An industry's actual rate of increase minus the average (weighted) rate of increase would be a measure of absolute mobility in this particular sense.

On this interpretation, the dispersion of rates of increase of assets measures also mobility, and the interpretation is in keeping with expectations. The greatest single year of mobility was 1946, when a large part of the demobilization of the economy took place. The two periods of mobilization, 1939–43 and 1949–51, witnessed almost as large a shift of capital. But even in years such as 1949, when capital was not increasing, the differential movements of capital were almost as large as in relatively prosperous years such as 1944 and 1948.

INSTABILITY OF INVESTMENT

The annual rate of investment is a relatively volatile magnitude even when it is restricted to durable goods, and the addition of inventories and other forms of working capital increases the instability. The average of the annual rates of increase of capital over the period is 8.43 per cent, but the standard deviation of these rates is 6.57 per cent. This instability is of course the Great Commonplace of all theories of business fluctuations.

The instability of investment rates is no less marked for individual industries. It would be possible for aggregate investment to fluctuate widely and at the same time for the industrial patterns of rate of investment to be stable: this would happen if the movements of general business dominated the investment of individual industries. But the industrial

[8] In 1950, for example, industry assets ranged from $40.6 million in millinery to $15.8 billion in petroleum refining—a range of 1 to 390.

[9] There is a modest positive rank correlation between 1950 size of industry and 1947–54 percentage increase of assets, however ($\rho = .23$, with 99 industries). In the 1938–47 period, no such correlation is present ($\rho = .02$ with 82 industries).

CHART 2

Frequency Distribution of Manufacturing Industries, by Annual Rate of Change of Capital, 1938–57

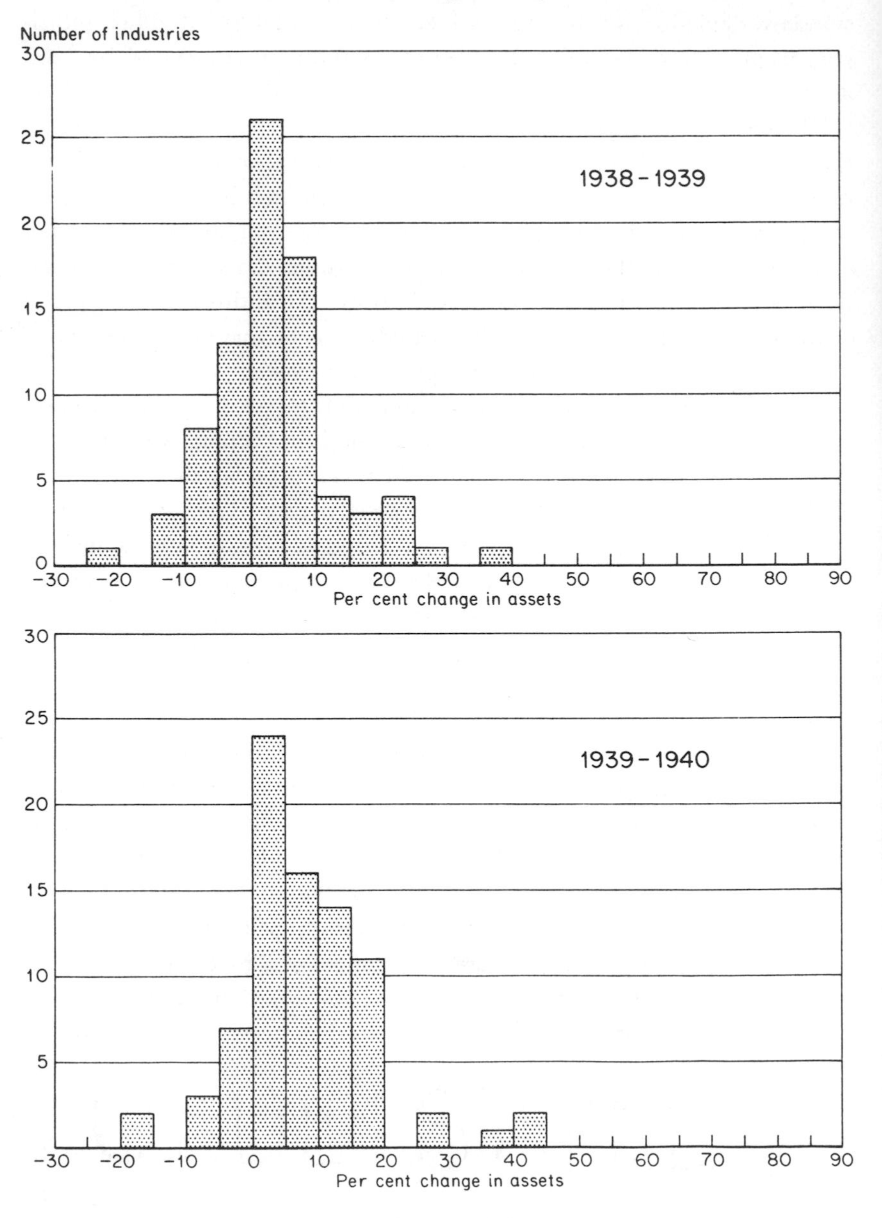

(continued)

CHART 2 (continued)

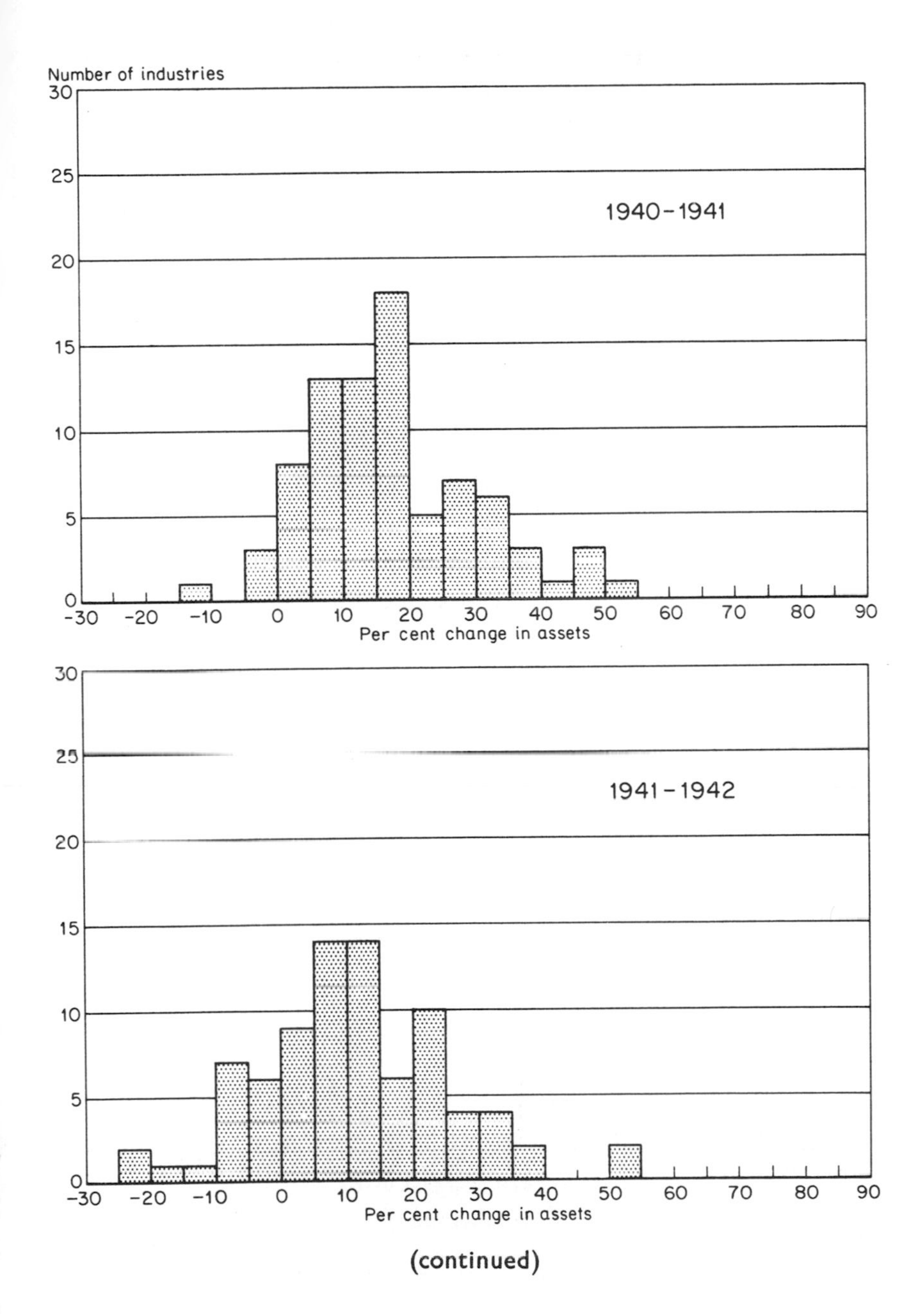

(continued)

CHART 2 (continued)

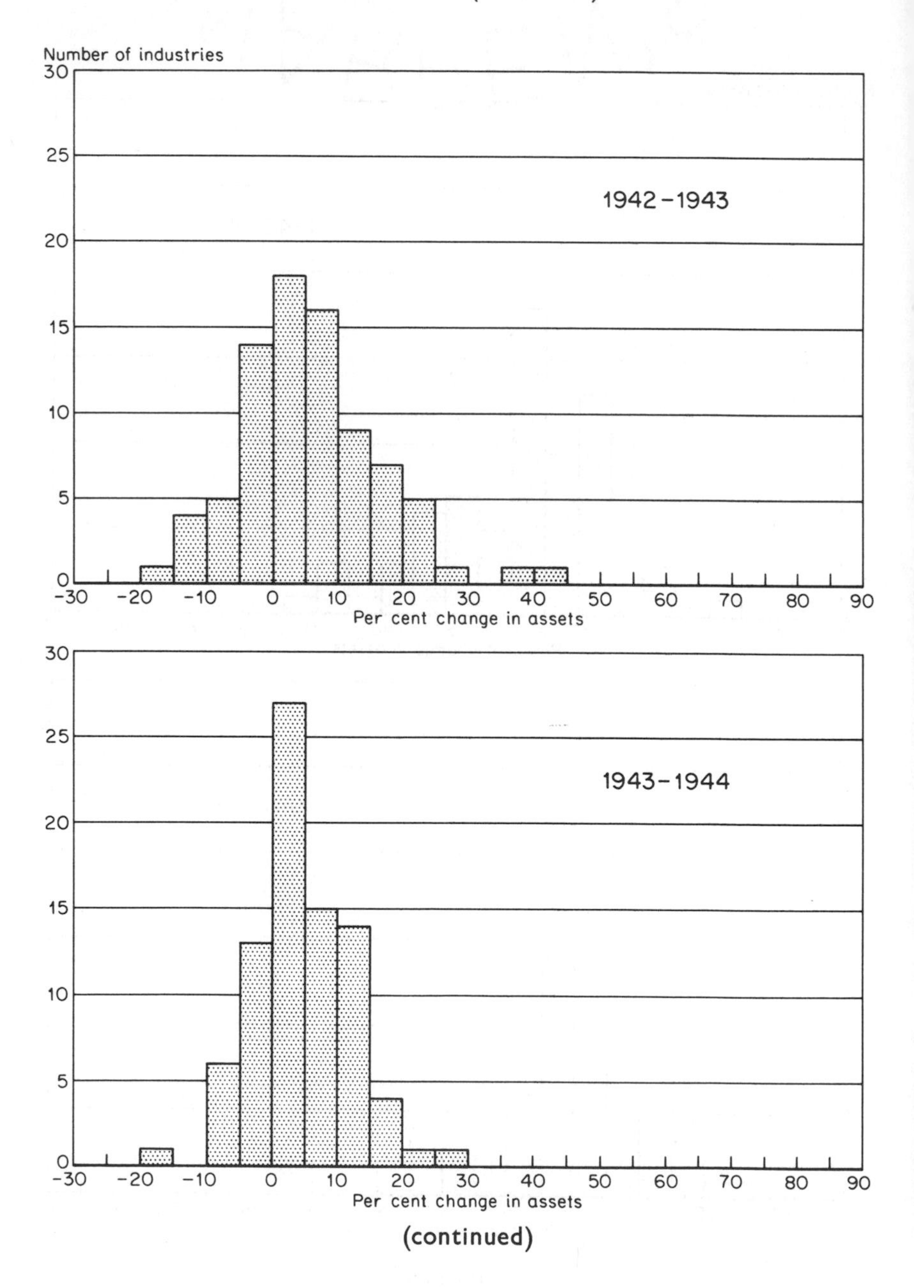

(continued)

CHART 2 (continued)

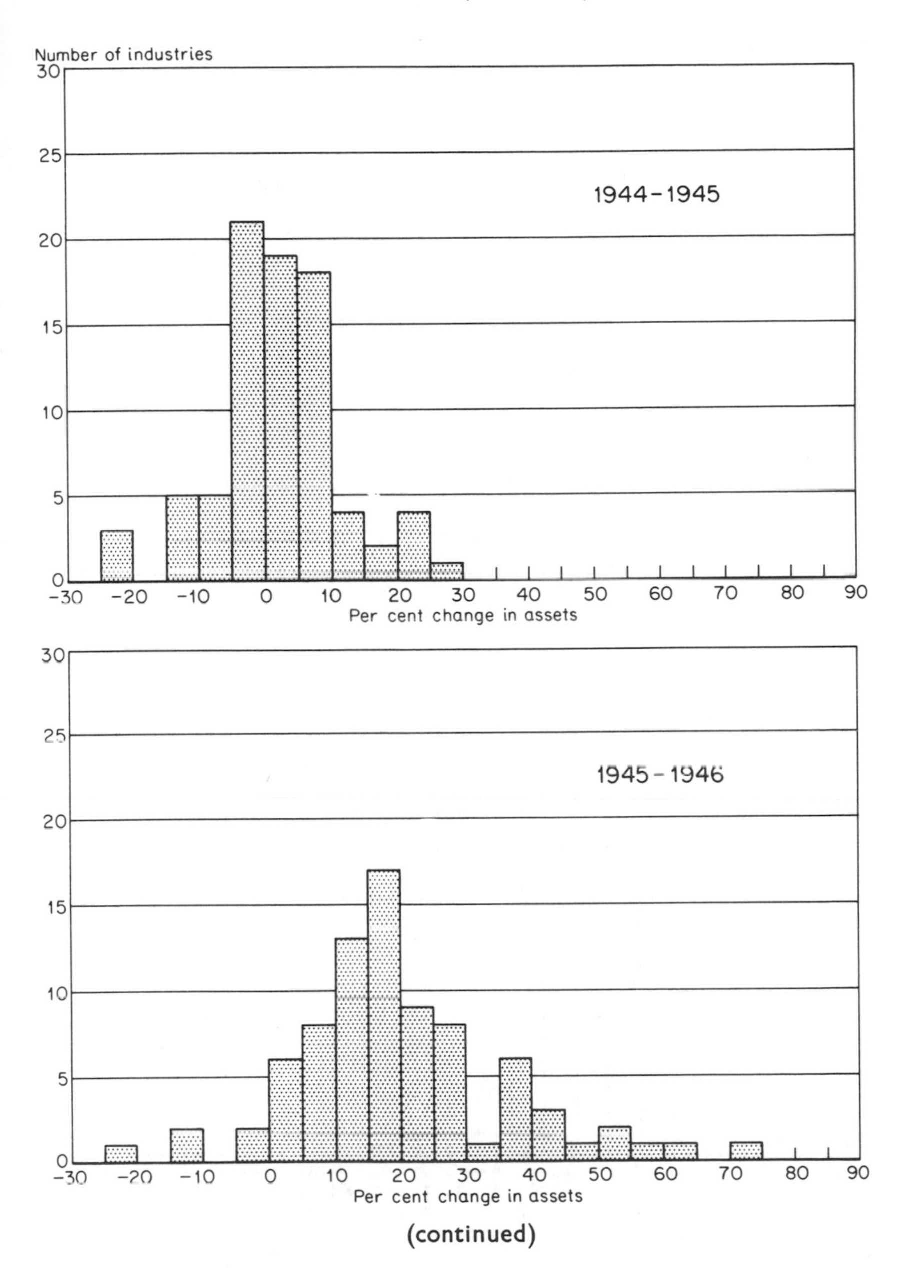

(continued)

CHART 2 (continued)

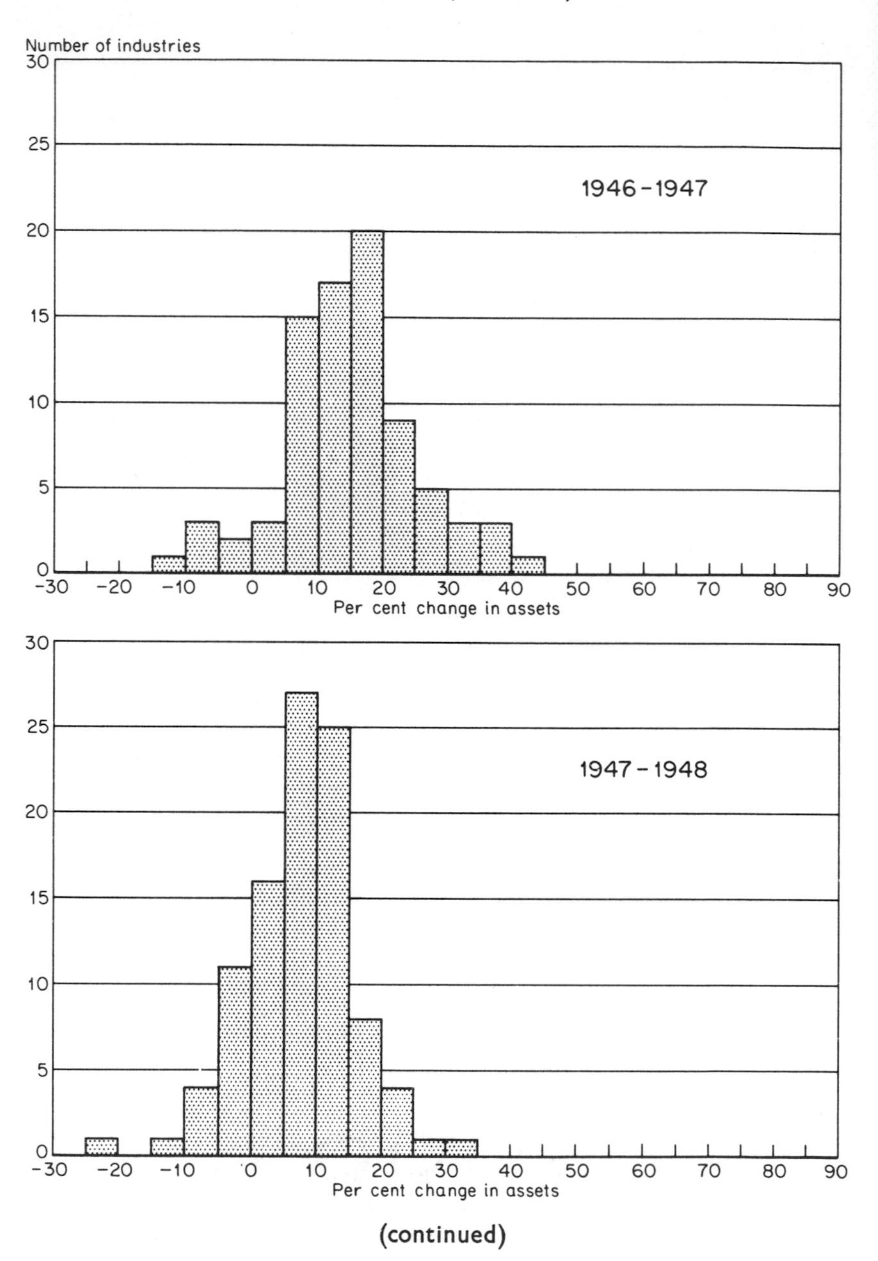

(continued)

CHART 2 (continued)

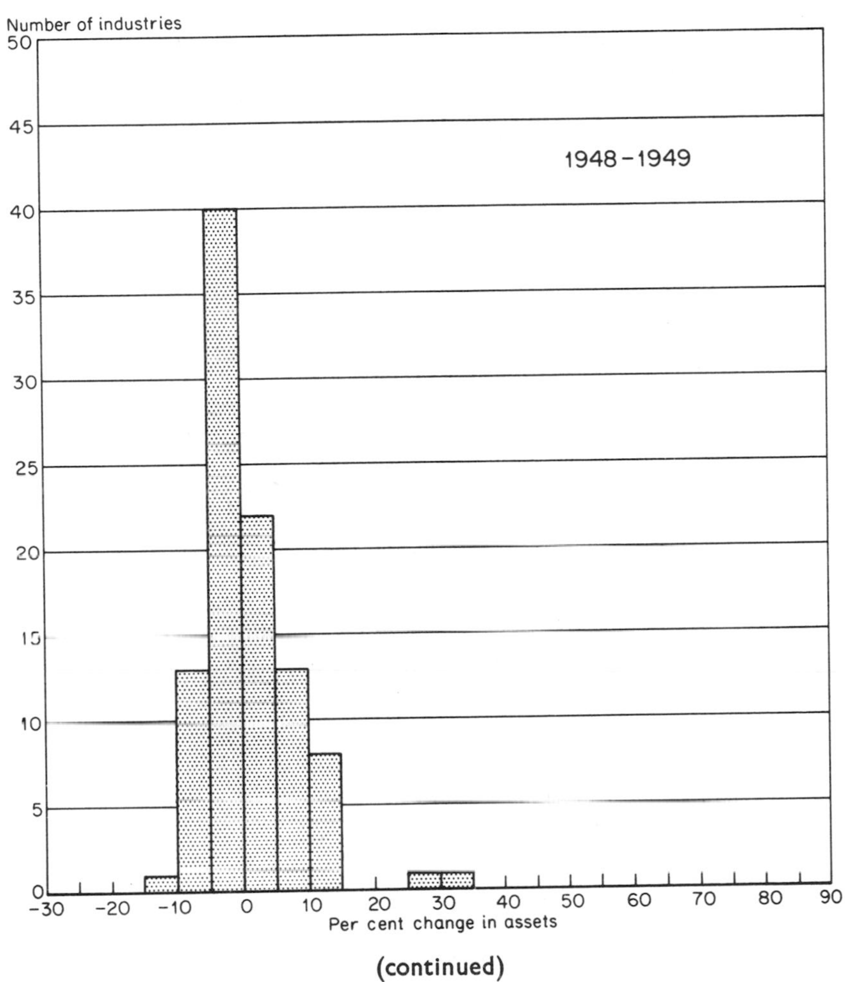

(continued)

CHART 2 (continued)

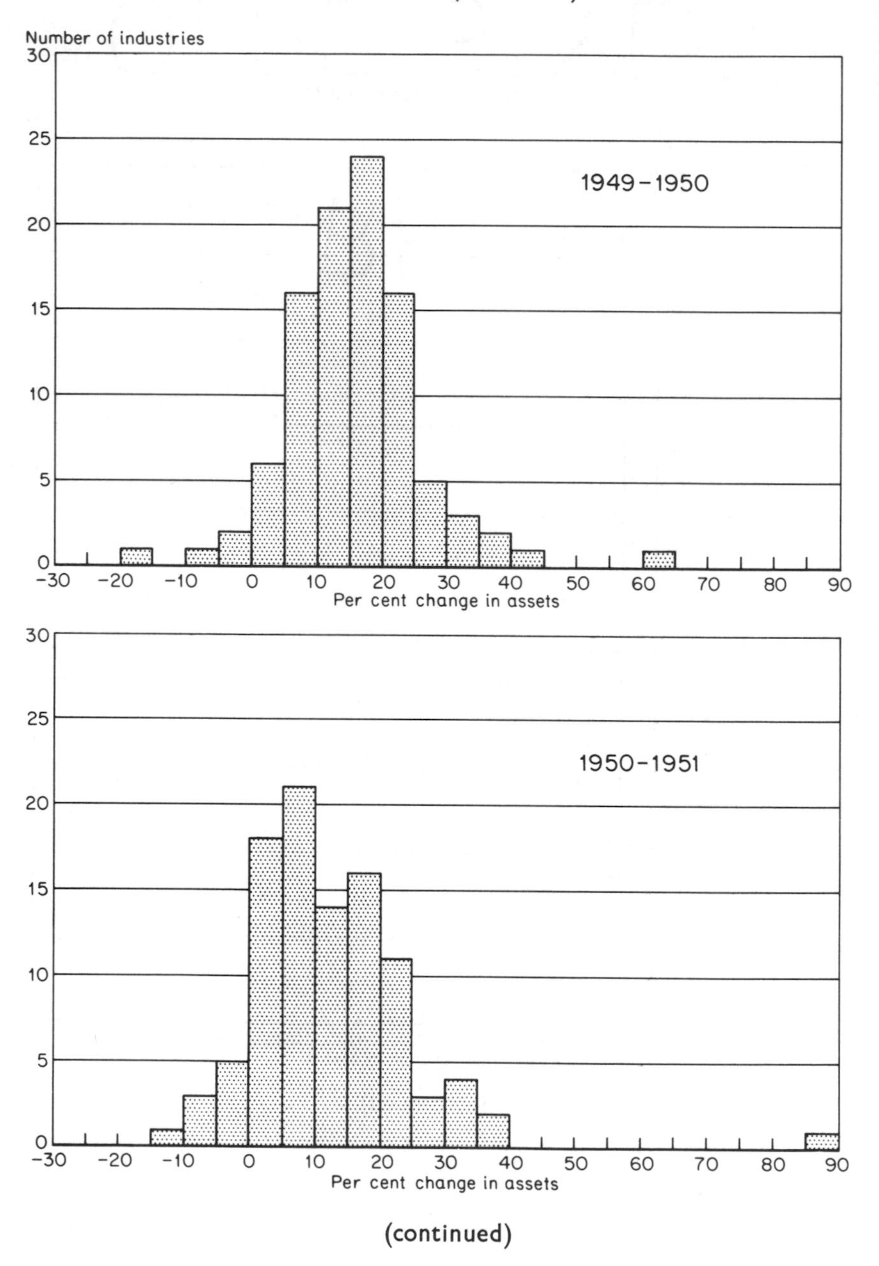

(continued)

CHART 2 (continued)

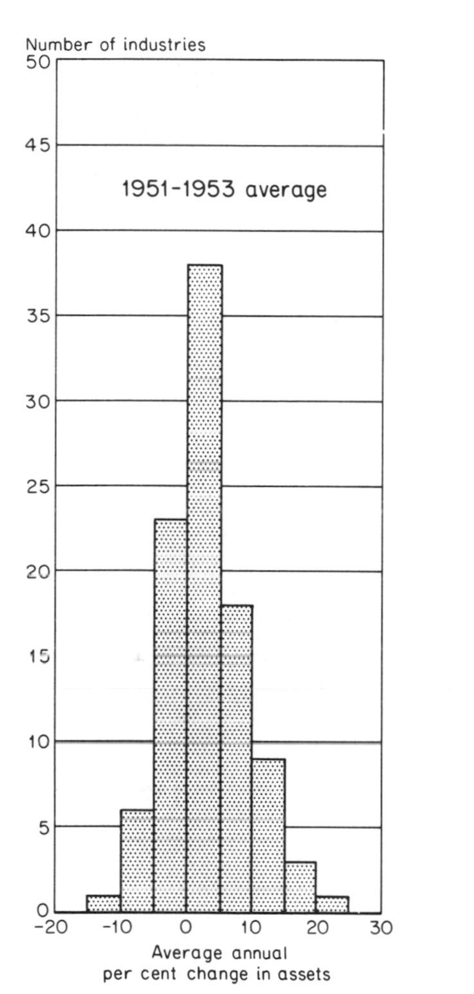

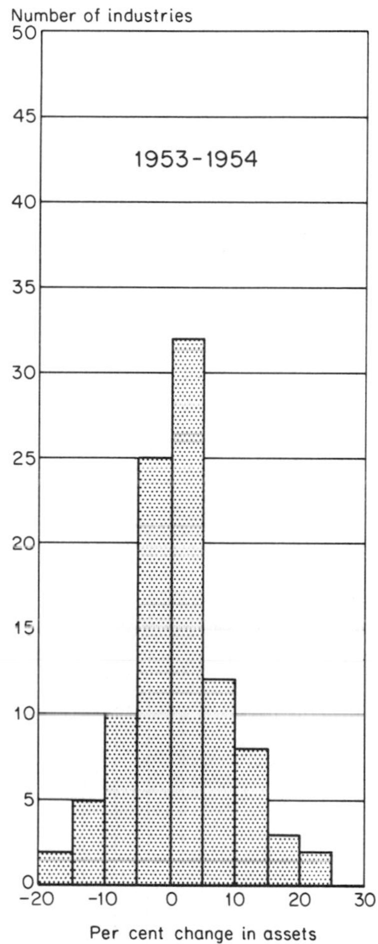

(continued)

CHART 2 (continued)

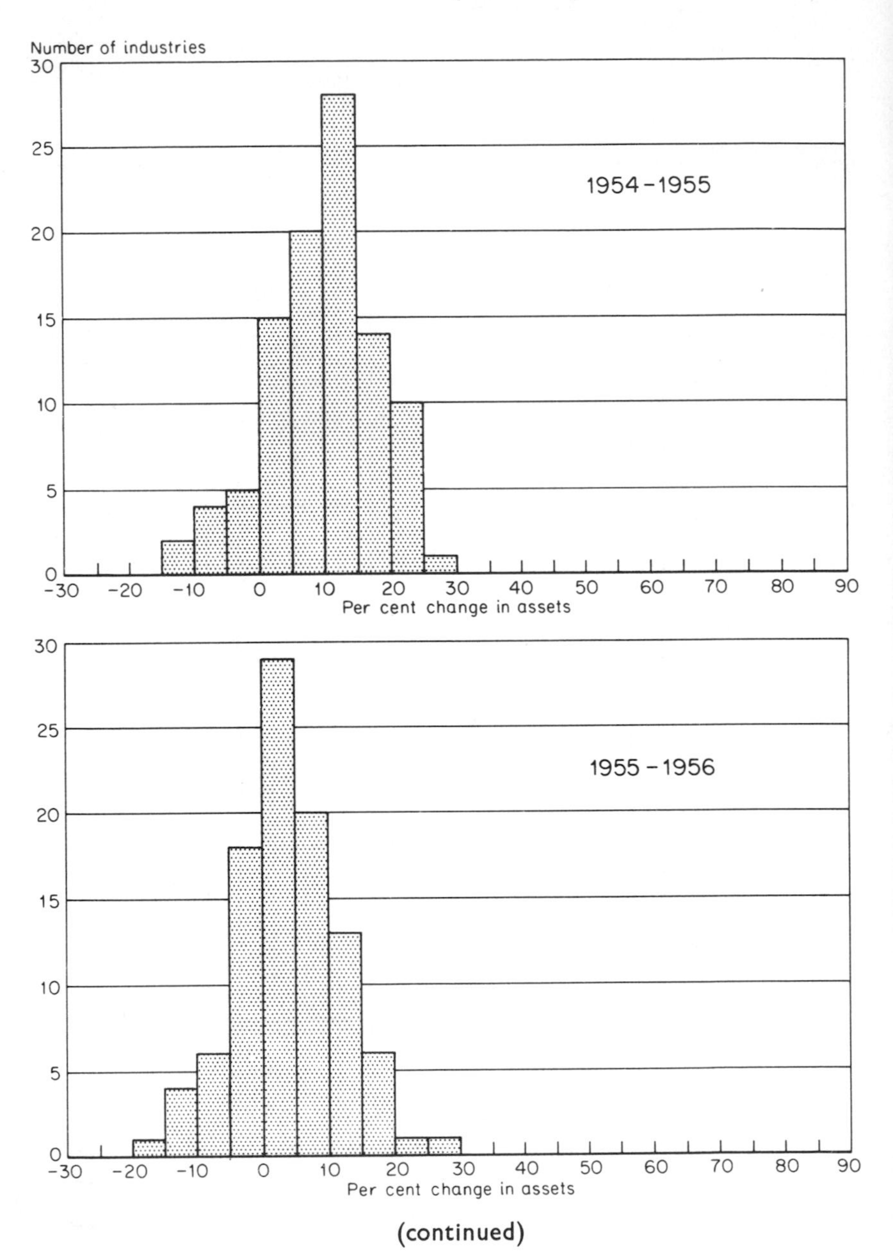

(continued)

CHART 2 (concluded)

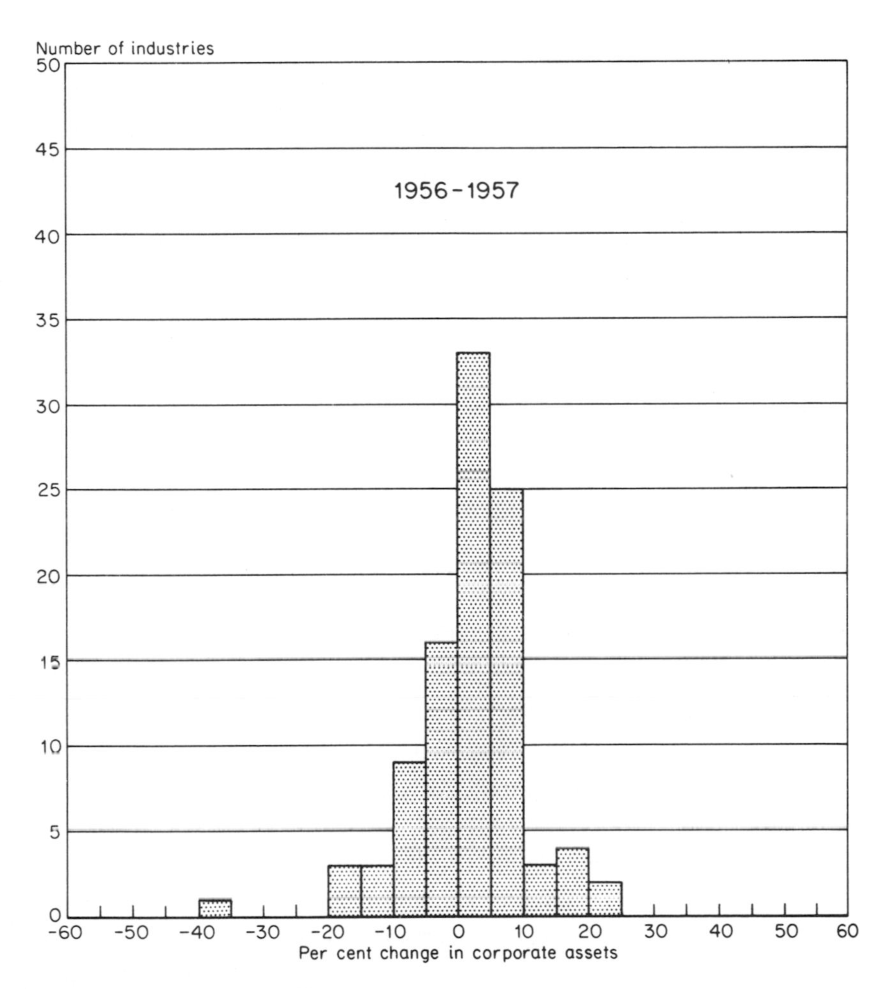

Source: Tables A-14 to A-59.

pattern is highly unstable (see Table 7); one is tempted to ask, not how strong the association is between successive annual rates of increase of capital, but whether there is any association. There is, in fact, a positive association in all but three years, but the correlations are nonsignificant in 13 out of 17 cases.

TABLE 7

RANK CORRELATION OF PERCENTAGE INCREASE IN ASSETS AMONG MANUFACTURING INDUSTRIES, PAIRS OF YEARS, 1938–57

Period	Correlation Coefficient	Number of Industries
1938–39 with 1939–40	−.104	82
1939–40 with 1940–41	.311	82
1940–41 with 1941–42	.290	82
1941–42 with 1942–43	.118	82
1942–43 with 1943–44	.254	82
1943–44 with 1944–45	.205	82
1944–45 with 1945–46	.138	82
1945–46 with 1946–47	.025	82
1946–47 with 1947–48	.116	75
1947–48 with 1948–49	.105	99
1948–49 with 1949–50	.067	99
1949–50 with 1950–51	.092	99
1950–51 with 1951–53[a]	.366	99
1951–53[a] with 1953–54	−.158	99
1953–54 with 1954–55	−.017	99
1954–55 with 1955–56	.011	99
1955–56 with 1956–57[b]	.153	99

[a] Two-year change.

[b] For 1956–57, percentage increase in corporate assets.

SOURCE: Tables A-14 to A-59.

One large source of variation in the industrial pattern of rates of investment is purely statistical. If we correlate

$$\log \text{capital}_t - \log \text{capital}_{t-1}$$

with

$$\log \text{capital}_{t-1} - \log \text{capital}_{t-2},$$

any error in the capital data for the intermediate year $(t - 1)$ works in opposite directions on the relative increases. It can be shown in fact that, even if the correlation between the precisely measured rates of capital increase were .75, the observed correlation could be as small as .125 if the variance of the errors in measuring capital in any year were half as large as the variance of the annual changes in capital.[10]

[10] Let $(C_i + \delta_i)$ be the logarithm of the observed capital in an industry in year i, where C_i is the "true" figure and δ_i is the error of measurement. The observed correlation between rates of increase in the two successive years will be:

$$r_0 = \text{correlation of } (C_2 + \delta_2 - C_1 - \delta_1) \text{ with } (C_3 + \delta_3 - C_2 - \delta_2).$$

This effect of errors of measurement can be reduced by lengthening the periods over which changes in capital are measured, for then the error in measurement is unaffected but the true change is increased. Taking a longer time span, the industrial pattern of rates of increase in capital becomes more stable. For example, the correlation between rates of increase in capital from 1949 to 1951 with 1951 to 1953 is .422, whereas the maximum correlation of successive annual rates in that period was only .366 (and it was based upon one two-year change).[11]

The magnitude of the errors in measurement of capital in a given year relative to the magnitude of annual changes in capital is unknown, but it is surely substantial and possibly the measurement errors are of the same order of magnitude as the annual changes in an industry's capital stock.[12] Since we can form no independent estimate of measurement errors, we deal usually with periods longer than one year in the analysis of rates of change of capital.

INCREASES IN ASSETS AND COMPANIES

The average assets of manufacturing industries grew by 60.3 per cent from 1948 to 1956, but assets of corporations of average size in each industry

---

The true correlation if there were no errors would be:

$$r_t = \text{correlation of } (C_2 - C_1) \text{ with } (C_3 - C_2).$$

By definition,

$$r_0 = \frac{\Sigma(C_3 + \delta_3 - C_2 - \delta_2)(C_2 + \delta_2 - C_1 - \delta_1)}{N\sigma_{C_3 + \delta_3 - C_2 - \delta_2}\,\sigma_{C_2 + \delta_2 - C_1 - \delta_1}}.$$

If the errors are not correlated with the C's or with one another,

$$\sigma^2_{C_3 + \delta_3 - C_2 - \delta_2} = \sigma^2_{C_3 - C_2} + \sigma^2_{\delta_3 - \delta_2}$$
$$= \sigma^2_C + 2\sigma^2_\delta, \text{ say.}$$

Substituting in the definition,

$$r_0 = \frac{\Sigma([C_3 - C_2] + [\delta_3 - \delta_2])([C_2 - C_1] + [\delta_2 - \delta_1])}{N(\sigma^2_C + 2\sigma^2_\delta)}$$
$$= \frac{\Sigma(C_3 - C_2)(C_2 - C_1) - \Sigma\delta^2}{N(\sigma^2_C + 2\sigma^2_\delta)}.$$

Using the definition of r_t,

$$r_0 = \frac{r_t\sigma^2_C - \sigma^2_\delta}{\sigma^2_C + 2\sigma^2_\delta}$$
$$= \frac{r_t - \lambda}{1 + 2\lambda}, \quad \text{if } \lambda = \frac{\sigma^2_\delta}{\sigma^2_C}.$$

[11] The correlation coefficient between relative changes in assets from 1947 to 1950 with those from 1950 to 1954 was .361.

[12] On the other hand, an error is likely to be correlated with the change in capital, and errors in successive years are surely also correlated, so the formula in footnote 10 is only a very rough approximation.

TABLE 8

INDUSTRIES WITH LARGEST RELATIVE INCREASE AND DECREASE IN NUMBER OF CORPORATIONS, 1948–56

Increase	*Per Cent Change* Number of Corporations	Industry Assets	*Decrease*	*Per Cent Change* Number of Corporations	Industry Assets
Aircraft and parts	194.7	394.8	Hats	–46.5	0.3
Fabricated structural steel	90.7	115.3	Tin cans	–44.1	106.3
Communications	90.4	167.3	Tires and tubes	–43.4	77.9
Costume jewelry	82.7	218.7	Cigars	–42.1	5.1
Metalworking machinery	77.0	104.6	Distilled beverages	–41.4	19.6
Electric generating equipment	68.4	113.0	Malt	–34.3	28.8
Miscellaneous petroleum products	65.2	3.3	Broad-woven wool	–34.1	–30.1
Metal stamping	64.9	81.4	Engines and turbines	–33.3	75.7
Professional and scientific instruments	62.2	200.3	Railroad equipment	–33.0	27.8
Insulated wire	59.5	116.2	Cereals	–30.6	91.3
Fabricated plastics	55.8	177.3	Sugar	–27.2	19.8
Fertilizers	54.0	89.8	Confectionery	–26.2	19.8
Commercial printing	53.3	103.4	Broad-woven cotton	–26.0	16.6
Miscellaneous machinery	47.9	85.1	Miscellaneous food and kindred	–22.0	52.9
Nonferrous foundries	47.0	47.7	Cut stone	–21.0	25.7

SOURCE: *Statistics of Income, Corporation Income Tax Returns*, for 1948 and 1956 (Internal Revenue Service); and Tables A-36 to A-59, below.

increased 65.3 per cent, showing the average number of corporations to have declined slightly.[13] Of course one expects average company size to rise (in current dollars of assets) in a period of rising prices, but deflated assets rose by more than one-third over this eight-year period.

TABLE 9

RELATIVE INCREASE IN ASSETS OF INDUSTRIES AND AVERAGE CORPORATE ASSETS, 1948–56

Decile of Relative Growth of Industry (1)	Number of Industries (2)	Average Increase in Assets $\left(\log \frac{\text{assets, 1956}}{\text{assets, 1948}}\right)$ (3)	Average Increase in Corporation Size $\left(\log \frac{\text{average size, 1956}}{\text{average size, 1948}}\right)$ (4)	(4) as Per Cent of (3) (5)	Average Assets per Corporation, 1956 ($ millions) (6)
(slowest)	9	—.03344	.01807	—	1.1
	10	.07675	.15753	205.3	3.4
I	10	.10576	.13360	126.3	5.3
	10	.14472	.16414	113.4	1.1
	10	.18458	.15854	85.9	1.0
I	10	.21842	.17769	81.4	8.3
II	10	.25653	.24912	97.1	10.6
III	10	.29841	.22542	75.5	12.3
	10	.32661	.26364	80.7	8.2
(fastest)	10	.44697	.28846	64.5	4.2
ll manufacturing industries	99	.20491	.21853	106.6	5.6

SOURCE: Same as for Table 8.

The stability in the total number of corporate tax returns during a period of rapid growth of manufactures occurred because industries ni which most corporations are found (food, textiles, and apparel) grew much less rapidly than the remainder of manufacturing industries did. The near-zero value of the (unweighted) average percentage change in the number of firms per industry, on the other hand, indicates that the phenomenon of stability in numbers was widespread. In fact, 48 of the 99 industries had a decline in the number of corporations.

The largest decreases in number of corporations occurred in a declining industry (broad-woven wool) and others which grew substantially (tin cans, cereals, engines and turbines, etc.), as Table 8 shows. But the industries with large increases in firms were those having unusually rapid

[13] The year 1948 is chosen as base because the 1947 number of tax returns cannot be estimated reliably on a basis comparable with the later years. These are unweighted averages of the industries. The number of returns in all manufacturing industries rose 4.6 per cent over the period.

growth—a relationship that was quite general. We may partition the relative increase of assets by the formula:

$$\log \frac{A_2}{A_1} = \log \frac{S_2}{S_1} + \log \frac{N_2}{N_1}$$

where A is industry corporate assets, S is average assets per corporation, and N is number of corporations, and the subscripts refer to dates. Then the share of industry increase ($\log A_2/A_1$) that is "accounted for" by increase of firm sizes ($\log S_2/S_1$) can be tabulated by deciles, as in Table 9.

The more rapidly an industry grew, the smaller the share accounted for by increased firm size and the larger the share accounted for by increased number of corporations. This is of course an eminently reasonable finding: that firms tend to leave slowly growing industries (often declining industries) and enter the most rapidly growing industries. Moreover, the rapidly growing industries had, on balance, larger average corporations (measured by assets in 1956) than the slowly growing industries had, but the relationship was very loose.

2. *Rates of Return*

The average rate of return on total assets was 7.2 per cent for the period 1938–56 (Table 10).[14] Aside from the only severe depression year, 1938, the average rate fluctuated between 5.4 and 10.4 per cent (after taxes), and averaged 7.5 per cent excluding that initial year. The rate of return when both income and asset data are converted to 1947 prices averaged 7.2 per cent, identical with the average of book-value rates. But if the process of deflation had no effect upon the average rate over the nineteen-year period, it had a noticeable influence upon its trend. The deflated rate fell below the book-value rate from 1939 to 1949, with peak differences in 1943 and 1947; from 1950 to 1957 the deflated rate exceeded the book-value rate by a steadily increasing amount. The effect of the adjustment for price changes is much smaller than its effect on capital, since a roughly parallel deflation of income is also made. The adjustment for accelerated depreciation (discussed in Appendix A) may have had as large an effect as that for inflation: calculations under admittedly extreme assumptions suggest that, in the absence of such depreciation, the rate of return would have been appreciably higher from 1942 through 1945, then lower through 1951, and higher again after 1951.

[14] The rates of return are calculated as total capital returns (excluding dividends received from other corporations) as a percentage of total assets (excluding investments in other companies) and therefore differ from the rates of return on stockholder's equity or net worth.

TABLE 10

PERCENTAGE RATE OF RETURN IN MANUFACTURING INDUSTRIES, 1938–57

Year	Average Rate of Return (weighted)	Average Rate in 1947 Prices (weighted)
1938	2.62	2.63
1939	6.00	5.77
1940	7.12	6.95
1941	8.56	8.36
1942	7.30	6.95
1943	7.30	6.80
1944	6.59	6.20
1945	5.43	5.26
1946	8.13	7.65
1947	10.34	9.84
1947[a]	10.38	9.85
1948	10.43	10.05
1949	7.93	7.92
1950	9.97	9.99
1951	7.34	7.78
1952	5.96	6.46
1953	6.05	6.54
1954	5.68	6.26
1955	7.47	7.97
1956	6.85	7.71
1957	6.29	7.40

[a] Comparable to subsequent years.

NOTE: Calculations are based upon two-digit industries. For a description of the computations, see Appendix A, p. 118.

The rate of return on capital, unlike the annual relative changes in the stock of capital, has been comparatively insensitive to business conditions. In our period there were four peak years (1944, 1948, 1953, and 1957) and four trough years (1938, 1946, 1949, and 1954), and in the peak years the rate of return averaged 7.34 per cent (see Table 10), whereas in the trough years it averaged 6.09 per cent.[15] The average rose more than a negligible amount in six of fifteen years of expansion, and fell in three of four years of contraction, so conformity to business conditions was closer in business declines. One gets the impression that changes in corporate income taxation were as important as business fluctuations in explaining fluctuations in rates of return.

The movements of the rate of return broadly paralleled those of the rate of investment. In both series the peak was reached in the immediate postwar period (1946–47), with lesser peaks coming early in World War II (1941) and the Korean War (1950). The rank correlation between annual

[15] Indeed, excluding 1938, the prewar trough, the latter average is 7.25 per cent.

rates of investment and the current annual rates of return in all manufactures was .67 for the eighteen-year period 1939 to 1956.[16]

What use was made of higher rates of return to obtain the vast expansion of the munitions industries during the war? The facts are given in the tabulation below.

	Average Rate of Return (per cent)	
Year	All Industries	Munitions[a]
1941	8.56	8.52
1942	7.30	7.39
1943	7.30	7.20
1944	6.59	6.65
1945	5.43	5.11
1946	8.13	–2.65

[a] Ships, aircraft, firearms, ammunition, tanks, sighting and firing equipment, munitions, n.e.c.

Among the many limitations of our data, one is especially important at this point: the rates of return are calculated upon end-of-year assets rather than average (or possibly mid-year) assets. When the rate of growth of assets was very high—and in the munitions industries it was reported as 356 per cent in 1942—the rate of return is seriously underestimated. The previous year-end assets are not strictly comparable to the current year-end assets because of the shifting of companies but, taking the data at face value, the rates of return may be recalculated on a mid-year asset basis. On the assumption that the increase of assets was linear, the adjusted rates of return will be as shown below.[17]

Year	*Rate of Return in Munitions Industries on Midyear Assets* (per cent)
1941	11.67
1942	12.12
1943	9.65
1944	6.18
1945	4.39

The effects of the adjustment are very marked: the rate of return is much higher in the earlier years, and somewhat lower in 1944 and 1945. If

[16] There is little evidence, in these aggregative data, of any relationship between the rate of investment and the profit rate of the preceding year ($\rho = .33$ for 1939 to 1954).

[17] That is, let A_0 and A_1 be assets at the beginning and end of year respectively, and R income. Then we can calculate $R/\frac{1}{2}(A_0 + A_1)$. A constant geometric rate of increase of assets would perhaps be more plausible.

proper allowance could be made for accelerated depreciation, the rate would be appreciably higher in the two latter years. Our data therefore do not deny that extensive use was made of profit incentives in the mobilization of resources during the war.

DISPERSION OF RATES OF RETURN

The unweighted average rate of return of individual industries followed a course closely similar to that of all manufacturing, but was generally higher during the war period and lower in the postwar period (Table 11).[18]

TABLE 11

DISPERSION OF RATES OF RETURN IN MANUFACTURING INDUSTRIES, 1938–57

Year	Number of Industries	Average Rate (per cent)	Standard Deviation (per cent)	*Quartile* Q_1 (per cent)	*Quartile* Q_3 (per cent)
1938	82	2.72	3.31	0.50	4.25
1939	82	6.21	3.16	4.11	7.69
1940	82	6.80	2.96	4.75	8.21
1941	82	8.49	2.37	6.86	9.85
1942	82	7.56	1.91	6.13	8.68
1943	82	7.40	2.02	6.19	8.56
1944	82	6.95	1.97	5.73	8.18
1945	82	6.18	1.99	5.03	7.50
1946	82	10.29	4.31	7.38	13.25
1947	82	10.93	3.01	8.92	12.68
1947	99	10.29	4.26	8.15	12.54
1948	99	9.40	3.22	6.97	11.89
1949	99	6.93	3.01	4.97	8.69
1950	99	9.07	2.58	7.44	10.81
1951	99	6.37	2.43	5.19	8.23
1953	99	5.16	2.12	4.05	6.61
1954	99	4.86	2.33	3.41	6.45
1955	99	6.34	2.40	4.85	8.81
1956	99	6.17	2.18	4.67	7.75
1957	99	5.41	2.49	3.79	6.94

NOTE: Calculations are based on three-digit industries. The average, unlike that of Table 10, excludes certain industries (munitions, and industries that could not be adjusted for reclassification of large companies).

SOURCE: Tables A-14 to A-59.

Aside from the initial depression year the rates never averaged below 4.9 per cent, and in all but five years fell between 6 and 10 per cent.

But the dispersion of industry rates was very great; the annual distributions are displayed in the panels of Chart 3. The dispersion was least in 1942–45, under the impact of very heavy corporate taxes but, these

[18] The averages are restricted to the "basic" set of industries, excluding munitions and industries excessively affected by reclassification of firms, described on p. 111.

CHART 3

Frequency Distribution of Manufacturing Industries, by Annual Rate of Return, 1938–57

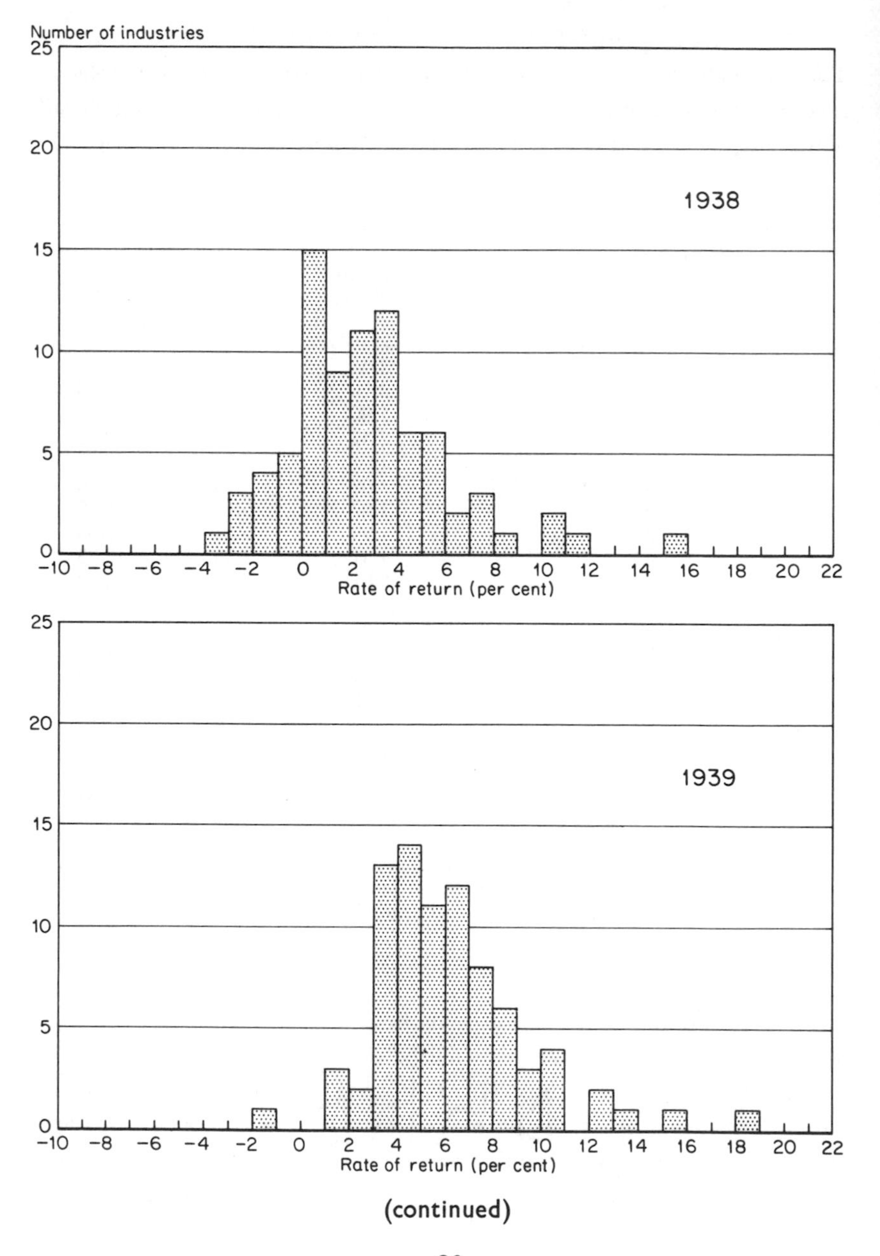

(continued)

CHART 3 (continued)

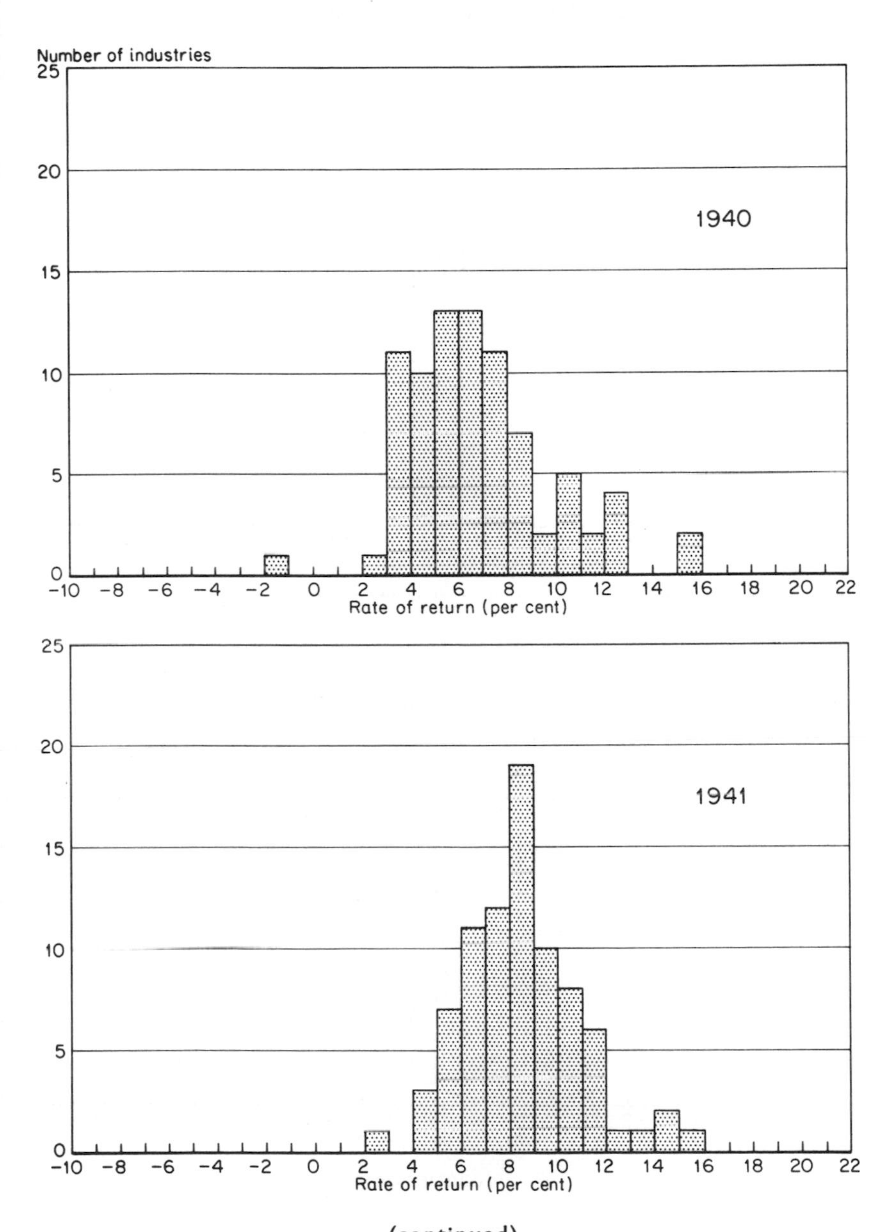

(continued)

CHART 3 (continued)

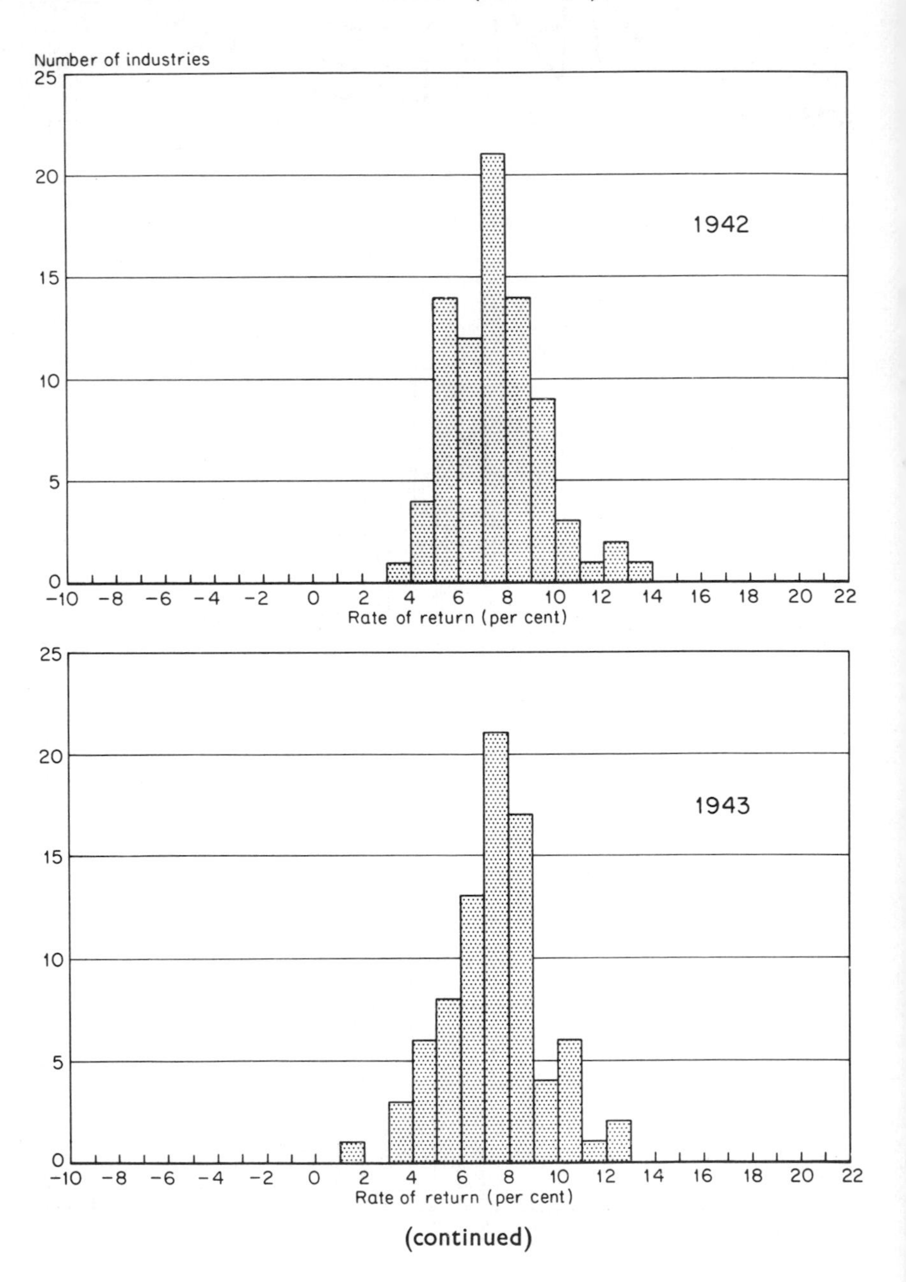

(continued)

CHART 3 (continued)

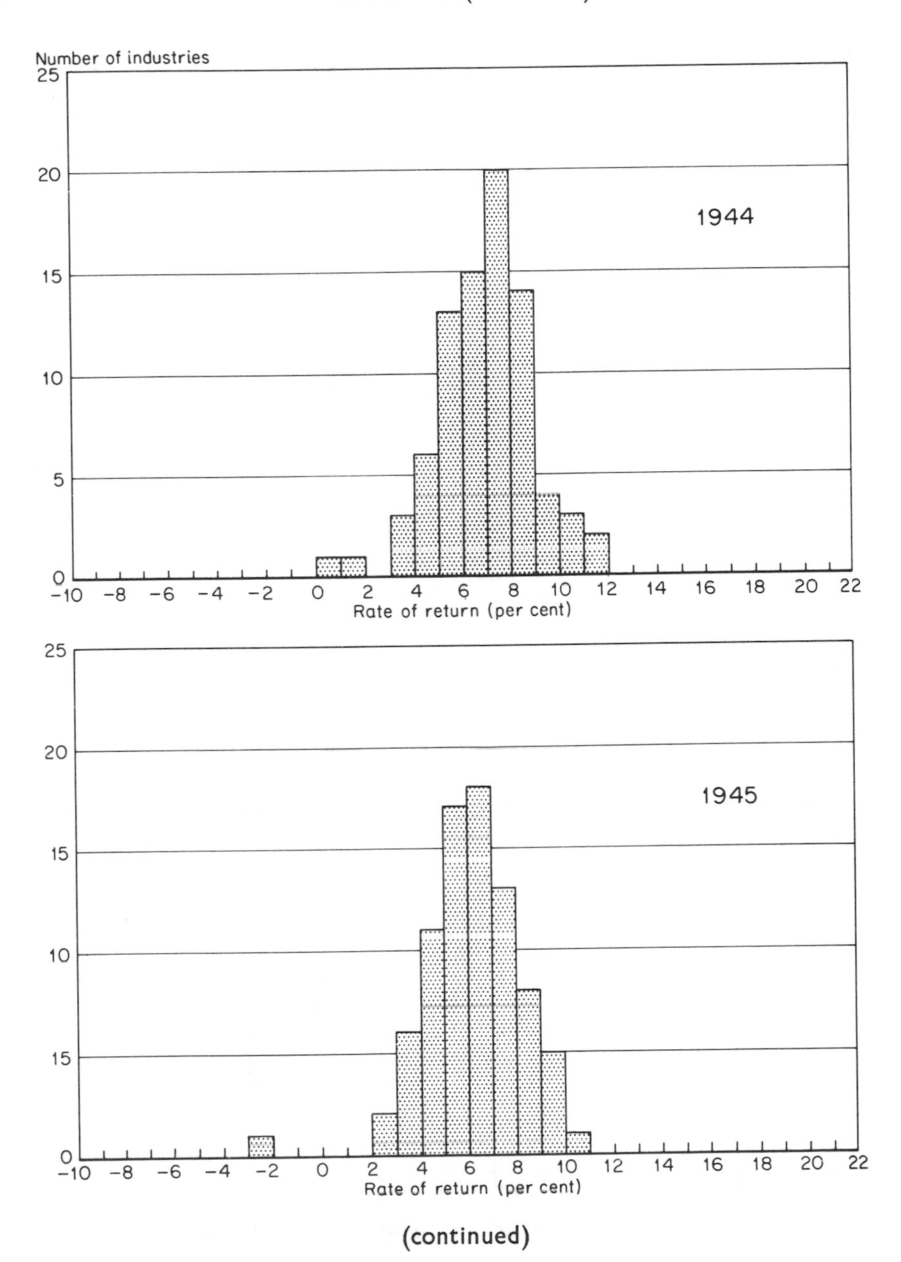

(continued)

CHART 3 (continued)

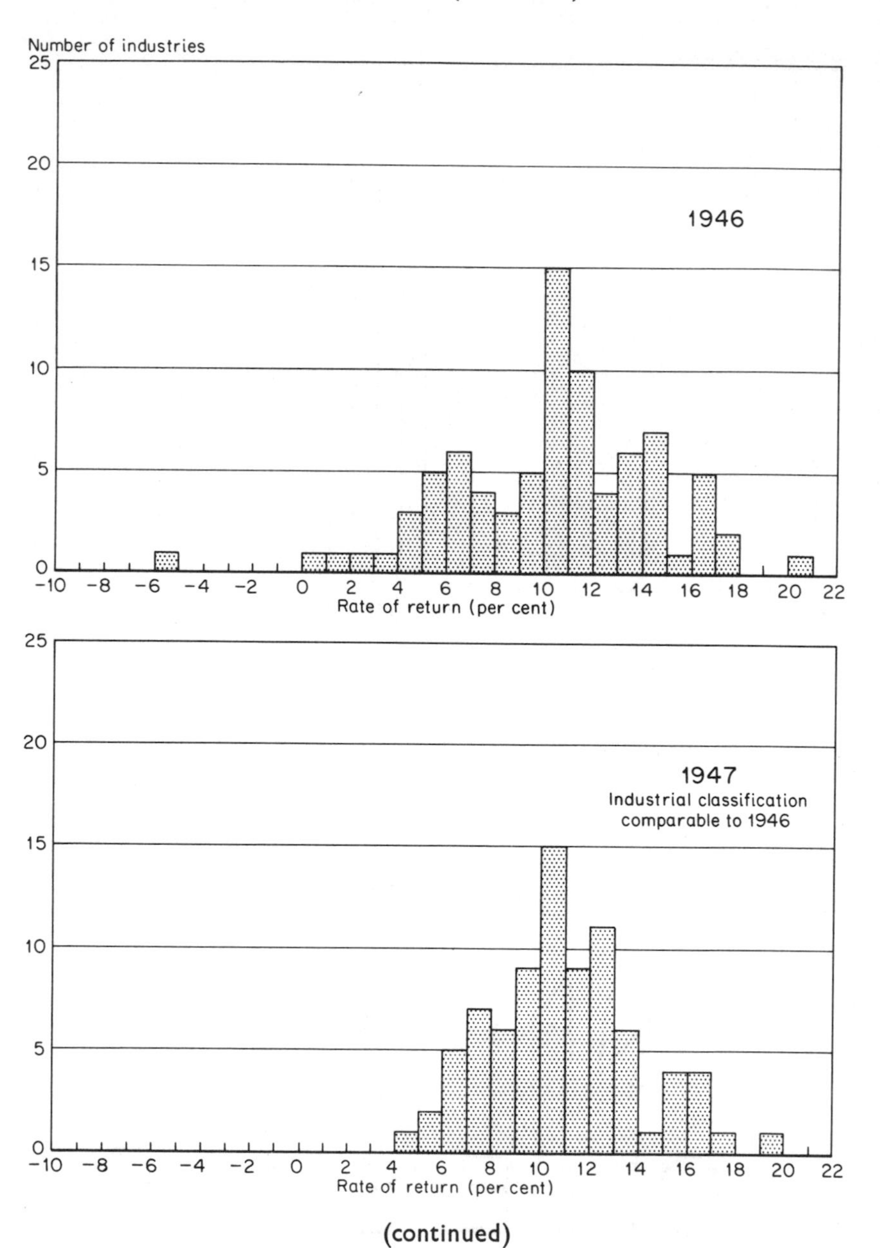

(continued)

CHART 3 (continued)

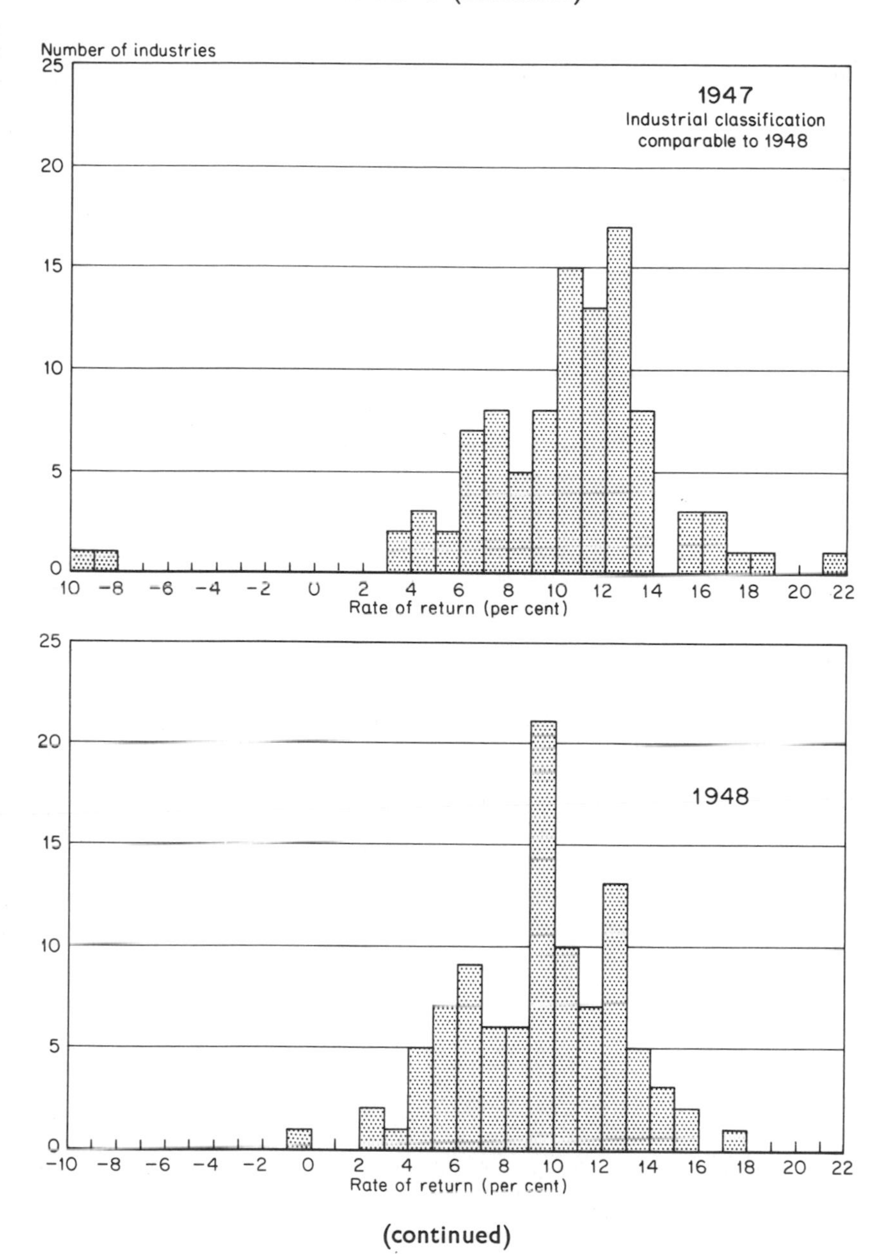

(continued)

CHART 3 (continued)

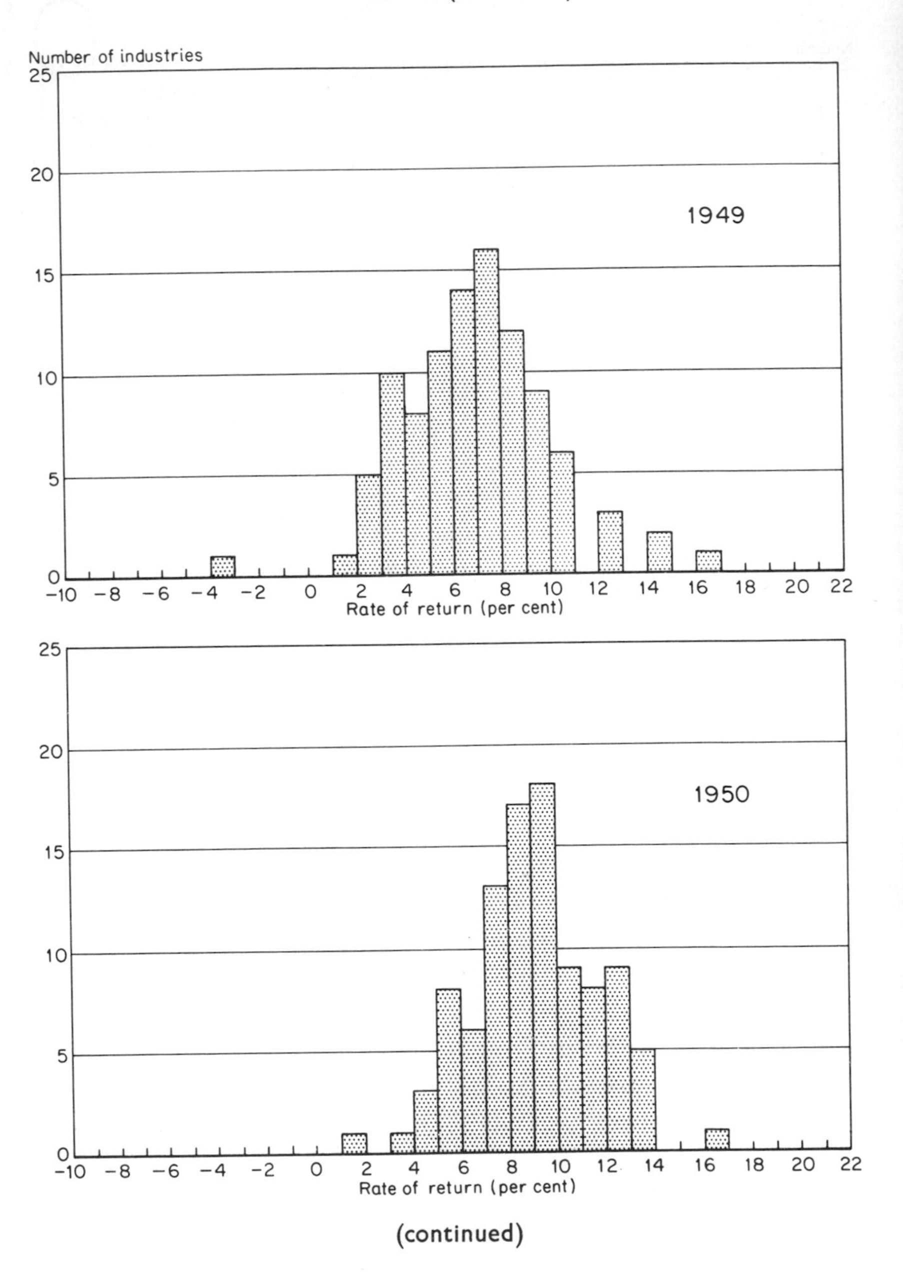

(continued)

CHART 3 (continued)

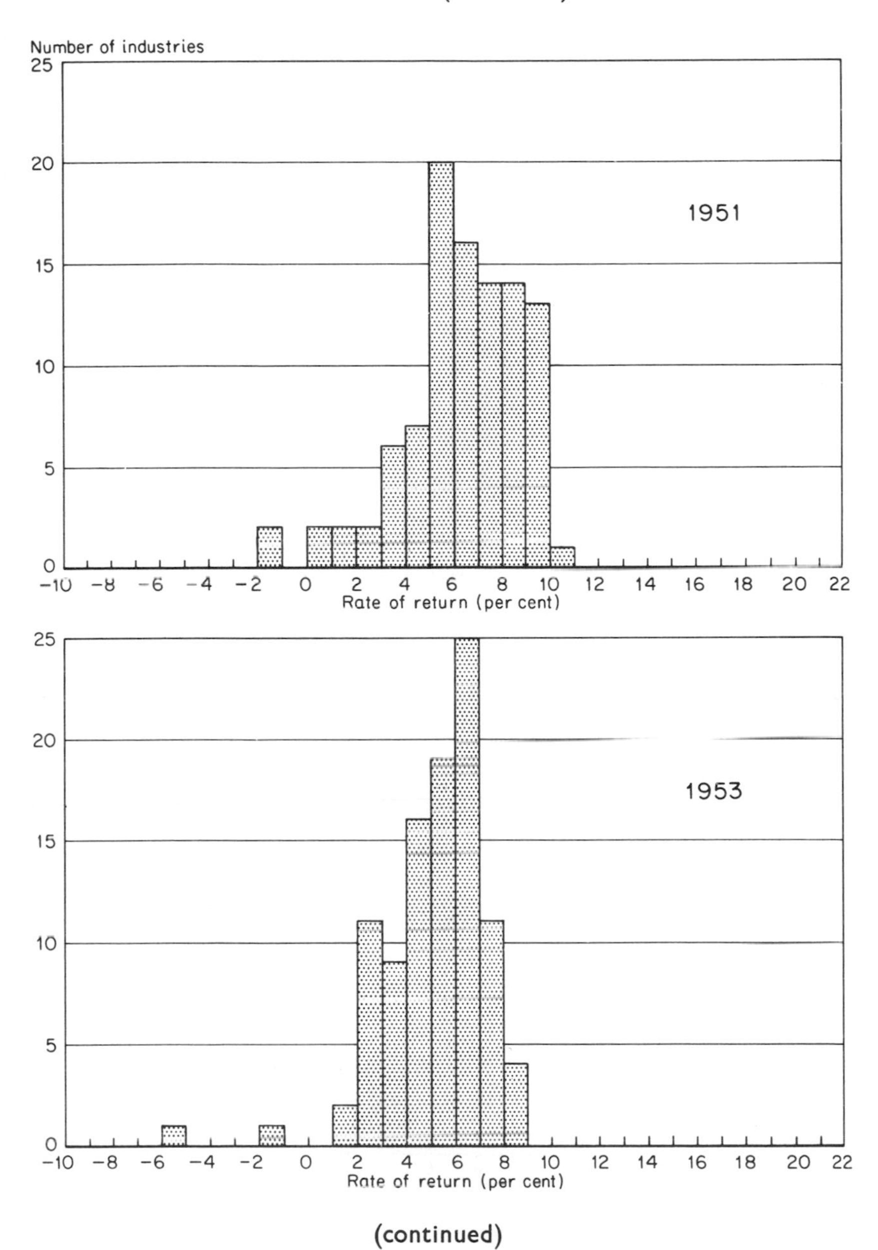

(continued)

CHART 3 (continued)

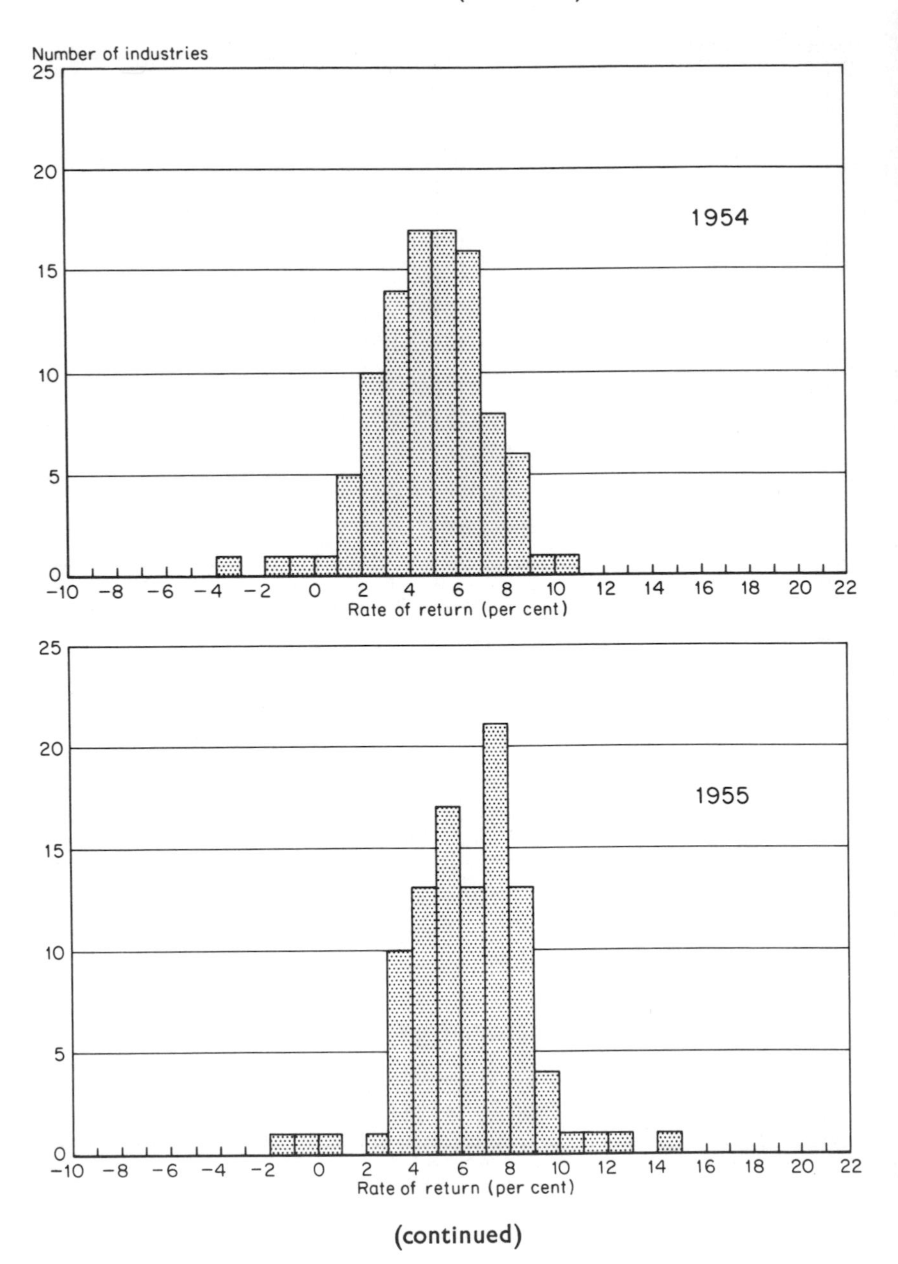

(continued)

CHART 3 (concluded)

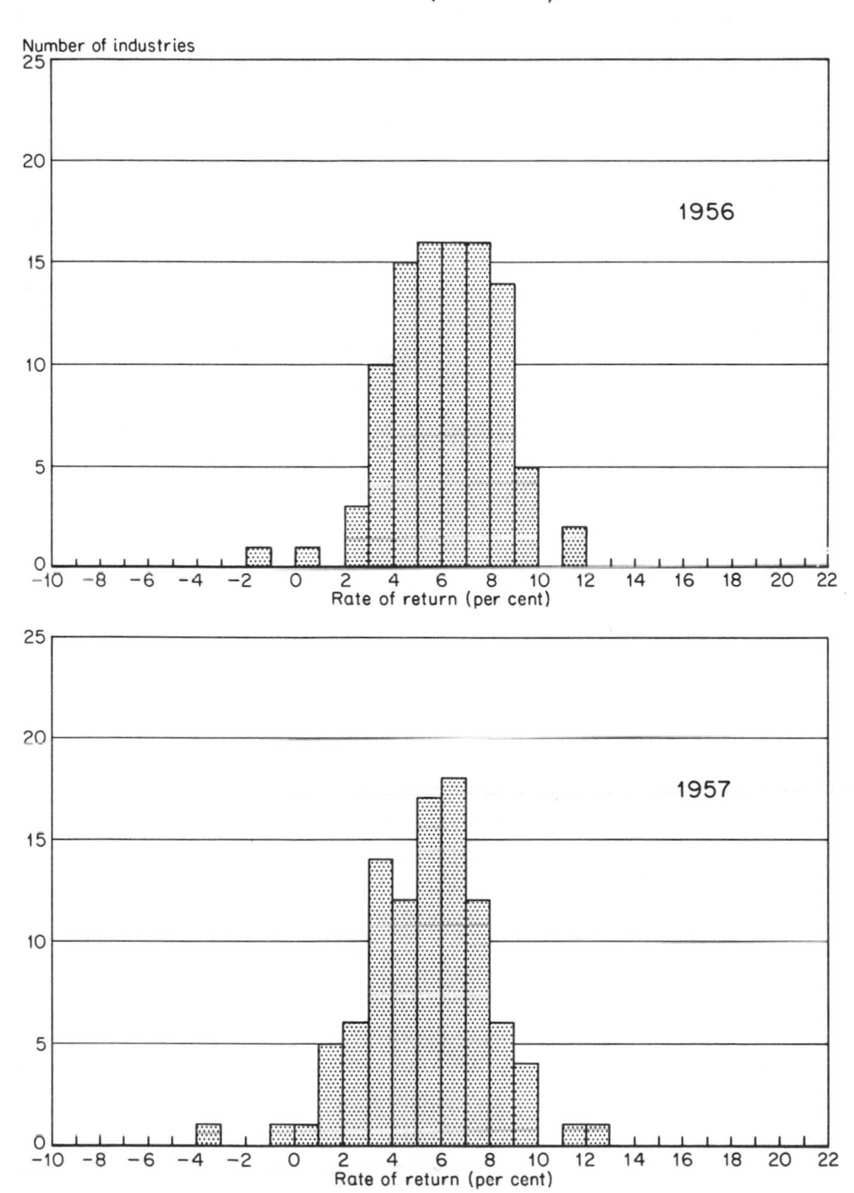

Source: Tables A-14 to A-59.

years aside, the standard deviation always exceeded 2 per cent. The empirical significance of the famous theorem that the rates of return tend to equality under competition, and the relevance of our data to this theorem, are discussed in detail in the next chapter.

These dispersions refer, of course, to interindustry differences in rates of return, and each industry average represents the weighted average of the firms' rates of return, ranging from 30 (cereals) to 6,989 (women's apparel) individual returns in 1950. For another purpose, described in Chapter 3, estimates were made of the dispersion of rates of return among firms within an industry,[19] and they are much larger. The standard deviations (calculated from 22 two-digit industry classes) in 1954, for example, are shown in the tabulation below.

Asset Class ($000's)	Standard Deviation (per cent) Minimum	Maximum	Median
0–50	18.6	37.0	23.4
50–100	11.4	48.4	15.8
100–250	10.2	20.2	14.4
250–500	8.6	22.1	12.0
500–1,000	7.8	17.9	12.3
1,000–5,000	7.5	18.7	11.4
5,000–10,000	6.1	16.3	10.0
10,000–50,000	6.6	14.2	9.3

Similar estimates for other years consistently shared both characteristics of these standard deviations: the absolute level was high, and it fell quite steadily as the size of the enterprise increased.

THE INDUSTRIAL PATTERN OF RATES OF RETURN

The industrial pattern of annual rates of increase of capital was found to be unstable over time, in considerable (and perhaps dominant) part because of measurement errors. The industrial pattern of rates of return, on the contrary, is relatively stable from year to year (Table 12): in every pair of years the correlation coefficient is highly significant. Aside from the years of demobilization after World War II, the coefficients are, in fact, always above .6 and average more than .7.[20] In the next chapter

[19] See Chapter 3, footnote 14.

[20] The statistical sources of instability that obscure the pattern of investment rates have much less influence upon the rates of return. A reclassification of companies, for example, will have at most a minor effect on an industry's rate of return because income is reclassified with assets.

TABLE 12

CORRELATION BETWEEN RATES OF RETURN IN MANUFACTURING INDUSTRIES IN SUCCESSIVE YEARS, 1938–57

Pair of Years	Number of Industries	Correlation Coefficient
1938 and 1939	82	.769
1939 and 1940	82	.848
1940 and 1941	82	.803
1941 and 1942	82	.782
1942 and 1943	82	.730
1943 and 1944	82	.885
1944 and 1945	82	.776
1945 and 1946	82	.494
1946 and 1947	82	.468
1947 and 1948	99	.689
1948 and 1949	99	.626
1949 and 1950	99	.677
1950 and 1951	99	.775
1951 and 1953	99	.738
1953 and 1954	99	.828
1954 and 1955	99	.826
1955 and 1956	99	.808
1956 and 1957	99	.790

the stability of the industry pattern over longer periods of time is explored.

The pattern is in general more stable—the correlation coefficients are larger—the less the dispersion of rates of return (see Table 11). During the war years, the dispersion of rates fell to a very low level due to heavy taxation, and the correlations of successive years were high; conversely in 1945–47, the dispersion of rates reached a peak and the correlations a trough. There is apparently a strong tendency toward at least short-run persistence of interindustry differentials in rates of return, and only very heavy impacts on this structure, arising out of major and sudden shifts of resources, are able to weaken this tendency appreciably. The implications of this characteristic for investment behavior are discussed in Chapter 4.

3. *Investment and Returns in Book Values Versus Stable Prices*

Throughout this chapter we have quietly assumed that changes in asset value were to be interpreted as changes in the volume of capital resources disposed of by an industry. Yet the period was one of inflation—and of substantial magnitude—upon which were superimposed highly diverse movements of individual prices. How can we know whether the industrial pattern of movement of book values of assets reflects movement of resources rather than of asset prices?

In order to give at least a partial answer to this question, deflated capital values have been calculated for the major industrial categories in each year.[21] Although corresponding price deflators for three-digit industries require assumptions that seem seriously unreasonable, the comparative behavior of "real" and book-value assets for the broader groups sheds considerable light on the effects of price movements.

A direct comparison of annual percentage increases in book-value and "real" assets yields very favorable results on the whole (Table 13). In

TABLE 13

CORRELATION OF PERCENTAGE CHANGE IN ASSETS, IN BOOK VALUES AND 1947 PRICES, MANUFACTURING INDUSTRIES, 1938–57

Year and Period	Coefficient of Rank Correlation
1938–39	.901
1939–40	.944
1940–41	.962
1941–42	.949
1942–43	.937
1943–44	.964
1944–45	.998
1945–46	.935
1946–47	.797
1947–48	.870
1948–49	.928
1949–50	.921
1950–51	.927
1951–52	.996
1952–53	.877
1953–54	.815
1954–55	.962
1955–56	.956
1956–57[a]	.940
1938–41	.979
1941–44	.965
1944–47	.945
1947–50	.989
1950–53	.950
1953–56	.963

NOTE: Based upon 20 two-digit industries through 1947, and 22 two-digit industries thereafter.

[a] For percentage changes in corporate assets only.

15 of 19 annual comparisons, the rank correlation exceeds .9 and in no year does it fall below .8. Moreover, if we compare movements over three-year periods, the correlations are all above .94. The deflation

[21] See Appendix A.

leaves the ranking of industrial categories by rates of increase of assets almost unchanged.

There is good reason to believe that a similar result would hold for minor industries if we could deflate the assets data. If we denote assets by A, and price indexes by P, the relative increase in book values from year 1 to year 2 is A_2/A_1, whereas the deflated relative increase is

$$\frac{A_2}{P_2}\Big/\frac{A_1}{P_1} = \frac{A_2}{A_1}\Big/\frac{P_1}{P_2}.$$

If we let

$$a = \log A_2/A_1$$
$$b = \log P_2/P_1$$

then we wish to know the correlation between a and $(a + b)$. Let a' and b' be the deviations of a and b from their means. Then

$$r_{a(a+b)} = \frac{\Sigma a'(a' + b')}{\sqrt{\Sigma(a')^2\,\Sigma(a' + b')^2}}$$
$$= \frac{N\sigma_a^2 + N\sigma_a\sigma_b r_{ab}}{N\sigma_a(\sigma_a^2 + \sigma_b^2 + 2\sigma_a\sigma_b r_{ab})^{1/2}}$$
$$= \frac{\sigma_a + \sigma_b r_{ab}}{(\sigma_a^2 + \sigma_b^2 + 2\sigma_a\sigma_b r_{ab})^{1/2}}.$$

If r_{ab} is small—if the movements of book values and price deflators are not closely correlated—

$$r_{a(a+b)} = \frac{1}{\left(1 + \frac{\sigma_b^2}{\sigma_a^2}\right)^{\frac{1}{2}}}, \text{ approximately,}$$

that is, increases in book values will be closely correlated with movements in deflated values, providing the standard deviation of the rates of price increase among industries is much smaller than the standard deviation of the rates of increase of assets in book values, and the two are not highly correlated. These conditions appear to hold.

The correlations between percentage change in book-value assets and percentage change in price deflators are usually fairly small for the two-digit industrial groups; and they are possibly smaller among the three-digit industries.[22] The variance of the percentage increases in capital is

[22] The correlation coefficients for the two-digit groups are:

1938–41	.152
1941–44	.202
1944–47	−.057
1947–50	.619
1950–54	.255

many times the variance of the price ratios for the two-digit groups.[23] We know the variance of the percentage rates of increase in the assets of minor industries is much larger than that of the major industrial groups. The price deflators are in good part (i.e., with respect to durable assets and working capital) based upon prices common to many industries, and in general one does not expect fairly broad price indexes appropriate to the deflation of assets of industries to display the diversity that rates of investment show.

TABLE 14

COMPARISON OF RATE OF RETURN, IN BOOK VALUES AND 1947 PRICES, TWO-DIGIT INDUSTRIES, SELECTED YEARS, 1938–56

Year	*Unweighted Average Rate of Return* Book Values (per cent)	1947 Prices	Coefficient of Rank Correlation	Average Absolute Deviation Between Book-Value Rate and 1947 Rate (per cent)
1938	2.87	2.88	.998	.20
1947	9.94	9.51	.968	.60
1954	5.50	6.04	.955	.53
1956	6.51	7.38	.963	.87

SOURCE: Tables A-14 to A-59.

These arguments apply much more weakly to comparisons of relative increases of assets at different times. A rise in book values of 1 per cent in 1933 would represent a larger increase in assets than a rise of 10 per cent in 1947 would (when the average price index rose 10.8 per cent). In our period, however, the movements of asset prices were sufficiently steady, so the general order of magnitude of the rates of increase of book values is fairly similar to those for deflated values; the rank coefficient of correlation for the two series in Table 3 is .895 for the period 1938–54.

The rates of return have been calculated in 1947 prices as well as in book values.[24] The agreement between the two, at the level of the major

The derivative of $r_{a(a+b)}$ with respect to (r_{ab}) has the sign of

$$\sigma_b/\sigma_a - r_{ab}.$$

Hence $r_{a(a+b)}$ will be decreased if r_{ab} is positive and moderately large.

[23] The variances are:

	σ^2_a	σ^2_b
1938–41	240.8	10.0
1941–44	2,195.5	41.6
1944–47	2,423.1	45.8
1947–50	161.2	3.5
1950–54	518.8	19.9

[24] In addition, rates of return were calculated in current prices (see Appendix A).

industrial groups, is in general very close (see the rank correlations in Table 14). The absolute levels of the two series are also fairly close, since we deflate income as well as assets: the absolute difference in rates in 1947 prices and book values averaged .38 percentage points during the period 1938–57.

CHAPTER 3

Competition and the Rate of Return

THERE is no more important proposition in economic theory than that, under competition, the rate of return on investment tends toward equality in all industries. Entrepreneurs will seek to leave relatively unprofitable industries and enter relatively profitable industries, and with competition there will be neither public nor private barriers to these movements. This mobility of capital is crucial to the efficiency and growth of the economy: in a world of unending change in types of products that consumers and businesses and governments desire, in methods of producing given products, and in the relative availabilities of various resources—in such a world the immobility of resources would lead to catastrophic inefficiency.[1]

Movements of capital are presumably dominated by the prospective rate of return to the owners of the capital. An entrepreneur will seek to maximize the present value of his equity in the enterprise. If he is dealing with competitive capital markets—markets which lend or borrow funds at interest rates (for given risks) which are constant to the individual entrepreneur—he will hold any type of investment up to the point where the last increment yields a rate of return equal to the market interest rate.

Lenders (whether short or long term) will act on the same principle: they will seek a maximum rate of return (for given risks), and in this respect they differ from entrepreneurs only in having less taste for risk.[2] But many lenders take large risks and many entrepreneurs take fairly small risks, so it is difficult clearly to distinguish the groups. The owner of American Telephone and Telegraph common stock functions more as a lender, in terms of risks and managerial responsibilities, than the owner of a convertible debenture in a mining company does. This fuzziness is in

[1] A considerable amount of mobility of resources is necessary even in the absence of changes in the size of industries required by changing tastes, resources, and technologies. Members of the labor force change their occupations and often their industries, partly as an expression of changing personal tastes, partly as a result of increasing age and knowledge. There is a similar movement of specific capital goods among industries, although it is presumably smaller because capital goods have shorter lives and are usually more specialized than workers are. Movement of baseball players over forty to other occupations, and sale of used cars by car rental agencies are instances of these movements. Since we have information only on net movements of aggregates of resources, we cannot trace the movements of individual resources.

[2] They also differ in having less desire to engage in management of a firm where this is required by the entrepreneurial role, as in farming. But this difference (like the taste for risk) is only a matter of degree: the lender must have some knowledge of the borrower's abilities and character; the entrepreneur must have some knowledge (no doubt, often more detailed) of the men he hires to manage his enterprise.

fact one reason for combining entrepreneurial income and interest on debt into a single return on capital in our statistical work.

Our primary object in this chapter is to examine the traditional theory of the effect of competition upon the rates of return in different industries in the light of empirical evidence. Then we examine differences between concentrated and unconcentrated industries in rates of return.

1. *Competition and Equality of Rates of Return*

What is the nature of the proposition that under competition there is a tendency for the rates of return on investments in various industries to approach equality? It has been taken by some economists as a *definition* of competition; persistently high profits in an industry would be proof that the industry is not competitive. But this usage is one-sided: no one would argue that the existence of the average rate of return in an industry proved that the industry is competitive.

More commonly, the proposition is viewed as a corollary of the main conditions of competition: a considerable number of firms (no one or few dominant in size) in the industry, and freedom of these firms to leave or of other firms to enter the industry. When competition is so defined, the proposition is evidently not a logically necessary corollary, for a lack of desire for profits or a lack of knowledge of returns in alternative ventures could render any tendency toward equality of rates so negligible as to be wholly unimportant. From this point of view, given the conditions of adequate numbers of firms and freedom of entry, the role of empirical data is to reveal the degree of knowledge, foresight, and enterprise possessed by entrepreneurs.

The role of the word "tendency" raises further issues. Economic analysis tells us that the rates of return in competitive industries will be strictly equal (in a sense to be noted shortly) in *long-run equilibrium*, that is, after a period long enough to allow (enough) entrepreneurs to move to the industry they favor and operate at the rate of output they desire. But this very concept of long-run equilibrium reminds us that, in a world where all events are not perfectly anticipated, there will be a stream of unexpected disturbances that call for a stream of changes in the allocation of resources: unanticipated shifts in consumers' desires; the impact upon international markets of wars and political events; the irregular march of major advances in technology, and others.

One could argue that these unexpected events are so frequent and so drastic in their effects that long before full adjustments have been made to one impact—before long-run equilibrium could be regained—a second large impact would superimpose reactions on the allocation of capital, and so on. At a given moment, we might observe in an industry:

1. Beginnings of an extensive investment program designed to provide a component to another industry which has just received vast orders from the Department of Defense
2. Continuation of an earlier investment program initiated in response to the discovery five years ago of large new deposits of resources
3. Retirement of capital goods rendered increasingly obsolete (but not yet physically worn out) by the introduction of much superior machines eight years ago

Neither of the earlier impacts will have been fully adjusted to when the recent expansion called for by military demands begins and, long before the new impulse is adjusted to, several new and large displacements of long-run equilibrium may have occurred.

If this were the case—if such unexpected and large disturbances occurred frequently within the period necessary to bring about a reasonably full adjustment to just one disturbance—the equality of rates of return would never be approached even distantly. Almost any amount of dispersion of rates of return in competitive industries would be consistent with the basic theoretical proposition, and it would lose most of its value. More precisely, if the effects of unexpected events on rates of return were very much larger and more persistent than the effects of competition were, the proposition on equality of rates would have almost no value in predicting the direction of investment.

I do not believe this is true: the large unexpected events are not so frequent relative to the speed with which competition equalizes rates as this argument implies (and the smaller events will largely cancel each other). This is an empirical question, however, and one to which we shall soon turn.

Finally, the strict reading of the proposition on equality of rates of return is that the returns entrepreneurs equalize are the total of all advantages and disadvantages—nonmonetary as well as monetary—of using resources in various fields. An example of such possible nonmonetary returns is the pleasures of rural life associated with farming; if they are widely and strongly appreciated, the equilibrium rate of return in agriculture would be lower than in other industries. Another example, more appropriate to our manufacturing universe, is the possible premiums demanded for investing in very risky industries. Risk premiums are indeed regarded in the literature of capital allocation as the chief supplement to average returns, although tax considerations are becoming an important rival. The fact that investment decisions depend upon more than the expected number of dollars of return is therefore still another source of dispersion in the realized rates of return. We should like to know the quantitative magnitude of this source of dispersion and to identify its source.

Let us now draw together these threads of discussion. We expect the rates of return in a set of competitive industries (defined independently of returns) to approach equality, but subject to several qualifications:

1. Some dispersion would exist because of imperfect knowledge of returns on alternative investments.
2. Dispersion of returns would arise because of unexpected developments and events which call for movements of resources requiring considerable time to be completed.
3. Dispersion would arise because of differences among industries in monetary and nonmonetary supplements to the average rate of return.
4. In any empirical study, there is also a fourth source of dispersion: the difference between the income concepts used in compiling the data and the income concepts relevant to the allocation of resources.

Before we turn to these various sources of dispersion, it is well to present the basic data on the rates of return. The distribution of the average rates for the periods 1938–47 and 1947–56 are presented in Table 15.[3] In each case the list of industries is restricted to the "unconcentrated" ones. This word is not a euphemism for "competitive" because it takes account (and then, none too well) of only one requisite of competition: the presence of numerous independent firms (none dominant in size) in the industry.[4] The condition of free entry, which is also a requisite of competition, is not taken into account because relevant data are not at hand, but there is some presumption that industries containing many firms are relatively free of contrived barriers to entry. (The rates of return in other than unconcentrated industries are considered later.)

The concentration of rates of return within narrow limits is quite marked

[3] The distribution for 1947–54 is also reported because it is used subsequently.

[4] The precise criteria of the class of unconcentrated industries turn on the "concentration ratio," that is, the fraction of the "shipments" of each industry produced by the four largest firms. This ratio is averaged for 1935 and 1947 for the earlier period, and for 1947 and 1954 for the later period. Unconcentrated industries meet one of two conditions: (1) the market is national, and the concentration ratio is less than 50 per cent; (2) the market is regional, and the concentration ratio is less than 20 per cent. The limitations of the measure are discussed in Appendix C.

TABLE 15

Distribution of Unconcentrated Manufacturing Industries, by Average Rate of Return, Three Periods, 1938–56

Average Rate of Return (per cent)	*Number of Industries* 1938–47	1947–54	1947–56
0–1	—	1	1
1–2	—	—	—
2–3	1	—	1
3–4	—	3	5
4–5	2	6	5
5–6	6	8	7
6–7	5	7	11
7–8	16	10	9
8–9	6	10	10
9–10	3	7	6
10–11	3	5	2
11–12	1	—	—
Total	43	57	57
Mean rate	7.43	7.10	6.73
Standard deviation	1.63	2.18	2.12
Coefficient of variation (per cent)	21.90	30.70	31.50

Source: Tables A-14 to A-59.

in the first period, and somewhat less so in the second period. The more protracted impact of extremely heavy corporate excess-profits taxation in the earlier period is doubtless a major cause of the smaller dispersion. Our task is to relate the traditional theorem on equalization of rates of return to these distributions.

STATISTICAL SOURCES OF DISPERSION IN RATES OF RETURN

The basic data of our study have a variety of defects which are discussed in detail in Chapter 1 and Appendix A. Perhaps the three most important defects for present purposes are those discussed below.

1. *The concept of income appropriate to the economic theory of resource allocation differs substantially from the concept underlying the corporate income tax.*

The most pervasive difference is that, in economic theory, a productive service is valued at its maximum product in any alternative use, whereas corporate income tax rules usually require that costs be actually (historically) incurred. Putting aside the effects of inflation (discussed below), we may say that, in a highly stable period, the historical costs of a firm should approximate the alternative products (or costs) in competitive industries: the firm will not acquire or retain resources that are more valuable in other uses. But the condition for equality of historical and alternative costs is very severe: the period of stability must be as long as the life of the most durable assets in the industry. The short-lived assets (such as inventories) will differ in historical cost from market values unless the period of stability is also one of rigidity, and the average difference between the two values will approach zero only over many accounting periods. In addition, there are a host of technical provisions of the tax regulations (and of general accounting practices) that have very uneven impact on different industries.[5] It would require an independent investigation of immense scope to ascertain the magnitude of this source of dispersion of rates of return, and we must be content simply to note its existence.

2. *Officers of small corporations who own much of the stock have considerable discretion in withdrawing income either as salaries or as returns on capital, but only the latter form of income enters our rates of return.*

There exists no satisfactory direct method of estimating "excess" salary withdrawals,[6] but we know that the problem is quantitatively important only in industries in which corporations with less than $250,000 of assets are relatively numerous. It is suggestive that the industry with the lowest rate of return for 1938–47, millinery (4.67 per cent), had 91.7 per cent of its corporate assets in the smallest asset classes. We have correlated average rates of return R with the percentage of industry receipts in companies having less than $250,000 of assets P.[7]

1938–47 period:

$$R = 7.566 - 0.0277\,P$$
$$r = -0.267 \quad (n = 82)$$

1947–54 period:

$$R = 8.237 - 0.0792\,P$$
$$r = -0.435 \quad (n = 99)$$

The reduction in dispersion is appreciable: the rates of return before and

[5] See D. T. Smith and J. K. Butters, *Taxable and Business Income*, New York, National Bureau of Economic Research, 1949.

[6] See Appendix A.

[7] P has been calculated for one year only in each period: 1943 in the 1938–47 period, and 1950 in 1947–54. The correlations are based upon all industries, rather than only unconcentrated industries, because this relationship should be present in all. However, here, as elsewhere in this chapter with the exception of Tables 15 and 16, those industries with severe large-company classification problems have been eliminated from the computations. These exclusions are described on p. 111.

TABLE 16

DISTRIBUTION OF UNCONCENTRATED INDUSTRIES, BY RATE OF RETURN, BEFORE AND AFTER ADJUSTMENT FOR SMALL BUSINESS SALARY WITHDRAWALS, TWO PERIODS, 1938–54

Average Rate of Return (per cent)	*Number of Industries* 1938–47 Original	1938–47 Adjusted	1947–54 Original	1947–54 Adjusted
0–1			1	
1–2				
2–3	1			2
3–4		1	3	3
4–5	2	2	6	2
5–6	6	3	8	6
6–7	5	10	7	14
7–8	16	14	10	11
8–9	6	7	10	8
9–10	3	3	7	11
10–11	3	2	5	
11–12	1	1		
Total	43	43	57	57
Mean	7.43	7.43	7.10	7.10
Standard deviation	1.63	1.48	2.18	1.80
Coefficient of variation (per cent)	21.90	19.90	30.70	25.40

NOTE: See the accompanying text for explanation of the method of computation.

after adjustment for the varying share of "small" businesses are given in Table 16.

A simple interpretation of the regression equation may be offered. Let P and R be defined as above, and let the subscripts u and l denote the asset classes above and below $250,000.

Then:

$$R = (1 - P)R_u + PR_l.$$

If W is the withdrawal of salaries by officers in the lower size class, b the fraction of withdrawals that are "excessive" (i.e., really property income), and I_l and A_l the respective property income and assets of this class, the true rate of return of the industry is:

$$R_t = \frac{(bW + I_l)}{A_l} P + (1 - P)R_u$$

$$= \left(b \frac{W}{I_l} + 1\right) R_l P + (1 - P)R_u$$

$$= R + b \frac{W}{I_l} R_l P$$

$$\text{or} \quad R = R_t - b \frac{W}{I_l} R_l P$$

If we equate the coefficient of P in the last term to .0792 and apply the equation to the men's clothing industry (see Appendix A), b is .47. Of course when this equation is estimated from a group of industries, it is implicitly assumed that the true rate of return is not correlated with P, i.e., it is assumed that the equilibrium rate of return is not lower in industries with a larger proportion of small businesses. We examine this question later.

Omission of noncorporate businesses from the calculations of the rates of return is a closely related source of dispersion. It is quite possibly an important source of dispersion because of the wide variations among industries in the relative importance within them of noncorporate businesses. If the noncorporate sector of an industry is declining, we can infer that its rate of return (including nonmonetary elements) is smaller than the return in the corporate sector and, conversely, that the rate is higher if the noncorporate sector is growing relatively. But an analysis of variance revealed no significant association of the share or trend of the noncorporate sector with the average rate of return of the corporate sector.

The noncorporate profit rate may also influence the average industry rate by fluctuating more or less over time. If we may judge the fluctuations of the noncorporate rate by that of small corporations, it is in fact somewhat more stable over time, so the average industry rate over time would also be more stable if we could measure noncorporate profits.[8]

3. *The asset values on which rates of return are calculated have not been adjusted for price changes.*

An industry that has relatively old assets will have a relatively smaller asset-value base in a period of inflation, and hence a relatively larger rate of return.[9] The period of our study was continuously inflationary in the sense that the book values of assets rose in every year relative to their values in 1947 prices. The difference between rates of return in constant prices and in book values was not large for the two-digit industries, however (see Chapter 2, section 3).

The only possible direct measure of the effect of price deflation of assets and returns on the dispersion of the rates of return is a comparison of the

[8] The standard deviations of the annual rates of return for 1947–57 are, in per cent:

	Corporations with Assets	
	Under $100,000	Over $100,000
All manufacturing	1.46	1.84
Food and kindred products	1.38	1.36
Apparel and related products	2.06	2.75

[9] Such a firm will also be charging depreciation on assets valued at lower prices, which works in the same direction.

two distributions for the broad two-digit industry groups, shown in the tabulation below.

	1938–47	*1947–54*
	(per cent)	
Average rate of return		
1947 prices	6.81	7.73
Book values	7.07	7.54
Standard deviation of rates		
1947 prices	1.23	1.54
Book values	1.17	1.66

The deflated rates of return thus show a larger dispersion in one period and a smaller dispersion in the other, but in neither period is the difference statistically significant. There is some presumption that the effect of deflation would be greater for the three-digit industries, but we have been unable to estimate it.[10]

RISK PREMIUMS

There exists a strong tradition in economics that a positive risk premium must be paid to investors in risky industries. More precisely, the realized rate of return, after full allowance for defaults and failures, is expected to be higher, the riskier the investment. Only a few economists have taken the opposite position that small prospects of large gains are so highly esteemed that the net risk premium is negative.[11]

The traditional view is supported by the findings on corporate bonds. Whether the risk of an issue is based upon ratings by investment agencies, the market (i.e., by promised yields at market prices), or criteria such as the number of times fixed charges are earned, the corporate bonds issued in the United States between 1900 and 1943 confirm this expectation.[12] Hickman leaves open the question whether this premium reflects risk aversion or institutional limitations upon investments by financial intermediaries.

The investors in corporate equities do not necessarily have the same attitude toward risk, and certainly not the same legal limitations on purchase of equities. Unfortunately our data do not allow us to contribute

[10] One might expect the difference between deflated and undeflated rates of return to be correlated with the percentage of fixed capital, but among two-digit industries no such correlation was found.

[11] See C. O. Hardy, *Risk and Risk Bearing*, University of Chicago Press, 1931, p. 38.

[12] See W. B. Hickman, *Corporate Bond Quality and Investor Experience*, Princeton University Press for National Bureau of Economic Research, 1958, pp. 10 ff.

much to this question. Two alternate measures of risk have failed to yield any reliable relationships.

The first measure is the standard deviation of the annual rates of return realized by all reporting corporations in each industry.[13] The relations between average return R and its standard deviation σ are:

1938–47

$$R = 8.44 - .231\sigma$$
$$r = -.151 \ (n = 38)$$

1947–54

$$R = 6.31 + .302\sigma$$
$$r = .165 \ (n = 54)$$

The results are not heartening: the risk premium coefficient is negative in the first period and statistically nonsignificant in both periods.

The fluctuations over time in an industry's rate of return are risks to investors as a group. The dispersion of rates of return among firms measures the risks to investors in one firm, and is at least equally relevant to entrepreneurial decisions. An estimate of firm dispersions can be constructed from *Statistics of Income*, which reports the share of returns with no net income, and the average rates of return of both income and deficit corporations. On the assumption that the distribution of rates of return is normal, one may estimate the standard deviation for an industry, by asset classes, in each year.[14] An average was calculated for the two prosperous years, 1948 and 1953, and the two recession years, 1949 and 1954. The average of these four standard deviations proves to have a nonsignificant (positive) relationship to average rates of return.

[13] This average includes corporations taking losses, so long as income tax returns are filed.

[14] The method may be illustrated by the data for the \$50,000 to \$100,000 asset class for all manufacturing industries, 1949:

	Per Cent of Returns	*Average Rate of Return Before Taxes* (per cent)
Income corporations	60.8	11.86
Deficit corporations	39.2	−15.44

From a table of mean deviates (H. M. Leverett, "Table of Mean Deviates for Various Portions of the Unit Normal Distribution," *Psychometrika*, June 1947), one finds that with a normal distribution the top 60.8 per cent of cases has a mean of .629 σ, and the bottom 38.2 per cent a mean of $-.984\ \sigma$, so

$$\begin{aligned} 11.86 &= .629\ \sigma \\ -15.44 &= -.984\ \sigma \\ \hline 27.30 &= 1.613\ \sigma \end{aligned}$$

or $\sigma = 16.92$ per cent, as a weighted average of the two estimates. The estimate for each asset class is in turn weighted, to strike an industry average, by the share of industry assets.

These two measures of risk are so crude that we are not entitled to conclude that no risk premiums are demanded. All that can be concluded is that we find no evidence of such premiums in our own restricted investigation.[15]

2. *Sources and Correction of Disequilibriums*

If the entrepreneurs in a competitive industry correctly anticipated all relevant future events and if they were able fully to adjust theirs plans, no disequilibriums could arise: the markets would be in full equilibrium at every moment of time. All disequilibriums arise out of imperfect or tardy anticipation of future events, and they persist only until the adjustment of rates of investment and output they call for can be made.

The sources of disequilibrium are infinitely varied—discovery of new mineral deposits or new techniques, closing or opening of foreign markets, new regulations by governmental bodies, increase of competition within an industry, and so forth. All leave their impact upon the rates of return, and we can, in fact, turn our analysis around and define the fluctuations in an industry's profit rate as the measure of the extent and duration of disequilibriums.[16]

The Marshallian theory, which is the parent of modern theories of the role of time in attaining equilibrium, emphasizes certain barriers to the immediate adaptation of a firm to new conditions. These barriers are usually subsumed under the headings of technological and contractual limitations.[17] Technological limitations arise out of the durability of certain capital forms, which delay the withdrawal of specialized resources, and the time required for construction of new capital, which delays expansion of productive capacity. Contractual obligations set limits upon the short-run discretion of the firm, for they fix prices or rates of purchase or sale. The speed of adaptation to new conditions will therefore

[15] If any further documentation of the elusiveness of the risk factor is needed, we may cite a related inquiry: is the average rate of return different in industries with relatively much borrowed capital from that in industries with relatively little borrowed capital? The "leverage" of high borrowings would argue that risks of equity holders were larger in the former type of industry. Again no statistically significant relationship was found. Of course the industries with more stable rates of return can safely borrow relatively more, which makes the interpretation of this finding difficult.

[16] Fluctuations in an industry's profit rate can be measured either in absolute terms or relative to the average rate in all industries. The former measure presumably records the total forces of disequilibrium, whereas the measure based upon annual deviations of the industry's rate from that of all industries will eliminate general business fluctuations to the extent that they affect all industries similarly.

[17] The word technological is not ideal, for the importance of technological factors depends upon the price a company is willing to pay: the construction period of a plant can be halved if it is willing to pay the extra costs of the speed.

be governed by the relative use of specialized and durable assets and the time required to produce them, and by the extent and nature of contractual obligations.

Most contractual obligations run for a year or less, and it is improbable that they are an important barrier to adaptations to market changes in so short a time. The growing practice of leasing plants (often financed by pension funds) is giving a larger role to long-run commitments, but this development is too recent to leave a large imprint upon rates of return in the period we study.

Consider, then, specialized and durable resources. Obviously, if resources are not specialized, they can be shifted among industries, and usually on a large scale within a year or two. If they are not durable, an industry can contract its productive capacity rapidly by failing to replace worn-out assets if demand falls. If resources are quickly producible, the industry can expand its capacity rapidly when demand rises or costs fall. We cannot identify specialized resources in our industries, but we can measure the variations among industries in the use of fixed (durable) capital. We would expect rates of return in relatively unprofitable industries to rise (toward the general level) more rapidly, the less the share of fixed assets in total capital.

This hypothesis has been tested by the following procedure. The trough (or peak) in the profit rate of an industry (relative to the average of all industries) in a given period is first identified. Then the magnitude of the differences in the profit rate in that and succeeding years is calculated, and the amount by which the profit rate approaches the average is correlated with the percentage of fixed to all assets.[18]

The results have not been in keeping with expectations. The amount by which an industry's rate of return moves toward the average of all industries proves to be positively correlated with the ratio of fixed to total capital, whereas Marshall's theory predicts a negative correlation. The correlation coefficients are not statistically significant, however. The introduction of an additional variable, change in sales, does not improve the situation.[19]

[18] This percentage is calculated for a year in the middle of the period, since it normally does not change much from year to year.

[19] For the period, 1947–54, the results may be summarized: let x_1 be the increase in the rate of return a year after the trough (or decrease after the peak); x_2 the ratio of fixed to total capital in 1950; and x_3 the percentage increase in sales receipts. Then

From troughs ($n = 27$)

$r_{12} = .330$ $\qquad$ $r_{12.3} = .329$

$r_{13} = .033$ $\qquad$ $r_{13.2} = .013$

Imperfect as our measures are, they suggest at least tentatively that Marshall's emphasis upon fixed capital as the prime determinant of the rate of return to equilibrium may be misplaced. The effect of specialized and durable resources is surely in the direction his theory describes, but it may be that the adjustments are completed largely within a year, or the effects of fixed plants are important only for very large displacements from equilibrium, or some other factor we have not isolated conceals the effects.

We have observed that the sources of disequilibrium are enormously diverse, but many of them operate upon the selling price of the industries on which they impinge. A shift in demand, a change in taxes, a change in foreign markets or international competition, higher prices of complementary or substitute products—all such forces will leave their mark on the price history of the industry in question.

Steady changes in prices should not occasion or mirror disequilibrium, however, for they can be fully anticipated. If prices rise 5 per cent a year, for whatever reason, the entrepreneurs will adjust their investment plans so the price rise will be no occasion for unusual profits. For the fifty-eight industries for which price indexes could be constructed, we have therefore taken as our measure of unanticipated price movements the standard deviation of the prices after elimination of a linear trend.[20] The unanticipated price fluctuations, so measured, are in fact correlated ($r = .336$) with the standard deviations of the industry profit rates over the period 1947–54. It is interesting to note that the magnitude of price fluctuations, when not corrected for trend, is wholly uncorrelated with fluctuations of profit rates ($r = -.001$).

3. *Returns in Concentrated and Unconcentrated Industries*

Economic theorists have long emphasized the differences in rates of return—and other aspects of business enterprise such as price behavior—between competitive and monopolistic industries. Some of these hypotheses will now be examined. But first, how are we to classify industries as competitive or monopolistic?

From peaks ($n = 23$)

$$r_{12} = .216 \qquad r_{12.3} = .182$$
$$r_{13} = -.680 \qquad r_{13.2} = -.675$$

Scatter diagrams of similar analyses for 1938–47 suggest similar findings, except that there is a weak negative correlation between x_1 and x_2 for decreases from peaks.

When the return to the mean is expressed as a percentage of the initial peak or trough, the relationships are generally even weaker.

[20] That is, if σ is the standard deviation of the price index over a given period, and r is the correlation of the index with time, $\sigma(1 - r^2)^{1/2}$ is the measure of unanticipated price fluctuations.

The definition of unconcentrated industries has already been given.[21] Concentrated industries are simply those in which the four leading firms produce 60 per cent or more of the value added, and for which the market is national. Industries falling in neither of these categories are labeled ambiguous. It should be noticed that some of the unclassified (ambiguous) industries, operating in smaller than national markets, may be effectively more concentrated than those we so designate. Readers who are acquainted with either the highly controversial literature on concentration ratios or the even more controversial literature on antitrust policy hardly need be told that a concentrated industry need not be monopolistic. High elasticity of demand for the industry's product, or ease of entry by new firms, or the extent of independent rivalry among firms may make the concentrated industry (in this definition) differ in, at most, trifling respects from a fully competitive industry. This difficulty of classification must be faced frankly, but it is not possible to attempt here a more refined classification. One can only give plain warning that discrepancies between the hypotheses of the traditional theory and the findings below may be due in some part to the deficiencies of industry classification.

THE LEVEL OF RATES OF RETURN

The average rate of return of monopolistic industries should, by hypothesis, be greater than that of competitive industries. A monopolist can always enter competitive industries, so he will not be content with less than a competitive rate of return on investment in the long run. On the other hand, there will normally be important barriers to entry of new competitors in a monopolistic industry, or it would not remain monopolistic. Is this expectation confirmed in our concentrated and unconcentrated industries?

The answer is somewhat ambiguous, but on the whole it is negative (see Table 17). The concentrated industries have a higher average rate in 1938–40 and after 1948 (but not in the eight intervening years), according to the annual data. The differences between concentrated and unconcentrated industries in the periods 1951–54 and 1955–57 were statistically significant at the 5 and 2 per cent levels, respectively. These findings suggest a weak affirmative answer, but a qualification undermines them. Over the period 1947–54, the average rate in the concentrated industries was 8.00 per cent, that in the unconcentrated industries 7.16 per cent. If one adjusts the returns for excess withdrawals of officers of small corpora-

[21] Footnote 4, this chapter, and Appendix C.

TABLE 17

AVERAGE RATE OF RETURN AND STANDARD DEVIATION OF RATES OF RETURN IN CONCENTRATED, UNCONCENTRATED, AND AMBIGUOUS INDUSTRIES, 1938–57

Period	*Industries* Concentrated	Unconcentrated	Ambiguous
		NUMBER	
	14	54	31
		AVERAGE RATE OF RETURN (per cent)	
1938–41	6.51	5.25	6.59
1942–44	6.23	7.68	7.19
1945–47	7.30	10.01	8.64
1948–50	9.11	8.02	8.90
1951–54	6.33	5.05	5.90
1955–57	7.05	5.44	6.35
		STANDARD DEVIATION OF RATE OF RETURN (per cent)	
1938–41	2.60	2.83	2.70
1942–44	1.48	1.40	2.01
1945–47	2.80	2.20	2.15
1948–50	2.82	2.52	2.46
1951–54	1.33	2.21	1.79
1955–57	2.10	2.29	1.75

SOURCE: Tables A-14 to A-59, and C-1 and C-2.

tions, which are important in the unconcentrated industries, the differences almost vanish.[22]

This same conclusion is reached by correlation analysis. Of our industries, twenty-five have national markets: in this group the coefficient of correlation of concentration ratios and average rate of return (corrected for withdrawals) was .130 in 1947–54. In fourteen industries with

[22] In the concentrated industries, the corporations with assets under $250,000 had on average 1.6 per cent of all receipts, whereas the corresponding percentage in unconcentrated industries was 12.7. On the basis of the regression equation (p. 59, above), this factor would account for 95 per cent, or almost all, of the observed difference.

Using data for registered companies, J. S. Bain found that, in the period 1936–40, when the concentration ratio (for the eight largest firms) exceeded 70 per cent, the average rate of return of the industry was substantially higher ("Relation of Profit Rate to Industry Concentration," *Quarterly Journal of Economics*, Aug. 1951). For the sixteen of his forty-two industries that can be approximately identified with our industries, the same result holds for 1938–40—the correlation coefficient between profit rates and concentration is .53. For the period 1947–54, however, neither the difference in means of the two classes (concentration ratios above and below 50 per cent for four firms, roughly corresponding to his 70 per cent level for eight firms) nor the correlation coefficient of profit rates and concentration differs significantly from zero.

regional markets the coefficient was —.085, and in nine industries with local markets, —.379. In no case was the correlation coefficient significant at the 10 per cent level.

It is possible, of course, that a higher level of profits will be reflected in the value of the assets of the industries receiving the profits, whereas the traditional theory predicts higher rates for monopolies on assets valued, not on the basis of earnings, but of alternative products of the assets. Before the economic theorist embraces this popular—and untestable—interpretation of these findings, he should consider the analysis in the next section.

THE DISPERSION OF RATES OF RETURN

Some monopolistic industries will have very high rates of return, if they can preserve their position, because of favorable demand and cost conditions, whereas others will earn only as much as competitive industries, because of unfavorable demand and cost conditions. These differences can persist in monopolistic industries, whose high profits will not be quickly eroded by new rivals, whereas the profits of competitive industries will be. Hence the traditional theory implies that the dispersion of average rates of return (over a substantial period) among competitive industries will be smaller than that of monopolistic industries.

At first glance, the data seem equally unkind to this hypothesis (Table 17). The standard deviation of average rates of return of the concentrated industries is higher in periods from 1942 to 1950, but the differences are not large, and the opposite relationship holds in the terminal periods. But here the adjustment for excess salary withdrawals of officers in small corporations plays an opposite role to that in the average rates of return. The share of assets held by small corporations varies widely among unconcentrated industries, but is always small in concentrated industries. If we adjust the average rates for this factor, the following variances are obtained:

1938–47

$$\frac{\text{variance of concentrated industries}}{\text{variance of unconcentrated industries}} = \frac{5.809}{1.513} = 3.84$$

with 10 and 36 degrees of freedom.

1947–54

$$\frac{\text{variance of concentrated industries}}{\text{variance of unconcentrated industries}} = \frac{4.841}{3.120} = 1.55$$

with 13 and 53 degrees of freedom. The former variance ratio is significant at the 1 per cent level, the latter only at the 20 per cent level.[23]

The larger dispersion of rates of return of concentrated industries demands reconciliation with the failure to find a higher rate of return, for both hypotheses rest upon the same theoretical argument. The reconciliation may simply be that the concentrated industries, which are few in number, include enough essentially competitive industries to mask the higher rates of return of the truly monopolistic industries. Alternately, it may be that concentration itself, quite aside from any monopoly power, is associated with characteristics (e.g., large cyclical fluctuations of output) which make for dispersion of profits.

STABILITY OF THE PATTERN OF RATES OF RETURN

The final hypothesis to be considered here is the stability of the industrial pattern of rates of return. The argument is intimately related to that of the previous hypotheses. Competitive industries will have a volatile pattern of rates of return, for the movements into high-profit industries and out of low-profit industries will—together with the flow of new disturbances of equilibrium—lead to a constantly changing hierarchy of rates of return. In the monopolistic industries, on the other hand, the unusually profitable industries will be able to preserve their preferential position for considerable periods of time.

The correlation coefficients between the rates of return at various time intervals are averaged in Table 18. On the whole, the pattern of coefficients agrees remarkably well with the hypothesis. The industrial pattern of rates is extremely stable in the concentrated industries: even after eight years it was still .5 in both periods. The industrial pattern is much more volatile in the unconcentrated industries, although here the record is somewhat different in the two periods. In the war period the correlation coefficients approached zero when the time span reached four years, whereas in the postwar period the correlation coefficient did not fall below .4 until six years had elapsed. It may be that the mobilization and demobilization affected the unconcentrated industries much more unevenly than they affected the concentrated industries, most of which became important producers of munitions.

[23] The ambiguous industries also have larger variances than the unconcentrated industries.

TABLE 18

CORRELATION OF RATES OF RETURN FOR CONCENTRATED, UNCONCENTRATED, AND AMBIGUOUS INDUSTRIES, TWO DECADES, 1938–57

Industry Structure	*1938–47* Number of Comparisons	Average Correlations	*1947–57* Number of Comparisons	Average Correlations
	RATES OF RETURN IN YEAR T AND (T + 1)			
Concentrated	9	.76	8	.74
Unconcentrated	9	.69	8	.72
Ambiguous	9	.82	8	.77
	RATES IN YEAR T AND (T + 2)			
Concentrated	8	.56	7	.72
Unconcentrated	8	.41	7	.61
Ambiguous	8	.58	7	.70
	RATES IN YEAR T AND (T + 3)			
Concentrated	7	.58	6	.66
Unconcentrated	7	.18	6	.57
Ambiguous	7	.40	6	.64
	RATES IN YEAR T AND (T + 4)			
Concentrated	6	.56	5	.69
Unconcentrated	6	.10	5	.53
Ambiguous	6	.30	5	.64
	RATES IN YEAR T AND (T + 5)			
Concentrated	5	.54	4	.71
Unconcentrated	5	.06	4	.47
Ambiguous	5	.20	4	.70
	RATES IN YEAR T AND (T + 6)			
Concentrated	1	.49	5	.57
Unconcentrated	4	.24	5	.36
Ambiguous	4	.15	5	.57
	RATES IN YEAR T AND (T + 7)			
Concentrated	3	.60	4	.57
Unconcentrated	3	.04	4	.26
Ambiguous	3	.16	4	.38
	RATES IN YEAR T AND (T + 8)			
Concentrated	2	.49	3	.53
Unconcentrated	2	.00	3	.27
Ambiguous	2	.04	3	.38
	RATES IN YEAR T AND (T + 9)			
Concentrated	1	.38	2	.35
Unconcentrated	1	.17	2	.20
Ambiguous	1	−.15	2	.37
	RATES IN YEAR T AND (T + 10)			
Concentrated			1	.40
Unconcentrated			1	.11
Ambiguous			1	.05

SOURCE: Same as for Table 17.

CHAPTER 4

The Rate of Investment

THE rate of investment is a surpassingly important factor in economic life. The short-run fluctuations in investment are large in amplitude, and they are commonly credited with a dominant influence upon the state of business conditions. The secular growth of capital was long considered to be the basic determinant of the progress of an economy. In modern times there has been a growing tendency to place more emphasis upon the state of technological development as the prime source of progress, but no one has argued that the provision of adequate capital is an unimportant part of growth and, in one view, expenditures on research are simply investment in knowledge.

The main focus of our inquiry is upon the influence of the rate of return on investment. This emphasis is not due to the belief that *realized* rates of return are of decisive influence—indeed their relative unimportance will be argued. The emphasis is due rather to the fact that our data on rates of return and capital are comprehensive and comparable, whereas most other explanatory variables influencing investment—for example, shifts of consumer demands and advances in technology—involve such large and difficult problems of data collection and analysis as to be beyond our reach. Estimation of prospective profit rates receives some attention, and the effects of wages upon investment are treated in Chapter 5.

1. *The Rate of Return and Investment*

The rate of investment in an industry is governed by its expected rate of return, but the rate of return is itself a summary of all the forces impinging upon the industry. Any change in costs—whether due to raw-material prices, wage rates, taxes, or changes in technology—and any change in consumer demands will affect prospective costs, revenues, and therefore rates of return.

If one possessed direct and precise knowledge of (schedules of) prospective rates of return, he could by-pass all these other considerations in predicting investment, with one qualification. Since we are dealing with *industries*, not individual firms, it is probable that there will be no single amount of capital corresponding to the weighted average of the firms' rates of return. An increase in demand, for example, may lead to a given average prospective rate of return (with present capital), but the amount of investment will depend upon how the increased demand is distributed among the firms. If the increase is directed primarily toward firms near capacity, it will have a different effect upon investment than if it is directed primarily toward firms with excess capacity.

But, of course, the prospective rates of profit are not known to an outside investigator, and even if anticipations of entrepreneurs are completely accurate, realized (ex post) rates of return will give only one point on the schedule of prospective rates. If it is correctly anticipated that without additional investment the rate of return next year will be 10 per cent, the long-run equilibrium rate being 7 per cent, then such an amount of investment may (and, if possible, will) be undertaken that the ex post rate will be only 7 per cent.

Realized rates of return will therefore be a clue to what they were previously and correctly anticipated to be (in the absence of additional investment) only to the extent that entrepreneurs were unable to make sufficient investment (or disinvestment) to bring the rate to the equilibrium level. If anticipations were in some degree incorrect, the ex post rate of return may be either higher or lower.

In an empirical study, therefore, we should not expect to find a high correlation between investment in year *T* and the realized rate of return in year *T*. If the anticipations were perfect and complete competitive adjustment could be made within a year (or other time period under study), the correlation would be zero. If anticipations were correct, but technological or other barriers prevented complete adjustment to the long-run competitive level, investment would be positively correlated with rates of return. Errors in anticipation, unless they were systematic, would presumably reduce any observed correlation. On the other hand, anticipations that were systematically conservative, in the sense of underestimating the departure of the anticipated rate of return from the competitive average, would increase the correlation between investment rates and realized rates of return: equilibrium would not be restored in the next time period, so ex post returns would be above average in expanding industries and below average in contracting industries.

To these possible reasons for a correlation between realized rates of return and investment, one must add a wholly different consideration. Profits fluctuate much more from year to year than dividends do, so unusually large profits lead to unusually large retained earnings, which are a substantial source of the increase in capital in manufacturing. In our postwar period, retained earnings were more than one-fourth of the increase in capital in every year, and were almost exactly one-half of the increase in capital for the period as a whole (Table 19). Hence one might argue

TABLE 19

INCOME, DIVIDENDS AND INTEREST PAID, RETAINED EARNINGS, AND INCREASE IN CAPITAL, ALL MANUFACTURING INDUSTRIES, 1947–58
(amounts in billions of dollars)

Year	Income	Dividends and Interest Paid	Retained Earnings	Increase in Capital	Retained Earnings as Per Cent of Increase in Capital
1947	10.5	4.4	6.2	13.6	45
1948	11.6	4.9	6.8	9.7	70
1949	9.0	5.0	4.0	2.1	190
1950	13.0	6.1	6.9	16.6	42
1951	10.9	5.9	5.0	18.5	27
1952	9.4	6.0	3.4	8.6	39
1953	9.9	6.3	3.6	6.6	55
1954	9.5	6.2	3.3	3.4	98
1955	13.8	7.3	6.5	17.1	38
1956	13.5	7.9	5.6	12.2	46
1957	12.8	8.3	4.5	6.9	65
1958	10.5	8.0	2.4	9.2	27

NOTE: Retained earnings and percentage calculated from unrounded data. Income excludes dividends received from other corporations, and dividends paid exclude a pro rata share of dividends received.

SOURCE: *Statistics of Income, Corporation Income Tax Returns*, for 1947 to 1958 (IRS).

that high profits automatically generated a large increase in capital in the same year.

The main defect in this argument is that it views the surplus of earnings over dividends and interest payments as an end-of-year residual which increases the firm's aggregate resources whether the firm wishes more capital or not. These earnings normally accrue over the year, not on December 31, and if the enterprise does not wish to increase (or decrease) dividends or investment commensurately, it can reduce its short-term (or, to some extent, long-term) liabilities. Only if the capital structure of the firm does not allow debt reduction (or increase) or if the capital markets are very imperfect (so retained earnings are a much cheaper source of capital than new borrowings or equity issues) will the current profits have a simple arithmetic effect upon total assets. The "arithmetic" influence of current profits upon current investment may therefore be quite small, and subsequent findings suggest that it is small.[1]

The preceding argument on the relationship between investment and ex post profits requires little modification if the industry is monopolized. There is less likelihood that the equilibrium rate of return will be stable

[1] See p. 76.

over time: this rate is set by the conditions of the particular industry, whereas the average rate in the competitive industries is set by the sum of their diverse conditions. But the equilibrium rate will be all that is observed ex post if the industry correctly anticipates and fully adjusts to changes in supply and demand conditions.[2]

Even if an industry were in long-run equilibrium each year so the rate of return was (approximately) constant, investment would be highly correlated with the factors that led to changes in the equilibrium position. If demand grew, the stock of capital would parallel the physical output of the industry. If changes in factor prices led to a substitution of capital for labor, the stock of capital would parallel increases in wages relative to the cost of capital. If technology advanced—and here we have no reliable quantitative measure—the stock of capital might either increase or decrease. Of course, to the extent that durable and specialized forms of capital were involved, long-run equilibrium could not be attained each year even with perfect foresight.[3]

Direct increases in demand (shifting of the industry's demand curve to the right) are measured approximately by receipts of the industry. If the increase in demand is not fully anticipated, prices will rise above their long-run equilibrium level, and receipts may increase in greater or less proportion than the horizontal shift of the demand schedule—normally a quantitatively minor complication.[4]

Reductions in cost are also measured, less perfectly, by changes in output. A reduction in costs will lead to a reduction in price and hence to an increase in output and, in general, the larger the reduction in costs, the greater the increase in output. If demand is elastic, increase in output will in turn be accompanied by an increase in receipts.

Since conditions of demand are usually less stable in the short run than those of cost, and since changes in receipts may measure changes in both demand and cost, receipts of the industry will be used as the primary index of the demand for capital.

[2] To the extent that monopoly declines over a period, investment and realized rates of return should be negatively related.

[3] For example, even if the future availability of an improved machine were known, an unimproved machine might have to be built this year.

[4] Let the industry have a constant long-run equilibrium price p_0, and let the demand shift to the right by a factor λ, i.e., the old demand curve is $q = f(p)$ and the new demand curve is $\lambda f(p)$. Then receipts will rise in the ratio

$$\frac{p\lambda f(p)}{p_0 f(p_0)} = \lambda + \lambda \frac{\Delta p(1 + \eta)}{p_0},$$

where Δp is the excess of price over p_0 and η is the elasticity of demand.

ANNUAL RELATIONSHIPS

Let us turn to the evidence. All the possible regressions of relative increase in capital on relative increase of receipts and either current or preceding year profit rates have been calculated for the period 1948 to 1957 (Table 20).[5] They agree almost too well with expectations! In every case, the overridingly important influence on the rate of investment is the change in receipts: this is the only consistently significant regression coefficient, and even its magnitude is remarkably stable. Except during the depression year, 1949, the relative change in capital was approximately six-tenths of the relative change in receipts. On average, somewhat over half the variance of relative changes in capital is explained by the relative change in receipts.

The current profit rate plays a negligible role in the regression equations: it is significantly different from zero only in 1950, 1951, and 1956, and in the former year it has a negative sign. The preceding year's profit rate is better behaved: it is almost consistently positive and is significant (at the 5 per cent level) in five (and almost so in 1957) of the nine years.[6] One possible interpretation of this finding is that this year's profit rate is used as predictor of next year's profit rate—which would be a sensible short-run rule, as our study of the stability of the industrial pattern of profit rates indicated. Investment in durable goods is, of course, less sensitive to short-run fluctuations in rates of return. There is another interpretation, however, which will be discussed shortly.

Our findings on the accelerator relation cannot readily be compared with those obtained (usually from data on individual companies) by others, because our capital concept (all assets except investments in other companies) is much broader than that usually employed. In fact, most investigations seek to relate gross investment in plant and equipment to changes in sales. This narrower concept is appropriate if it is believed that

[5] The considerable degree of direct control over investment during the war makes the earlier period less interesting; however, it is analyzed in the longer period regressions (see below). In the postwar period the aircraft industry, which underwent extreme fluctuations, was omitted, usually with little effect upon the regressions for three-digit industries.

[6] These two sets of regressions seem to support the argument (text accompanying Table 19) that the "arithmetic" effect of retained earnings on the increase of assets need not be of much importance. If it were, the relationship of investment to profit rates should not only be substantial but also larger for current than for preceding year profit rates.

As a further test of the arithmetic effect of retained earnings on investment, the residuals from the regressions of relative investment on current profits and relative change in receipts were correlated with the ratio of retained earnings to income, for 98 industries. In neither 1949 nor 1950 was there any correlation.

TABLE 20

ANNUAL REGRESSION OF RELATIVE CHANGE IN CORPORATE CAPITAL ON RELATIVE CHANGE IN RECEIPTS AND PROFIT RATE, NINETY-EIGHT INDUSTRIES, 1948–57

X_1 = log capital$_t$ − log capital$_{t-1}$
X_2 = log receipts$_t$ − log receipts$_{t-1}$
X_3 = profit rate, year t
X_4 = profit rate, year $(t-1)$

Year	*Regression Coefficient, and Standard Error, of X_1 on:* X_2	X_3	Coefficient of Multiple Correlation
1948	.633	.000161	.776
	(.0556)	(.000724)	
1949	.402	.000602	.671
	(.0491)	(.000784)	
1950	.627	−.00371	.744
	(.0594)	(.00112)	
1951	.466	.00476	.794
	(.0572)	(.00111)	
1953	.654	−.000725	.837
	(.0473)	(.00144)	
1954	.583	−.00144	.726
	(.0570)	(.00104)	
1955	.471	.00272	.726
	(.0564)	(.00108)	
1956	.650	.00262	.778
	(.0636)	(.00108)	
1957	.772	−.000120	.744
	(.0775)	(.00118)	

Year	*Regression Coefficient, and Standard Error, of X_1 on:* X_2	X_4	Coefficient of Multiple Correlation
1948	.637	.000200	.776
	(.0530)	(.000583)	
1949	.438	.00149	.686
	(.0477)	(.000722)	
1950	.523	−.000988	.713
	(.0536)	(.000886)	
1951	.555	.00177	.820
	(.0470)	(.000835)	
1953	.627	.00269	.847
	(.0440)	(.00115)	
1954	.561	.00106	.722
	(.0556)	(.00112)	
1955	.515	.00418	.758
	(.0497)	(.000987)	
1956	.609	.00402	.812
	(.0554)	(.000851)	
1957	.739	.00239	.756
	(.0711)	(.00124)	

SOURCE: Tables A-36 to A-59; and *Statistics of Income*, for 1947 to 1957.

the technological ties between output and fixed capital are closer than those between output and total capital. But there is no presumption that this is true: it is almost certainly not true in the short run, when the relationship of fixed plant to output is highly variable; and it is not very plausible even in the long run. If fixed and working capital are substitutable, as of course they are, the presumption will in fact be that total capital has a more stable relationship than fixed capital has to output. The same presumption holds with respect to rates of return: we should expect net investment to be more sensitive than gross fixed investment is to changes in profit prospects. For gross investment will be influenced by replacement needs as well as by profits, and again the substitution between fixed and working capital enters to weaken the relationship, especially in the short run.

Eisner's estimates of the accelerator relation are based upon a distributed lag model, in which investment in durable goods this year is related to changes in sales in this and each of several previous years.[7] The sum of these coefficients for 1955 is .72, or .48 if firms making gross fixed investments of more than 40 per cent of their total fixed assets are excluded. Current and earlier profit rates had no systematic relationship to investment. The profit rates in this study are highly ambiguous, however: they are total earnings divided by fixed assets, which are a variable and minor fraction of total assets. The better performance of profits in the study of separate industries, where this profit measure is somewhat less dubious, suggests that the measure may have had an important effect on the results.

The well-known study of Meyer and Kuh is even more difficult to compare with our work. The net profit variable is again measured on gross fixed investment, and the change in sales enters into two of their variables—directly, and in a capacity measure.[8] Their finding that change in sales has no important effect on investment,[9] while the "capacity effect" is positive,[10] may arise in part from this multiple use of change in sales.

[7] Robert Eisner, "A Distributed Lag Investment Function," *Econometrica*, Jan. 1960, pp. 1–29.

[8] The change in sales relative to gross fixed investment is also measured. The capacity measure is defined as follows: let $(K/S)_m$ be the minimum ratio of fixed capital to sales during 1946–49. The capacity measure is then $(K/S)_m S_t$, where S_t is sales in the given year. If $(S_t - S_{t-1})/K_t$ is the direct measure of sales change, clearly this variable and $S_t K_t / S_{t-1}$ are not independent.

[9] The partial correlation coefficients are often negative, and significant in only 5 of 75 cases (John R. Meyer and Edwin Kuh, *The Investment Decision: An Empirical Study*, Harvard University Press, 1957).

[10] The correlation coefficients are generally significant and positive in 1946 and 1947, but not in the next three years (*ibid.*, p. 122).

Meyer and Kuh kindly supplied the simple correlations for their sample, and these were used to calculate for each of fifteen industries equations of the form,

$$\frac{\Delta F}{F} = a + b\frac{\pi}{F} + c\frac{\Delta S}{S},$$

where F is fixed investment, π is previous year's profits, and ΔS is change in sales in the given year. The lagged profit variable was much more influential than the change in sales, as shown below.

	Number of Significant Regression Coefficients, .05 level	
Year	Profits	Sales
1947	6	2
1948	7	3
1949	7	2
1950	8	5

All significant regression coefficients were positive. The relatively poor performance of changes in sales suggests that the sales of individual firms contain random fluctuations which are large relative to changes in sales, so industry sales may be a better index, even for a firm, of changes in its demand.[11]

LONGER-PERIOD RELATIONSHIPS

One source of ambiguity in the interpretation of annual rates of investment is that they are subject to large errors of measurement. We have no direct measure of their magnitude, but the instability of the year-to-year industrial pattern of rates of investment, and the greater stability of this pattern over longer periods, suggest that the errors are not negligible.[12] What should we expect when the period of investment is lengthened?

[11] The correlations of successive profit rates of individual firms are very high:

Pairs of Years	*Average Correlations of Profit Rates* (15 industries)
1945 and 1946	.59
1946 and 1947	.78
1947 and 1948	.81
1948 and 1949	.78
1949 and 1950	.72

[12] Note that the errors in measurement of capital should be at least in part positively correlated with the errors in measurement of receipts. When companies are reclassified, both their assets and receipts are allocated to the same industry.

On our previous argument, lengthening the period over which investment is measured should reduce the correlation between investment rates and profit rates. The presence of correlation in the short run is presumably due to one of two factors: either the expectations of future profit rates were systematically biased—the strength of the forces making for high or low rates was underestimated—or technological or other limitations on the firm's ability to adapt to new conditions prevented a complete elimination of unusual profits or losses. And both of these causes of correlation are surely weaker in a longer period: errors in expectations can be corrected; and any limitations on the firm's freedom to adjust investment diminish with time.

This argument assumes that a misjudgment of the demand for capital next year cannot be fully corrected next year, that it will require more than a year to recognize the error in expectations or to make the appropriate investment or disinvestment to restore the industry's profit rate to equilibrium, or both.[13] This is perhaps a plausible assumption, but its plausibility (which rests on the most casual empirical observation) surely varies from industry to industry.

This is of course an ex ante view: we are asking why the equilibirium amount of investment may not be attained next year. To the extent that the entrepreneurs misjudge the new demand for capital (the shifts of which we roughly measure by receipts), of course, profit rates will in actual fact not be at equilibrium next year. They will be higher or lower, but (in the absence of systematic errors of expectation) they will not be correlated with investment.

When the period is lengthened to several years, however, surely it will embrace both unanticipated changes in profit rates and the investment adjustments they in turn call forth. An unanticipated high profit rate next year will lead to larger investment the year (or two or three) thereafter and, conversely, an unexpectedly low profit rate will lead to smaller investment thereafter. This effect will be realized even if, on average, expectations are correct—it can be the result of unsystematic errors in anticipation.

The finding that investment in a year is correlated positively with the previous year's rate of return could be interpreted to support this view. In year t, the firm invested I_t expecting a realized rate of return, π^*_t. If in the event the realized rate was π_t, investment was too large or too small, and the excess or deficiency was larger, the larger the difference

[13] Recall that in our interindustry universe, equilibrium is defined by the profit rate in an industry relative to that of other industries.

between expected and realized rates of return. Say the deficiency or excess was $\Delta I_t = \lambda(\pi^*{}_t - \pi_t)$, with $\lambda > 0$. Then this amount of investment should be added to or subtracted from that amount called for by next year's shift in the demand for capital, and $\lambda(\pi_t^* - \pi_t)$ becomes one of the determinants of next year's total investment. This interpretation is not independent of that given in the previous subsection, for unexpectedly high profits this year are a relevant basis for predicting larger profits (with given capital) next year.

In sum, either larger or smaller correlations between investment and profit rates are therefore possible as the period of time is lengthened.

The regression equations for the two periods used in our study are given in Table 21. They display the usual strong relationship between invest-

TABLE 21

REGRESSION OF PERCENTAGE CHANGE IN CAPITAL ON PERCENTAGE CHANGE IN RECEIPTS AND ON PROFIT RATE, 1938–56

X_1 = percentage change in total capital
X_2 = percentage change in corporate receipts
X_3 = average profit rate

1938–47 ($n = 82$)	$X_1 = -54.86 + \underset{(.051)}{.527X_2} + \underset{(3.26)}{6.12X_3}$	$R = .765$
1947–54 ($n = 98$)	$X_1 = .212 + \underset{(.037)}{.808X_2} + \underset{(.732)}{2.12X_3}$	$R = .924$
1947–56 ($n = 98$)	$X_1 = -31.70 + \underset{(.029)}{.858X_2} + \underset{(.816)}{6.64X_3}$	$R = .957$

SOURCE: Data employed from Tables A-14 to A-59; and from *Statistics of Income*, for 1938, 1947, 1954, and 1956.

ment and receipts,[14] and they also give substantially more weight to the profit rate. Even in the earlier period the regression of relative investment on profit rates was significant, and in the postwar period it was highly significant. In both periods, however, introduction of profit rates does not add appreciably to the "explanation" of the variance of investment

[14] The relative changes in capital and receipts for the longer period were calculated with relative changes expressed as percentages; in the annual regressions (which were calculated subsequently), the differences in successive logarithms were used.

rates.[15] The elasticity of relative investment with respect to relative receipts was .6 in the annual postwar regressions; it was .9 in the corresponding long-period regression. The difference between the annual and long-term elasticities is in keeping with expectations:[16] entrepreneurs will make a fuller adjustment of capital to a permanent than to a transitory change in demand.

EFFECTS OF PRICE CHANGES

Since our three-digit industry data were not deflated, it is necessary to turn to the two-digit industries for information on the effects of price

TABLE 22

REGRESSION OF PERCENTAGE CHANGE IN CAPITAL ON PERCENTAGE CHANGE IN OUTPUT AND ON PROFIT RATES, TWENTY-ONE MAJOR INDUSTRIES, 1947–54

X_1 = percentage change in total capital
X_2 = percentage change in output
X_3 = average profit rate

Book values

$$X_1 = -9.641 + \underset{(.098)}{.743X_2} + \underset{(1.92)}{4.03X_3} \qquad R = .937$$

1947 prices

$$X_1 = -45.34 + \underset{(.158)}{.396X_2} + \underset{(2.14)}{7.55X_3} \qquad R = .811$$

SOURCE: Tables A-36 to A-59; and *Census of Manufactures, 1954*, Vol. IV, Part 4.

changes on the relationships between investment, receipts, and profit rates. The basic equations for this set of major industry groups are given in Table 22.[17] Elimination of price changes has a radical effect upon the

[15] If X_1 and X_2 are relative changes in investment and receipts, respectively, and X_3 is profit rates, the correlation coefficients are:

	1938–47	1947–54	1947–56
r_{12}	.753	.917	.926
r_{13}	.181	.325	.393
r_{23}	.060	.234	.167
$r_{12.3}$	.756	.915	.949
$r_{13.2}$	.207	.285	.640
$R_{1.23}$	.765	.924	.957

[16] A minor difference arises because the long-term regression is based upon percentage changes, whereas the annual regressions are based upon differences in logarithms. The exclusion of a single, highly abnormal industry (aircraft) increased the long-term elasticity from .5 to .8 for the 1947–54 period.

[17] The output measure is a ("cross") weighted average of output indexes in the *Census of Manufactures, 1954*, Vol. IV, Part 4. The transportation sector is omitted because the extremely unusual behavior of aircraft greatly affects the regressions.

relative importance of the two independent variables. The dominant part previously played by changes in receipts no longer holds: in fact, the coefficient of determination of profit rates becomes larger than that of physical output.[18] Since investment and receipts are similarly influenced by movements of prices much more than profit rates are, it is of course natural that deflation of the data reduces the role of receipts.[19] On the whole, the regression fits the data remarkably well even after deflation.

EXPECTED PROFIT RATES

The role of *expected* profit rates is crucial in determining the direction and volume of investment, in the traditional theory. We should naturally like to observe this variable and introduce it into our analysis, less to test its relevance (for this can hardly be doubted) than to form a notion of the quantitative effect of expected rates on investment. Expectations, however, are fully as difficult to quantify here as elsewhere in economics and, in particular, the popular method of questionnaire, even were it possible in our context, would yield results difficult to interpret or to trust. So we are thrown back on methods of constructing what may be more or less plausible measures of expectations.

Yehuda Grunfeld proposed the use of the market value of securities of a firm as an index of expectations of its future earnings.[20] There are substantial forces working to bring the expectations of management and market together: outside investors will profit by a more accurate set of predictions of future demands and costs, and management will profit by sale or purchase of securities if its expectations are superior to and different from those of the market.

Only modest use can be made of this index of future profits because of the limitations of data. Market values are available only for large firms whose securities are listed on exchanges (Grunfeld's work is based on such companies), and this requirement excludes many industries and raises doubts concerning the representativeness of the data for others. The available industry indexes of stock-market values have two other deficiencies for

[18] The correlation coefficients, in the notation of Table 22, are:

	Book Value	1947 *Prices*
r_{12}	.921	.648
r_{13}	.697	.733
$r_{12.3}$	.873	.509
$r_{13.2}$	.444	.640

[19] The same price indexes, in fact, enter into output and inventory deflations.

[20] "The Determinants of Corporate Investment," in *The Demand for Durable Goods*, Arnold C. Harberger, Ed., University of Chicago Press, 1960.

our purposes: only market values of common stocks are reported; and yearly values are the means of high and low quotations (of variable date) rather than those at a fixed time of year.[21] Yet the variable is sufficiently promising to make even a crude application worthwhile.

The time periods involved in the use of market value as a measure of expected profits are not self-evident. A given movement of market value reflects a change in expected earnings sometime in the future, and all one can say in general is that a given expected change in earnings will have a larger effect on present market value, the nearer in the future it is to occur.[22] It is possible that profit expectations for the near future dominate *movements* of stock-market values, or that the whole level of expected future earnings is decisive. We use *differences* among industries in movements of market value to measure *differences* in expected future earnings, and to this extent remove the effects of changes in the general level of security prices. Both annual and longer-period regressions will be examined.

The predictions of relative investment in a year by the preceding year's change in market value turn out rather poorly: in only one year is the correlation coefficient significantly greater than zero, and it is negative in two recession years (Table 23).[23] The predictions provided by the rate of return in the preceding year are considerably better, although only in 1951 and 1954 are they significant. The introduction of the preceding year's relative change in receipts does not appreciably affect either relationship.

This is of course a severe test to impose, for the predictions are unconditional in the sense that no data from the year in which investment occurs are employed.[24] Even changes in receipts, which are so successful in all analyses in which they are simultaneous with investment, have no predictive power: the correlation coefficient is negative in the only year in which it is statistically significant.

To test the role of market-value changes over a longer period, the market values in 1947 and 1948 (averaged) were compared with those of 1949 and 1950 (averaged), and the relative change in market value over

[21] See S. Cottle and T. Whitman, *Corporate Earning Power and Market Valuation, 1935–1955*, Duke University Press, 1959, p. 12. We are indebted to Cottle and Whitman for supplying supplementary information.

[22] Grunfeld used successive annual time periods for both market value and gross investment, where the latter is the dependent variable in a regression on market value and beginning-of-year stock of capital.

[23] A larger sample of rates of change in industry stock price indexes compiled by Standard and Poor were also analyzed for 1948–49 and 1949–50 against the subsequent year's investment rate, without a significant change in the results. These stock indexes were taken at the end of year.

[24] But it should be noted that $r_{12.3}$, in the notation of Table 23, is not very different if the change of receipts in the year of investment is used.

TABLE 23

CORRELATION BETWEEN INVESTMENT AND PROFIT RATES, CHANGE IN MARKET VALUE AND RECEIPTS, TWENTY-ONE INDUSTRIES, SELECTED YEARS, 1949–54

X_1 = investment = log capital$_t$ − log capital$_{t-1}$
X_2 = change in market value = log value$_{t-1}$ − log value$_{t-2}$
X_3 = change in receipts = log receipts$_{t-1}$ − log receipts$_{t-2}$
X_4 = profit rate, year $(t-1)$

Year	r_{12}	r_{13}	r_{14}	r_{23}	r_{24}	$r_{12.3}$	$r_{14.3}$
1949	−.077	.107	−.010	.348	.273	−.123	−.033
1950	.351	−.006	.295	.351	.350	.377	.345
1951	.481	.269	.499	.600	.382	.414	.437
1953[a]	.118	−.412	.154	.398	.462	.337	.169
1954[b]	−.161	−.114	.476	.205	−.150	−.142	.464

[a] Because 1952 data are not available, X_1 for 1953 is ½ (log capital 1953 − log capital 1951).
[b] For the same reason, X_3 is ½ (log receipts 1953 − log receipts 1951).

SOURCE: For market value data, Cottle and Whitman, *Corporate Earning Power*; other figures from Tables A-36 to A-59 and *Statistics of Income*.

that period was correlated with relative investment from 1950 to 1954. The simple correlation coefficient was .315 (for twenty-one industries). This result is also less than impressive, but in the light of the deficiencies of the data it cannot be viewed as wholly unpromising. The performance of market value as a predictor of investment demand appears to be about as good in this four-year analysis as it is in the annual analyses.

An alternative method of predicting ex ante profit rates is the extrapolation of recent profit rates. If the industry had previously been in long-run equilibrium, there would be no basis in past experience for estimating future returns, which would presumably also be at the equilibrium level after appropriate investment. But this is only a simple instance of the general rule that only if a system gets out of equilibrium can one discover the forces that restore equilibrium. If recent profit rates have not been at the equilibrium level, they possess predictive value for future profit rates. If profit rates have been above the average, and rising, the industry will have rosy profit prospects; if profit rates have been below average, and falling, the industry's near future is unattractive.

In this interpretation, one might assume that relative investment $(\Delta C/C)$ will be some function such as

$$\frac{\Delta C_{t+1}}{C_t} = a + b\,(\pi_t - \bar{\pi}_t) + c(\pi_t - \pi_{t-1}) + d\left(\frac{\Delta R_t}{R_{t-1}}\right)$$

where π is the profit rate, $\bar{\pi}$ the average of industries, R is receipts, and the subscripts refer to time. The coefficient b should be positive since a profit rate above average encourages investment, and c should be positive because rising profit rates should work the same way. Finally, d should be positive because rising sales also suggest a large investment demand. The equation can be written

$$\frac{\Delta C_{t+1}}{C_t} = (a - b\bar{\pi}_t) + (b + c)\pi_t - c\pi_{t-1} + d\left(\frac{\Delta R_t}{R_{t-1}}\right)$$

$$= A + B\pi_t + C\pi_{t-1} + d\left(\frac{\Delta R_t}{R_{t-1}}\right),$$

with the expectation that B and d are positive and C negative. In this form, the equation differs from a simple regression of the rate of investment on previous years' profit rate and increase in receipts only by the presence of the profit rate two years before. It is in this form that the regression equation has been calculated, with differences in logarithms replacing percentage changes in corporate capital and receipts.

The predictions are again unconditional, in the sense that no data from the predicted year enter as independent variables so, at best, only modest results can be expected, and even they are not forthcoming (see Table 24). In the one year (1950), in which the profit rate of the preceding year has a statistically significant regression coefficient, it has the wrong sign. The regression coefficients for the profit rate lagged two years are significant in 1950 and 1956, but in other years are statistically nonsignificant and erratic in sign.

The results of both these profit expectation analyses are calculated to remind one that investment rates are among the most difficult of all economic magnitudes to predict. One must use very lenient standards of success in judging unconditional predictions, but even by these standards one can say only that both market value changes and lagged profit rates deserve further exploration.

2. *Other Possible Determinants of Investment Rates*

Although the level of demand (here measured by receipts) and profit rates are taken as the leading determinants of investment in the literature on the subject, there are a host of other variables which have been regarded as relevant. In general no strongly influential variables were found in this canvass, which was severely restricted by data limitations.

CONCENTRATION OF INDUSTRY

The effects of monopoly on the amount of capital invested in an industry are debated in an extensive literature. The most popular conclusions are

TABLE 24

REGRESSION OF RELATIVE INVESTMENT ON PREVIOUS RELATIVE CHANGE IN RECEIPTS AND PROFIT RATES, NINETY-EIGHT INDUSTRIES, 1949–57

$X_1 = \log \text{capital}_t - \log \text{capital}_{t-1}$
$X_2 = \log \text{receipts}_{t-1} - \log \text{receipts}_{t-2}$
$X_3 = \text{profit rate}_{t-1}$
$X_4 = \text{profit rate}_{t-2}$

1949

$$\begin{array}{lllll} X_1 = .0085 + & .149X_2 - & .00035X_3 - & .00052X_4 & \quad R = .220 \\ & (.081) & (.0015) & (.0012) & \end{array}$$

1950

$$\begin{array}{lllll} X_1 = .0629 + & .124X_2 - & .0044X_3 + & .0036X_4 & \quad R = .233 \\ & (.099) & (.0020) & (.0018) & \end{array}$$

1951

$$\begin{array}{lllll} X_1 = -.0079 + & .020X_2 + & .0051X_3 + & .0010X_4 & \quad R = .437 \\ & (.103) & (.0026) & (.0020) & \end{array}$$

1953[a]

$$\begin{array}{lllll} X_1 = -.0289 - & .107X_2 + & .0061X_3 + & .0022X_4 & \quad R = .364 \\ & (.134) & (.0041) & (.0033) & \end{array}$$

1954[b]

$$\begin{array}{lllll} X_1 = -.00084 - & .090X_2 + & .0048X_3 - & .0026X_4 & \quad R = .223 \\ & (.057) & (.0025) & (.0020) & \end{array}$$

1955

$$\begin{array}{lllll} X_1 = .0125 & .062X_2 + & .0031X_3 + & .0023X_4 & \quad R = .331 \\ & (.085) & (.0028) & (.0030) & \end{array}$$

1956

$$\begin{array}{lllll} X_1 = -.0118 + & .072X_2 - & .0041X_3 + & .0103X_4 & \quad R = .481 \\ & (.084) & (.0029) & (.0028) & \end{array}$$

1957

$$\begin{array}{lllll} X_1 = -.0309 & .149X_2 + & .0039X_3 + & .0024X_4 & \quad R = .343 \\ & (.120) & (.0035) & (.0030) & \end{array}$$

NOTE: 1952 data not available.
[a] 1951 substituted for $t - 1$; 1950 substituted for $t - 2$.
[b] 1951 substituted for $t - 2$.

SOURCE: Tables A-36 to A-59 and *Statistics of Income*.

that: (1) under monopoly proper or oligopoly there will be less capital, given demand and cost conditions, than there would be under competition; and (2) under most cartel systems there will be more capital per unit of output than under competition. But even if these conclusions are accepted, they do not settle the question of the effect of monopoly on investment. It would be quite possible for a monopoly to have 10 per cent less capital than a competitive industry would have, at each point in time, but clearly the percentage increase in capital (or investment relative to initial capital stock) would be identical in the two situations.

The long-term regressions of investment rates on profit rates and changes in receipts are given in Table 25. In the earlier period there is a considerable difference within both sets of regression coefficients, but

TABLE 25

REGRESSION OF RELATIVE CHANGE IN CAPITAL ON RELATIVE CHANGE IN RECEIPTS AND PROFIT RATE, BY INDUSTRY STRUCTURE, TWO PERIODS, 1938–56

X_1 = percentage increase in total capital
X_2 = percentage increase of corporate receipts
X_3 = average rate of return

Industry Structure	Number of Industries	Regression Coefficient of X_1 on:		Coefficient of Multiple Correlation
		X_2	X_3	
1938–47				
Unconcentrated	37	.313 (.105)	.41 (6.32)	.467
Ambiguous	34	.685 (.052)	12.14 (3.89)	.924
Concentrated	11	.294 (.125)	4.52 (5.77)	.651
1947–56				
Unconcentrated	54	.894 (.042)	2.89 (1.26)	.952
Ambiguous	30	.903 (.103)	−2.15 (2.83)	.905
Concentrated	14	.851 (.122)	8.62 (2.46)	.946

SOURCE: Tables A-14 to A-59; and C-1 and C-2.

there are no significant differences between the concentrated and unconcentrated industries. The impact of the war on that period, however, is such that its results are much less relevant than those of the later period. In the later period the relationships not only fit the data better, in the sense of higher coefficients of multiple correlation, but the parameters for the concentrated and unconcentrated industries seem much more stable.

In the later period, there appears to be one significant difference between the concentrated and unconcentrated industries. The unconcentrated industries' investment rates are considerably less responsive to changes in profit rates than the concentrated industries' rates are; the responsiveness to changes in receipts does not differ between the two classes. The lesser dependence, ex post, of investment on rates of return in unconcentrated industries may be due to the fact that investment adjusts more quickly to changes in demand under competition. This pattern may indeed be viewed as another aspect of the finding (in Chapter 3) that the industrial pattern of profit rates is more stable in concentrated than in unconcentrated industries; given that fact, the differences in long-run average rates of return in unconcentrated industries will be much smaller and their observed effect on long-run investment rates also smaller.

A closely related question is whether the number of firms in an industry exerts an independent influence on investment. The hypothesis runs as follows: the more numerous the firms in an industry, the greater the dispersion of their rates of operation relative to "capacity." Therefore, even if the industry on average is at (say) 80 per cent of capacity, a given increase in demand will lead those firms at higher rates of operation to expand investment to handle their share of the increase in demand. This is presumably a short-run phenomenon—indeed the very notion of capacity of a firm loses any meaning in the long run.

A rigorous testing of this argument cannot be made with our data. Only if firms are making the same products in the same geographical market does the conclusion follow, and we cannot isolate these complicating influences. A rough test was made by comparing the residuals from our regression equations (Table 20) relating relative investment to profit rates and relative changes in receipts, for the years 1949 and 1950, with the number of corporate tax returns in each industry. No relationship was found.[25]

IDLE CAPACITY

A permanent increase in demand for an industry's product will lead to increased investment if the industry has previously been in long-run equilibrium. For the "capacity"—meaning by this elusive term the rate of investment fully appropriate to the previous rate of output—must be enlarged: more intensive working of the existing plants will almost always be more expensive than making a suitable expansion of investment.

Our regression equations relating investment to percentage change in receipts are, in effect, estimates of this relationship for industries whose outputs are growing. But for industries whose demands are declining, the relationship will often be much looser. It may require more time to withdraw capital than expectations and events have allowed, and the question arises: do industries that have experienced more or less persistent declines in output display a different investment behavior?

In order to answer this question we have segregated those industries whose receipts in a given year were smaller than they were two or three years earlier. In 1950, for example, there were twenty-eight such

[25] The correlation coefficients between residuals and number of returns for 98 industries are −.091 for 1949 and .100 for 1950.

industries, and the declines from the previous peak receipts[26] are compared with the residuals from the regression equation relating 1950 investment to 1950 profit rates and to 1950 changes in receipts. This analysis is possible for four postwar years, and yields the correlation coefficients shown below.

Year	*Rank Correlation: Residuals and Idle Capacity*	*N*
1949	–.343	17
1950	–.297	28
1951	–.829	6
1954	–.026	29

None of these correlations is impressive, but their consistency suggests that delayed withdrawal of capital has been present in even the fairly broad industrial categories with which we had to deal. Apparently our

TABLE 26

TECHNICAL PROGRESS, INVESTMENT, AND RATE OF RETURN, 1947–54

Industry	Percentage Increase in Output per Unit of Input[a]	Average Rate of Return	Percentage Increase in Assets (book value)
Electric machinery and equipment	28.1	8.50	72.29
Fabricated metal products	28.0	8.68	62.14
Chemicals and allied products	22.5	8.92	65.64
Basic lumber	27.0	9.09	46.86
Petroleum and coal products	16.1	8.01	91.34
Textile mill products	14.4	7.13	27.83
Machinery, except transportation and electric	13.6	8.26	67.44
Stone, clay, and glass products	12.5	9.05	87.35
Food and kindred products	11.4	6.72	34.01
Rubber products	10.7	6.24	54.69
Furniture and finished lumber	8.8	7.23	54.70
Paper and allied products	8.5	9.93	81.10
Printing and publishing	7.7	7.51	45.34
Apparel and fabric products	6.9	4.51	19.49
Beverages	4.5	7.48	45.08
Tobacco products	3.5	6.46	35.84
Primary metal products	2.7	7.59	66.45
Leather products	0.1	5.52	4.40

[a] 1948–53.

SOURCE: Based on data from John W. Kendrick, *Productivity Trends in the United States*, Princeton for National Bureau of Economic Research, 1961, Appendix D, Table D-IV, pp. 468–475; and Tables A-36 to A-59, below.

[26] The decline in receipts is log receipts_{49} – log receipts_{48} or log receipts_{49} – log receipts_{47}, whichever is numerically larger.

regressions would be somewhat improved by introducing a lagged as well as a current relative change in receipts.

OTHER INFLUENCES ON INVESTMENT

Some of the most widely discussed influences on investment are already implicitly recognized in our analysis.[27] Shifts in consumer demand, for example, are already reflected in our receipts measure.

One economic influence on investment, which lurks behind our summary variables, is technical progress—the reductions in real costs, or improvements in quality or kind of goods. This influence is of the highest interest to contemporary economists, and certain comparisons of Kendrick's measures—unfortunately available only at a fairly broad level—with investments and rates of return are given in Table 26. There are moderately strong relationships of this measure of progress with investment and rates of return.[28] The former of these results is wholly in keeping with expectations—large reductions in cost and price will induce large sales and investment. The relationship between this measure of progress and rates of return is equally strong, and rather less expected. The inference may be that the adjustment of investment has not kept pace with the technical progress in these industries, or that the write-off of research expenditures leads to an appreciable understatement of capital.

[27] The influence of wage rates is discussed in the next chapter.
[28] The respective rank correlation coefficients are +.46 and +.57.

CHAPTER 5

Labor and Capital

In our comprehensive view of capital, which includes land, there are only two productive agents—capital and labor. They necessarily receive the total net product after taxes, and the division of this product (or income) between them gives rise to some of the most important questions of public policy. Since labor and capital constitute the productive agents, their allocation among industries is equally important in relation to the productive process.

For many purposes it is necessary to study individual workers and pieces of capital, but we shall restrict our discussion to industry aggregates. Even on this summary level, our material on the number and remuneration of workers is much less complete than that on amount and returns to capital. Comprehensive data are available (from the *Census of Manufactures*) only for 1939, 1947, and 1954, but they are reported on an establishment basis rather than a company basis, so discrepancies in the capital figures will arise because many companies operate in more than one (three-digit) industry.[1] Even with these limitations, some interesting problems can be examined.

1. *Wages and Returns to Capital*

The predominant part of the total income in manufacturing, as we know, goes to labor. The main percentage distributive shares are shown in the tabulation below.

	Payroll	*Return to Capital* (after taxes)
1939	80.1	19.9
1947	77.6	22.4
1954	85.9	14.4

These precise numbers are sensitive to the state of business because rates of return fluctuate more widely than wage rates do. If, for example, we had used the 1953 rate of return this share would have been 17.8 per cent. But with the rates of return of the last decade, wages have been more than four-fifths of the total income.

The division of income varies widely among industries: in 1954 labor's

[1] An attempt is made to reduce this source of discrepancy by (1) using two-digit classifications, or (2) excluding the industries where discrepancies (measured by receipts) are large, or (3) adjusting the labor data on the basis of receipts data. But the distortion that remains may be appreciable.

TABLE 27

AGGREGATE PAYROLL AS PERCENTAGE OF TOTAL DISTRIBUTIVE SHARES IN MANUFACTURING INDUSTRIES, SELECTED YEARS, 1939–54

Industry	*Payroll as Per Cent of Total*			*Total Payroll and Return to Capital, After Taxes* (billions of dollars)		
	1939	1947	1954	1939	1947	1954
d and kindred products	77.2	76.7	86.2[a]	1.61	4.16	5.30[a]
erages	63.0	66.3	81.9	0.35	0.90	1.06
acco products	43.8	60.1	58.9	0.20	0.34	0.44
tile mill products	88.7	74.0	95.6	1.23	3.83	3.17
arel, fabric products	95.2	86.8	96.8	0.90	2.91	3.31
c lumber	93.1	70.9	86.1[b]	0.41	1.52	2.00[b]
niture, finished lumber	91.0[c]	87.1	93.8	0.41[c]	1.34	1.28
er, allied products	81.5	68.5	82.8	0.55	1.87	2.68
ting, publishing	89.5	83.8	91.9	1.09	2.72	3.94
micals, allied products	60.4	64.7	76.3	1.02	3.05	4.47
roleum, coal products	54.5	37.2	43.8	0.46	1.93	2.51
ber products	81.2	86.0	89.0	0.28	0.91	1.19
ther products	91.6	86.0	94.1	0.40	1.02	1.09
ne, clay, glass products	76.1	80.5	82.9	0.53	1.50	2.34
tals, metal products	83.5[d]	81.2	88.2	2.43[d]	8.18	10.77
chinery, except transportation, electrical	81.2	82.8	88.9	1.37	5.58	8.09
ctric machinery, equipment	78.7	82.4	87.6	0.66	2.82	4.51
nsportation equipment, except vehicles	83.4	104.1[e]	92.1	0.36	1.45[e]	5.31
tor vehicles	76.7	74.7	78.9	1.03	2.95	4.32
cellaneous manufactures, including instruments	83.4[f]	86.3	89.0	0.57[f]	1.86	3.17
manufactures	80.1	77.6	85.9	16.02[g]	51.16[g]	72.17[g]

NOTE. Total distributive shares is defined as payroll plus return to capital, after taxes.
[a] Excludes fluid milk.
[b] Excludes logging.
[c] Excludes matches, for comparability with IRS.
[d] Excludes clocks and jewelry.
[e] Losses in 1947.
[f] Includes matches, clocks, and jewelry.
[g] Independently calculated, not equal to sum of two-digit entries.

SOURCE: *United States Census of Manufactures, 1939, 1947,* and *1954* (Bureau of the Census), and *Statistics of Income, Corporation Income Tax Returns,* for 1939, 1947, and 1954 (Internal Revenue Service).

share ranged from 43.8 per cent (petroleum) to 96.8 per cent (apparel), as shown in Table 27.[2] We shall see later that average wage *rates* do not differ greatly among industries, so the functional distribution of income is dominated by the amounts of capital per worker in the various industries. Since the differences among industries in the relative use of capital are

[2] The wage share in petroleum products is depressed by the inclusion of the mining operations of the integrated petroleum refining companies.

persistent over long periods, we expect, and find, that the share of wages in total income has a stable industrial pattern (the rank correlation coefficient between 1947 and 1954 was .82).

There is a large literature on the alleged constancy over time of the share of wages in the distribution of total income. Even the concept of constancy is in dispute: if the attraction of bodies were an inverse function of the 1.99 power of distance on weekdays and the 2.01 power on Sunday, the physical world would be rather eccentric; but if the percentage of consumer income spent on a commodity never exceeded these limits, the constancy would be astonishing. Our own data certainly suggest no such order of constancy. Even within our broad industry categories, from 1947 to 1954 the share of wages rose 10 or more per cent in half the industries. The fluctuations are possibly even larger in more precisely defined industries.

When we turn to income per worker and per thousand dollars of capital, we are faced with a dimensional problem. A doubling of prices all around, leaving relative prices unchanged, would double earnings per worker but leave the rate of return on capital (measured in dollars) unchanged. Broadly, that is what happened between 1939 and 1954: average earnings tripled while average rates of return rose slightly, in 1947 prices (and fell slightly, in book values). The average dollar of 1939 capital roughly doubled in nominal value over that period, so the return to the owner of that dollar fell by one-third relative to the earnings of a worker.

The differences among industries in average annual earnings per worker are largely due to differences in the use of skilled labor, location in large or small communities, and so on. These differences tend to persist over substantial periods, since they are compatible with long-run equilibrium. The rank correlations of average earnings (see Table 28) were, in fact, quite high: 1939 and 1947, .95; and 1947 and 1954, .91. As a result, the dispersion of average earnings in one year is a fairly good estimate of the dispersion over longer periods: the coefficient of variation was 22.2 per cent in 1939, 15.5 per cent in 1947, and 19.5 per cent in 1954—approximately 20 per cent on average.

The differences among industries in rates of return, on the contrary, are considerably larger in the short run than over long periods. The short-run fluctuations in business impose large fluctuations on returns to capital, which are a residual share in the short run (although not in the long run). The coefficient of variation of rates of return was 24.4 per cent in 1947, for example, when the coefficient of annual earnings was 15.5 per cent. As the period over which returns are calculated is lengthened, the dispersion

TABLE 28

ANNUAL EARNINGS PER WORKER AND RATE OF RETURN ON CAPITAL IN MANUFACTURING INDUSTRIES, SELECTED YEARS AND PERIODS, 1938–55

Industry	*Annual Earnings* (dollars)			*Rates of Return* (annual average, per cent)		
	1939	1947	1954	1938–40	1946–48	1953–55
l and kindred products	1,242	2,575	4,279	5.36	9.45	5.60
rages	1,690	2,955	3,645	8.74	11.22	5.37
acco products	904	1,841	2,738	10.25	6.74	6.39
tile mill products	941	2,299	2,923	2.87	14.74	2.72
arel, fabric products	1,014	2,336	2,690	2.68	10.51	2.90
c lumber	955	2,104	3,020	1.72	13.05[a]	—
					12.86[b]	6.55
niture, finished lumber	1,107	2,556	3,515	3.42	9.78[a]	—
					10.28[b]	5.32
er, allied products	1,375	2,847	4,182	5.33	13.70	7.50
ting, publishing	1,770	3,183	4,507	4.60	11.18	6.29
micals, allied products	1,536	3,021	4,608	8.46	11.20	7.43
oleum, coal products	1,791	3,487	5,105	2.79	9.16	6.59
ber products	1,515	3,024	4,297	4.81	8.66	5.43
ther products	1,018	2,280	2,881	3.32	9.63	4.82
ne, clay, and glass products	1,303	2,620	3,941	5.72	10.40	7.99
tals, metal products	1,507	3,019	4,444	4.41	8.94[a]	—
					9.00[b]	6.23
chinery, except transportation, electrical	1,631	3,109	4,664	6.90	8.75	6.02
ctrical machinery, equipment	1,551	2,834	4,119	8.95	7.24	6.54
nsportation equipment, except vehicles	1,639	3,147	4,844	4.40	0.01	5.96
tor vehicles	1,723	3,148	4,900	6.46	8.88	9.71
scellaneous manufactures, including instruments	1,321	2,695	3,843	6.28	7.75[a]	—
					7.83[b]	5.74
manufactures	1,334	2,777	4,025	5.25	9.63[a]	—
					9.65[b]	6.41

[a] Using 1947 profit rate on 1946 classification basis.
[b] Using 1947 profit rate on 1948 classification basis.

SOURCE: *Census of Manufactures, 1939, 1947,* and *1954*; and Tables A-14 to A-59.

of rates is reduced,[3] and the coefficient of variation approaches that of annual earnings (see Chapter 3).

Industries that have high rates of return tend also to have high annual earnings per worker, although the correspondence is only moderate.[4] Let us consider this relationship more closely.

[3] The rank correlations of three-year average rates of return in Table 28 are —.45 in 1939 and 1947 (compared with .95 for earnings), and —.09 in 1947 and 1954 (compared with .91).

[4] The rank correlations (Table 28) were .30 in 1939 and .55 in 1954. There was no correlation in 1947, but that period was much affected by postwar demobilization of the economy.

2. *The Capital-Labor Ratio*

The average employee in manufacturing worked with $12,320 of capital in 1939, when much capital was underemployed because of depressed business conditions, $10,614 in 1947, and $13,031 in 1954 (all measured in 1947 prices). Thus he was supplied with capital equal to the equivalent of two to three years' wages, or twenty to thirty times his own annual savings. This capital-labor ratio has of course been rising secularly in manufacturing industries.

The capital-labor ratio varies widely among industries: even in the limited group of industries for which capital and labor data are fairly comparable, the range in 1954 was from $1,900 in millinery to $39,300 in "other tobacco" (chiefly cigarettes).[5] The relative dispersion of the ratios has been diminishing in recent years.[6]

		Capital Per Worker		
Year	Number of Industries	Average Capital	Standard Deviation	Coefficient of Variation (per cent)
1939	38	$4,340	$3,090	71.2
1947	49	6,930	4,840	69.8
1954	53	10,500	7,200	68.6

Our concept of capital extends to working capital and inventories, so only in a correspondingly enlarged sense can we speak of differences in "technology" as underlying the capital-labor ratios. Even so, the pattern among industries of these ratios is remarkably stable: the correlation coefficient between 1939 and 1947 ratios was .83 (thirty-seven industries) and that between the 1947 and 1954 ratios was .96 (forty-nine industries).[7]

[5] The asset data are adjusted by the ratio of receipts as reported in *Census of Manufactures* to receipts as reported in *Statistics of Income*, and industries in which the unadjusted ratio of receipts from these two sources fell outside the range of 4 to 5 and 5 to 4 are excluded. In subsequent analyses the wider range, 2 to 3 to 3 to 2, is used. See Tables D-1 and D-2 for list of Internal Revenue Service industries for which comparable Census data are available.

[6] If one restricts the 1939 and 1947 comparison to 30 identical industries, the coefficient of variation falls from 71.8 per cent to 62.1 per cent.

[7] The regression equations are:

$$(C/L)_{47} = 1{,}680 + \underset{(.12)}{1.11}\ (C/L)_{39},$$

$$(C/L)_{54} = 630 + \underset{(.06)}{1.40}\ (C/L)_{47}.$$

In each period the industries are those for which the Census to IRS-receipts ratio falls between 3 to 2 and 2 to 3 in *both* years.

The stability of technology is the basic determinant of the short-run industry structure of capital-labor ratios.

Workers in industries with larger capital-labor ratios on average receive somewhat higher than average annual earnings (see Table 29).[8] One can

TABLE 29

ANNUAL EARNINGS AND CAPITAL PER WORKER, MANUFACTURING INDUSTRIES, 1939 AND 1954

(dollar amounts in thousands)

Approximate Deciles	Average Capital Per Worker	Number of Industries	Average Annual Earnings
	1939		
1	$0.94	3	$1.08
2	1.84	4	0.98
3	2.38	3	1.12
4	3.16	4	1.26
5	3.71	4	1.09
6	4.04	4	1.48
7	4.88	4	1.50
8	7.22	4	1.36
9	8.52	4	1.50
10	14.06	3	1.47
Total	5.02	37	1.29
	1954		
1	3.21	5	3.01
2	5.07	5	3.34
3	6.20	5	3.81
4	6.94	5	3.54
5	7.83	5	4.54
6	8.51	5	4.07
7	11.61	5	3.90
8	14.33	5	4.68
9	18.92	5	4.01
10	27.81	4	3.91
Total	10.70	49	3.88

SOURCE: Tables D-1 and D-2.

interpret this association as indicating that industries with larger capital per worker employ slightly better-trained workers on average; this interpretation is more appealing than the alternative that higher wage *rates* are paid to comparable workers in these industries. We do not possess data on a comparable basis for wage *rates* for given types of workers, but

[8] The correlation coefficients for capital-labor ratio and average earnings were .365 for 1939 and .215 in 1954. No such relationship was present in 1947.

the composition of workers by sex suggests that the moderate differences in earnings can be accounted for by differences in type of labor.[9]

Since capital-labor ratios have a tolerably stable industrial pattern, it is not surprising that those industries in which capital grew most rapidly are also those in which the number of workers increased most rapidly.[10] Moreover, industries with unusually large relative increases in their capital stock also had the larger relative increases in annual earnings ($r = .641$ in 1947–54). And again, those industries in which capital per worker rose most over the period 1947 to 1954 had the largest relative increases in annual earnings ($r = .501$).[11] All these relationships reflect one basic force: the differing rates of expansion of industries imply differing rates of increase in both labor and capital inputs, and higher remuneration for both inputs is a part of the mechanism of drawing in these resources.[12]

3. *Substitution of Capital for Labor*

The principle of substitution has been in neoclassical economics the basis of the theories of both production and distribution:

> Every agent of production, land, machinery, skilled labour, unskilled labour, etc., tends to be applied in production as far as it profitably can be. If employers, and other business men, think they can get a better result by using a little more of any one agent they will do so. They estimate the net product (that is, the net increase of the money value of their total output after allowing for incidental expenses) that will be got by a little more outlay in this direction, or a little more outlay in that; and if they can gain by shifting a little of their outlay from one direction to another, they will do so.[13]

The empirically minded economist is naturally concerned with how strong this principle is—how completely, and how rapidly, one resource is substituted for another if their relative costs or marginal productivities change.

[9] Seven out of the fifteen lowest-earnings industries in 1954 could be approximately matched in the *1950 Census of Population*; they had an average of 49.6 per cent female employees. The corresponding figure for six of the fifteen highest-earnings industries was 19.0 per cent.

[10] In the 1939–47 period, the correlation between log (C_{47}/C_{39}) and log (N_{47}/N_{39}) was only .278 (for thirty-seven industries) but in the 1947–54 period it was .617 (for forty-nine industries).

[11] This relationship, unlike that between relative increases in total capital and annual earnings, held also over 1939 to 1947 ($r = .502$).

[12] The correlation between relative increases in profit rates (1947–49 to 1951–54) with the relative increase in annual earnings was .618; the corresponding coefficient for the earlier period is .560 (where profit-rate averages were calculated for 1938–40 and 1945–47).

[13] Alfred Marshall, *Principles of Economics*, 8th ed., London, Macmillan, 1938, p. 521.

The quantification of the principle is elusive when the available information pertains to industries rather than firms. If we observe the relationship between wage rates and capital per worker in a group of industries at one time, we need not expect to find that there is more capital per worker in those industries in which wage rates are higher.[14] The industries have different techniques of production, which exert a large (and, at least over the moderate time periods, independent) influence upon the proportions between inputs. Moreover, labor is not homogeneous, and just as a steam shovel is more capital than a shovel, so is a skilled worker more labor than an unskilled worker.

Evidence of the importance of technological differences among industries in the ratio of capital to labor has already been provided by the comparison of capital per worker and average annual wages for 1939 and 1954 (in Table 29). There is in fact a weak positive relationship between annual wages and the amount of capital per worker (except in 1947), but it is attributable to differences in the quality of labor.

A more precise analysis encounters formidable difficulties in attaching a meaning to the cost of capital services. A given machine, for example, has costs composed of (1) interest on its purchase price, (2) depreciation, and (3) maintenance. Each component is obviously influenced by wage rates—original cost and depreciation, by wage rates in the machine building industry; maintenance, by wage rates in the industry in question. A proportional rise in wage rates for all types of labor raises simultaneously the cost of a given machine, and hence the cost of capital.

If product prices are proportional to the wage outlays which directly or indirectly go into the production of a piece of capital equipment, then a universal rise in wage rates by a given percentage will raise the price of the equipment in the same proportion. In this case, we should not expect a rise in wage rates—interest rates unchanged—to affect the optimum combination of capital and labor appreciably. In fact, however, there is reason for believing that a rise in wage rates would lead to a less than proportional rise in capital costs for a firm. Some outlays of capital goods are not resolvable into labor costs. This is clearly true of raw materials, cash balances, etc., and since these are essential to produce capital goods, it is therefore true also of capital goods. Yet there is no reason to believe that a 25 per cent rise in wage rates relative to interest rates will lead to anything like so large a rise in labor costs relative to the costs of capital.

We cannot test this argument for it rests on something we have never experienced, an equal proportional rise in wage rates throughout the

[14] Assuming that the cost of capital is the same for the industries.

economy. When wage rates rise at substantially different rates in different industries, substitution of capital for labor in the industries in which wages have risen relatively more is to be expected, because on average the prices of capital items to these industries will have fallen relative to wage rates.

The extent of substitution between capital and labor can be estimated from the changes in the capital-labor ratio over a period. There is, however, the usual problem of disentangling substitution from other forces, such as technology, which also affect the ratio. There has been some substitution due to the rising relative cost of labor, but changes in technology may have concealed or exaggerated the substitutability. Of course, the advances in technology may fundamentally be directed also by factor price changes.

If we attribute all of the substitution of capital for labor to relative factor price movements, we can estimate the elasticity of substitution by the regression equation: $(C/L)' = a + bE'$, where $(C/L)'$ is the percentage change in the capital-labor ratio and E' is the percentage change in earnings per worker. Here b is numerically equal to the elasticity of substitution,[15] on the assumption that capital costs are constant. For 1947–54, the equation is:[16]

$$(C/L)' = 10.939 + \underset{(.234)}{.931}\, E', \qquad (n = 49)$$

These gross comparisons indicate that the elasticity of substitution is roughly of the order of unity—a 1 per cent rise in earnings leads to a 1 per cent increase in the capital-labor ratio.

Two serious objections may be raised against the foregoing estimates of the elasticity of substitution. At best, analysis of different industries yields an average elasticity, about which the elasticities of individual industries may vary widely. The estimate of the average itself may be biased because of the operation of forces not taken into account. For example, if the quality of workers was rising in industries in which earnings rose most, the relative increase in the capital-labor ratio is overstated (and with it the elasticity). Or changes in technology could be acting to exaggerate (or conceal) substitution. Such possible extraneous influences can always be invented for any empirical relationship, of course.

[15] The elasticity of substitution of capital for labor is defined as $\Delta\left(\frac{C}{L}\right)\Big/\frac{C}{L}$ divided by $\Delta\left(\frac{E}{i}\right)\Big/\frac{E}{i}$, where i is the cost of capital (assumed to be constant).

[16] The corresponding equation for 1939–47 is:

$$(C/L)' = -57.74 + \underset{(.313)}{1.076}\, E', \quad (n = 37)$$

Estimates of elasticities of substitution for individual industries have been made by various economists for individual (usually two-digit) industries, chiefly by comparing capital-labor (value added-labor) ratios by states.[17] The method assumes that differences in the price of labor reveal true differences in labor costs, and not differences in quality of labor. Our data permit an alternative set of estimates, by comparing the capital-output ratios of large and small companies with differences in average earnings of workers.[18] This approach assumes that the differences in earnings of workers of large and small companies represent real differences in labor costs, and that capital costs are the same for both sizes of company. The costs of capital are probably somewhat less for larger companies,[19] and some of their higher wage costs may represent higher quality of workers. Both possible biases work in the direction of exaggerating the elasticity of substitution, so our procedure yields a maximum estimate of the elasticity.

The procedure consists of comparing the ratio of capital to receipts in two company sizes (capital under $250,000 and over $5 million) with annual earnings in small and large *plants* (less than 50 and more than 500 employees). The comparison can be converted into an elasticity of substitution, which is reported in Table 30.[20]

[17] These studies include K. J. Arrow, H. B. Chenery, B. S. Minhaus, and R. M. Solow, "Capital-Labor Substitution and Economic Efficiency," *Review of Economics and Statistics*, Aug. 1961, pp. 225–251; J. Minasian, "Elasticities of Substitution and Constant-output Demand Curves for Labor," *Journal of Political Economy*, June 1961, pp. 261–270; and an unpublished study by Phillip Nelson.

[18] Direct capital labor ratios cannot be computed, because no data are available on employees of large and small companies.

[19] The common findings of much lower interest rates for large bank loans, and much lower flotation costs on large security issues, are not conclusive. These capital sources clearly favor large companies, but small companies have other sources (trade credit, retained earnings) for which the differential may be much smaller.

[20] Let C be capital, M materials, L labor, and R receipts. Then

$$R = M + Lw + Ci,$$

where w is annual earnings and i is the rate of yield of capital services. If $M = \lambda R$ (so materials are proportional to sales), value added is

$$V = R(1 - \lambda) = Lw + Ci.$$

The elasticity of substitution between L and C is defined as

$$\sigma = - \frac{\partial \left(\frac{L}{C}\right)}{\partial w} \cdot \frac{wC}{L},$$

that is, the relative change in L to C divided by the relative change in the prices (= marginal products) of the factors, assuming that i is constant. Since

$$V = Ci + Lw,$$

The estimated elasticities are generally large, and are fairly similar for 1947 and 1954, which increases somewhat our confidence in them. The average elasticity is about 4 in both years. Although this is an upwardly biased estimate, the elasticity of substitution obtained from comparisons of large and small firms should exceed the average elasticity of unity obtained from the 1947–54 regression, and not merely because our procedure exaggerates the former elasticity. The differentials in factor prices to large and small firms are persistent and should have been adjusted to more fully than industries were able to adjust to wage changes within a seven-year period.

These estimates of the long-run elasticity of substitution between capital and labor are highly tentative, but if more refined data and analyses confirm the high elasticities we find, this result will have a large import for economics. High substitution elasticities lead one to predict that movements in relative wage rates or returns to capital—whether induced by state or private action—will lead to larger changes in the relative roles of labor and capital in the production process. Many important policies rest upon some assumption as to the effects of prices of resources on their employment, and few would be unaffected by the facts of substitution. It is the long-run substitution that dominates the questions of employment and income, and refinements of our procedure may contribute to its determination.

---

and

$$\frac{V}{C} = i + \frac{L}{C} w,$$

$$\frac{\partial \left(\frac{V}{C}\right)}{\partial w} = \frac{L}{C} + w \frac{\partial \left(\frac{L}{C}\right)}{\partial w}$$

$$= \frac{L}{C} (1 - \sigma)$$

and

$$\sigma' = \frac{\partial \frac{V}{C}}{\partial w} \cdot \frac{wC}{V} = \frac{Lw}{V} (1 - \sigma)$$

Let

$$\log \left(\frac{V}{C}\right) = \sigma' \log w - \text{constant},$$

where σ' is defined above. Our estimate of σ' is

$$\frac{\log \left(\frac{R}{C}\right)_u - \log \left(\frac{R}{C}\right)_l}{\log w_u - \log w_l},$$

where u and l denote upper and lower size classes.

TABLE 30

Annual Earnings of Employees, and Capital-Receipts Ratio, for Small and Large Plants and Firms, 1947 and 1954

Industry	Earnings[a] Small[c]	Earnings[a] Large[d]	Ratio, Capital to Receipts[b] Small[c]	Ratio, Capital to Receipts[b] Large[d]	Ratio Value Added to Payroll	Elasticity of Substitution
			1947			
ialt beverages	1.23	1.58	.531	.482	2.86	−0.11
leat products	1.11	1.29	.144	.149	1.64	1.38
akery products	0.95	1.12	.264	.404	1.78	5.68
onfectionery	0.83	1.10	.346	.488	2.74	4.34
len's clothing	1.09	1.12	.290	.463	1.72	e
ulp, paper, and allied products	1.17	1.31	.368	.753	2.41	16.25
aints	1.19	1.42	.395	.471	2.55	3.55
ructural clay products	0.97	1.18	.661	.896	1.66	3.57
ottery	0.84	1.31	.534	.511	1.53	0.85
in cans	1.08	1.31	.464	.728	1.82	5.15
and tools, hardware	1.10	1.31	.521	.771	1.68	4.77
gricultural machinery	1.04	1.41	.489	.725	1.52	2.97
onstruction machinery	1.23	1.40	.484	.671	1.80	5.49
pecial industry machinery	1.38	1.40	.535	.894	1.60	e
welry, except costume	1.35	1.35	.455	.516	1.81	e
nly 1947 Data Available						
anning and preserving	0.83	1.16	.541	.628	2.19	1.98
road-woven wool	1.07	1.21	.409	.609	1.76	6.70
nit goods	1.00	1.07	.428	.597	1.73	e
ewspapers	1.13	2.01	.566	.835	1.88	2.28
riodicals	1.30	1.72	.383	.656	2.82	6.42
rugs and medicines	0.97	1.29	.607	.836	3.18	4.56
eather tanning	1.20	1.37	.355	.468	2.58	6.39
ootwear	0.98	1.08	.294	.422	1.55	6.75

(continued)

TABLE 30 (concluded)

Industry	Earnings[a] Small[c]	Earnings[a] Large[d]	Ratio, Capital to Receipts[b] Small[c]	Ratio, Capital to Receipts[b] Large[d]	Ratio Value Added to Payroll	Elasticity of Substitution
			1954			
Malt beverages	1.87	2.64	.276	.576	2.64	6.62
Meat products	1.55	2.08	.159	.167	1.56	1.27
Bakery products	1.35	1.78	.247	.421	1.76	4.36
Confectionery	1.16	1.50	.339	.494	2.34	4.41
Men's clothing	1.36	1.35	.299	.531	1.52	e
Pulp, paper, and allied products	1.72	1.97	.429	.923	2.35	14.27
Paints	1.70	2.19	.414	.557	2.62	4.12
Structural clay products	1.43	1.75	.634	.934	1.59	4.06
Pottery	1.24	1.80	.459	.690	1.50	2.63
Tin cans	1.65	2.16	.347	.593	1.97	4.91
Hand tools, hardware	1.59	2.05	.554	.732	1.74	2.92
Agricultural machinery	1.54	2.21	.613	.826	1.74	2.45
Construction machinery	1.81	2.14	.476	.816	1.77	6.78
Special industry machinery	1.81	2.18	.589	.889	1.61	4.56
Jewelry, except costume	1.63	1.82	.500	.672	1.63	5.36
Only 1954 Data Available						
Broad-woven cotton	1.42	1.32	.432	.719	1.44	e
Narrow-woven fabrics	1.28	1.25	.451	.832	1.54	e
Hats	1.40	1.99	.418	.849	1.51	4.06
Drugs and medicines[f]	1.39	2.00	.550	.897	3.13	5.20
Perfumes	1.33	1.59	.522	.583	4.43	3.75
Industrial and miscellaneous chemicals	1.78	2.23	.435	1.029	2.58	10.88
Footwear[f]	1.31	1.45	.266	.556	1.59	12.56
Iron and steel foundries	1.70	2.18	.444	.787	1.50	4.44
Nonferrous foundries	1.79	2.28	.406	.615	1.46	3.50
Fabricated structural products	1.86	2.16	.397	.575	1.72	5.27
Metal stamping	1.70	2.20	.451	.588	1.60	2.65
Fabricated wire	1.52	2.13	.431	.616	1.69	2.80
Metalworking machinery	2.15	2.31	.523	.744	1.68	e
General industry machinery	1.82	2.11	.471	.669	1.75	5.16
Electric generating machinery	1.65	2.11	.421	.590	1.87	3.56
Appliances	1.48	2.07	.440	.535	2.10	2.22
Automotive electric equipment	1.64	2.13	.329	.600	1.69	4.90

[a] Wages per production worker man-hour.

[b] Ratio of assets, excluding other investments, to total compiled receipts for corporations submitting balance sheets to the IRS.

[c] Earnings are for establishments with less than 50 employees; capital-receipts ratios are for firms with assets under $250,000.

[d] Earnings are for establishments with over 500 employees; capital-receipts ratios are for firms with assets over $5 million.

[e] Difference in wage rates of large and small plants not considered significant.

[f] Not comparable to 1947 industry with same title.

SOURCE: *Census of Manufactures, 1947* and *1954*; and *Statistics of Income Source Book*, for 1947 and 1954. The method of computation is described in footnote 20.

APPENDIXES

APPENDIX A

Construction of the Basic Tables on Capital and Rates of Return

CONSTRUCTION of tables of annual changes in capital and of rates of return in more than 100 manufacturing industries for a period of nineteen years is an intricate and varied task. A variety of ad hoc decisions are demanded by deficiencies in data, peculiarities of industrial structure, and deviations of tax law concepts from those of economics. Yet a fairly detailed knowledge of the procedures we have employed is necessary if the nature and limitations of the data are to be appreciated, and we set this information forth in this appendix.

The ideal goal in constructing the basic tables for a study is, of course, to make every adjustment in the data which can with reasonable confidence be expected to improve them for the problems being investigated. We hasten to add that this goal was not reached—probably it never is fully attained. A fuller knowledge of the correct specifications of economic variables usually comes from their use, so in a kinder world it would be eminently appropriate to collect the data only after a study was completed. In addition one must take some account of costs—and returns: some adjustments that may be minor in their effects may be stupendous in their costs. Compromises with the goal will be found strewn through the appendix.

The basic data we start with are the corporate income tax returns for the "minor" industries reported in the *Statistics of Income Source Book*. The first main task was the construction of the tables of total assets, in which three chief problems were encountered. First, the industrial classification of firms changed several times (most radically in 1948) and therefore adjustments were necessary to achieve comparability through time. Second, an estimate was necessary for the noncorporate part of each industry. Finally, the capital figures reflect changing price levels and pose the problem of deflation, to approximate capital in stable prices. The second main task was the construction of rates of return tables, and here the chief problem was the treatment of depreciation. These and many minor matters are now discussed. The 1958 data, which became available after the study was completed, are presented in Appendix E.

1. *The Capital Tables*

The entire corporate sector of an industry does not report its balance sheets. Normally companies reporting balance sheets account for almost all receipts (about 98 per cent in many industries), but sometimes as much as 25 or 30 per cent of receipts are received by companies not reporting balance sheets. We therefore increase all balance sheet accounts by the ratio of all receipts to receipts of companies reporting balance sheets. This was done at both the "minor" or three-digit industry level and at the two-digit industry level.[1]

COMPARABILITY OF INDUSTRIES THROUGH TIME

The industry classification employed in the *Source Book* was revised in 1940, 1941, 1942, and 1948. The changes in the first three years were moderate, and it has been possible to revise the data for 1938–42 to achieve tolerable comparability with the succeeding period. The reclassification in 1948 was much more extensive and numerous breaks in the series had to be accepted, but an overlap between 1947 and 1948 was constructed.

For the earlier period, it was necessary to use the data on value of product from the *1939 Census of Manufactures* to adjust the individual industry data. The procedure may be illustrated by the reclassification in 1940 of the 1939 industry, "other electrical machinery," from which (1) the wire and cable class was transferred to "electrical equipment for utilities"; (2) telephone and telegraph apparatus was transferred to "communication equipment and phonographs"; and (3) the remainder was retained as "other electrical machinery" (*Statistics of Income*, for 1940, Part 2, pp. 312–13). According to the *1939 Census of Manufactures* (Vol. II, Part 2, p. 363), these components had the values of products shown below.

Product Class	*Value* ($000's)	*Per Cent of Total*
Wire and cable	120,390	21
Telephone and telegraph equipment	191,326	34
Other electrical machinery	259,405	45
Total	571,121	100

The percentages in the last column were used to redistribute the 1938 and 1939 capital figures into the industry categories of 1940 and later years. In a few cases the effects of the reclassification were so small (affecting well under 5 per cent of receipts) that no adjustments were made.

[1] In 1938–41, receipts of companies that report balance sheets were not reported at the three-digit level and must be estimated from the corresponding information at the two-digit level. The estimates were made on the assumption that the difference between: (1) receipts of all corporations, and (2) receipts of those reporting balance sheets was distributed among three-digit industries in 1938–41 in the same proportions as the average of 1942–43.

One of these early-year adjustments was both important and troublesome, and needs separate mention. In 1942 five ordnance series were split off from nonordnance series; for example, "ammunition" was taken out of "other chemicals". For the three years, 1938–40, these ordnance components were arbitrarily taken to be zero, but they were so small relative to the groups in which they were classified that it involves no great error. The ordnance components for 1941 were estimated on the basis of the ratio of their outputs in 1941 to outputs in 1942, as reported by the War Production Board.[2]

The sweeping changes in industrial classification in 1948 were fortunately accompanied by series of tables which present the 1948 data classified simultaneously by the 1947 and 1948 industry classes. A sample transition table is reproduced as Table A-1. The italicized figures, lines 1–7, are the absolute amount of receipts in 1948, in thousands of dollars. Italicized totals of columns are totals for the 1948 industry classes, and the totals of lines are the 1948 totals for the 1947 industry classes, so tables for 1938–47 may be directly continued to the next year.

It is also possible to estimate the 1947 figures for the 1948 industry classes on the assumption that the relative composition of each industry was the same in both years. The figure in parenthesis in each cell of Table A-1 is the percentage of the receipts in the first line to the line total. If these percentages are applied to the corresponding line totals for 1947, we get an estimate of receipts in 1947—the third figure in each cell, which permits reconstitution of the 1947 figures on a 1948 industry basis. Such transition tables are given also for total assets, fixed assets, total compiled receipts, short-term credit, and long-term credit.

No cross-classification was given for certain of the industries for which a change was made. In these cases we reverted to the method employed for the earlier years: value of product data from the *1947 Census of Manufactures* was used to estimate the 1948 figures on a 1947 industry basis. This method was also employed for a few industries in which a cross-classification was available in order to determine whether it led to important errors; the agreement between the two sets of data was reasonably close.

Despite the breadth of the three-digit industry classes, the asset data sometimes display large erratic fluctuations due to the reclassification of one or a few major companies to another industry. No fully satisfactory

[2] *Wartime Production Achievements and the Reconversion Outlook*, Oct. 9, 1945. The classification in this report (p. 105) is somewhat different from that of *Statistics of Income* so the adjustments are especially rough.

TABLE A-1

TEXTILE MILL PRODUCTS: RECEIPTS, CROSS-CLASSIFIED BY 1948 AND 1947 INDUSTRY CLASSES
(receipts in thousands of dollars)

Receipts	Yarn and Thread (1)	Broad-woven, Wool (2)	Broad-woven, Cotton (3)	Narrow Fabrics (4)	Dyeing, Except Knit Goods (5)	Other (6)	Non-allocable (7)	1948 Total for 1947 Classes (8)
1. Cotton manufactures, 1948	*723,498*		*3,118,583*	*145,586*		*31,365*	*120,832*	*4,139,864*
Per cent of (8), line 1	(17.48)		(75.33)	(3.52)		(0.76)	(2.92)	(100.01)
1947	770,409		3,320,073	155,139		33,496	128,695	4,407,372
2. Woolen manufactures, 1948	*375,779*	*1,313,505*		*1,240*	*14,194*		*44,914*	*1,749,632*
Per cent of (8), line 2	(21.48)	(75.07)		(0.07)	(0.81)		(2.57)	(100.00)
1947	364,438	1,273,665		1,188	13,743		43,604	1,696,637
3. Silk and synthetics, 1948	*390,931*			*103,794*		*948,360*	*40,996*	*1,484,081*
Per cent of (8), line 3	(26.34)			(6.99)		(63.90)	(2.76)	(99.99)
1947	334,098			88,661		810,510	35,008	1,268,404
4. Dyeing, except wool, 1948					*681,129*	*12,682*		*693,811*
Per cent of (8), line 4					(98.17)	(1.83)		(100.00)
1947					650,473	12,126		662,599
5. Other, 1948						*688,793*		*688,793*
Per cent of (8), line 5						(100.00)		(100.00)
1947						615,426		615,426
6. Nonallocable, 1948	*41,236*			*30,591*	*4,677*	*3,902*	*864,076*	*944,482*
Per cent of (8), line 6	(4.37)			(3.24)	(0.50)	(0.41)	(91.49)	(100.01)
1947	31,897			23,649	3,650	2,993	667,788	729,903
7. Total, for 1948 classes	*1,531,444*	*1,313,505*	*3,118,583*	*281,211*	*700,000*	*1,685,102*	*1,070,818*	*12,443,892*
for 1947 classes	1,500,842	1,273,665	3,320,073	268,637	667,866	1,474,551	875,095	

NOTE: For explanation of the classification of industries, see the accompanying text.

method was found to cope with this problem, but the following procedure was employed to detect and correct the most flagrant cases.

Each annual relative change in assets that deviated from the mean by two or more times the standard deviation of annual relative changes in assets for that year was examined, by means of the asset-size distribution data in the *Source Book*. Where the changes seemed reasonable in light of trend and large-company data, they were accepted. Where the changes were improbable and incapable of adjustment, the industry was omitted from most three-digit analyses; for example, "electric lamps" was omitted because it contained no major lamp producer after 1950. In the remaining cases, where only one or an occasional year was involved, the asset data were adjusted by the interpolated ratio of assets in the largest asset-size classes to assets in the smaller size classes. These various decisions presumably offer some protection against very large spurious changes, but of course they do not cope at all with minor fluctuations due to classification changes of firms.

The Basic Set of Industries

Our statistical analyses are usually restricted to a "basic" set of industries. This basic set includes all industries except (1) those bearing a footnote reference a in Tables A-14 to A-59 and (2) furs, where the noncorporate share of assets is very large. The basic set contains 82 industries in 1938–47, and 99 in 1947–57. In the analyses, especially of rates of investment, aircraft is usually omitted. Other ordnance is omitted from all statistical analyses.

Rented Assets

The part of capital assets rented rather than owned by the industry using them escapes our measure of assets. We can form some estimate of the amount and industrial composition of such assets from the data on rents paid on business property reported in *Statistics of Income*.

The rental paid on a piece of property is the gross yield of the property to the owner, and therefore contains depreciation, property and income taxes, and return on investment—and often also payments for repairs and maintenance of the property. If we compare rentals paid with depreciation plus return on investment, we obtain at least a crude estimate of the value of rented assets as compared with the value of owned assets, on the assumption that the costs of property services are equal for rented and owned property. For example, in 1953 rentals in all manufacturing industries were $1,177 million, depreciation was $4,614 million, and compiled net income before taxes plus interest paid was $22,370 million. The capital value of rented assets relative to owned assets is therefore approximately $1,177/($4,614 + $22,370), or 4.36 per cent. Comparable ratios are given for all years in Table A-2.

TABLE A-2

RATIO OF INDUSTRY RENTED ASSETS TO OWNED ASSETS, 1938–57

Year	Ratio, Rented Assets to Owned Assets[a]
1938	8.75
1939	5.59
1940	4.25
1941	2.66
1942	2.65
1943	2.74
1944	3.41
1945	4.70
1946	4.20
1947	3.44
1948	3.51
1949	4.31
1950	3.03
1951	3.23
1952	4.22
1953	4.36
1954	5.20[b]
1955	4.38
1956	4.83
1957	5.66

[a] Estimated by rentals divided by depreciation + interest + compiled net income.
[b] Depreciation estimated from 1955 relation of depreciation and amortization.

SOURCE: Data on rents paid on business property from *Statistics of Income, Corporation Income Tax Returns*, for each year.

This estimate of the relative importance of rented assets is of course rough, and probably underestimates moderately the role of rented assets.[3] Yet the data strongly suggest that rented assets are a rather minor part of total assets, and that their relative quantity has not fluctuated greatly over the period of our study.

The question of the differential role of rented assets in various industries is more relevant to our discussion of differential capital movements, and some exploratory calculations are given in Table A-3. Here we use only depreciation as our annual measure of owned capital because annual

[3] The noncorporate sector makes larger use of rental property, if we may judge by the ratio of rentals to depreciation in the smallest asset-size class of corporations (under $50,000). In 1953, for example, the ratio of rentals to depreciation was 0.255 for all corporations, 1.38 for the lowest asset-size class.

TABLE A-3

ESTIMATE OF RENTED PROPERTY AS SHARE OF OWNED ASSETS, BY INDUSTRY CLASS, 1948 AND 1953

Industry Class	*Rentals as Per Cent of Depreciation*[a] 1948	1953
Beverages	19.08	15.39
Food and kindred products	28.53	25.77
Tobacco products	17.86	16.57
Textile mill products	23.86	19.37
Apparel and fabric products	190.92	163.48
Lumber and wood products	16.55	14.18
Furniture, fixtures	64.59	64.48
Paper and allied products	19.93	18.45
Printing, publishing	75.45	64.41
Chemicals and allied products	16.06	13.17
Petroleum and coal products	26.26	28.38
Rubber products	24.67	27.44
Leather and products	93.55	89.20
Stone, clay, and glass products	13.41	14.23
Primary metals and products	15.75	16.61
Fabricated metal products	27.42	29.74
Machinery, except transportation and electrical	21.35	24.43
Electrical machinery	28.03	26.39
Transportation equipment, except motor vehicles	32.14	45.73
Motor vehicles	13.43	7.10
Ordnance	11.21	12.63
Scientific instruments	35.87	35.63
Miscellaneous manufactures	55.09	57.20
Total manufactures	26.87	25.53

[a] Depreciation, as reported on corporate income tax returns (*Statistics of Income*), is used as the measure of industry-owned property.

fluctuations in net income are so large as to obscure the question we are investigating. These calculations suggest that the industrial pattern of relative use of rented assets is also fairly stable, at least for two-digit groups: the rank correlation of the ratios at the two dates is .96.

Average Versus Year-End Balance Sheets

The balance sheets reported in *Statistics of Income* pertain to the end of the fiscal year, which on average is approximately that of the calendar year. A preferable measure of assets would be provided by the average of assets in four quarters, but it appears from one small investigation that the differences would not be significant. The average of four quarterly reports was correlated with the fourth-quarter report, on the basis of the sample of 9,000 company reports in the *Quarterly Financial Report* of the

Federal Trade Commission and the Securities and Exchange Commission.[4] The correlations are moderately good: $r = .9996$ for 1952; $r = .9998$ for 1953. If the percentage increase in assets is calculated from annual average and from fourth-quarter reports, the correlation between them is smaller, .896. We cannot say how much of this decrease is due to sampling fluctuations, and how much to the fact that perfect linear correlation of variates does not insure perfect linear correlation of relative changes.[5]

THE NONCORPORATE SECTOR

Statistics of Income does not give balance-sheet information on noncorporate enterprises and, because this type of enterprise plays widely differing roles in the various industries, capital data for the industries would not be comparable unless the noncorporate sectors were added.

In the years in which a census of manufactures was taken—1939, 1947, 1954, and 1958—information is given on the value added by corporate and noncorporate establishments, and these data can be arranged in the industry categories used in *Statistics of Income.*[6] These data can be employed, in connection with the receipts and balance-sheet information of corporations in those years, to estimate the share of assets of each industry held by noncorporate enterprises. Value added is not identical with receipts, but value of product data contain much duplication in the interplant shipments within a company; they were not available in 1947.

Information of an incomplete sort is available for the noncensus years, and it indicates that a simple interpolation between the census years would often be seriously in error. We therefore interpolate the intercensus years by the ratio of receipts reported by individuals (*Statistics of Income*, Part I) to the receipts of corporations, by two-digit industry classes. The individual tax returns are not complete for single proprietors, and do not include partnerships (whose returns are not tabulated each year), but it is believed that they display a much more realistic year-to-year pattern.

[4] The first-quarter 1953 and first-quarter 1954 reports were used. In all cases $n = 23$.

[5] Let $y = ax + b$, where y is the average of four quarters and x the fourth quarter, and let subscripts denote periods. Then, if $a_1 = a_2$ (as is approximately true),

$$\frac{y_2 - y_1}{y_1} = \frac{x_2 - x_1}{x_1 + \frac{b_1}{a_1}} + \frac{b_2 - b_1}{ax_1 + b_1},$$

which is a linear relationship only if $b_1 = b_2 = 0$.

[6] We are indebted to Harold Goldstein for making available the unpublished form of legal organization data in 1947 at the three-digit industry level.

TABLE A-4

PROCEDURE FOR ESTIMATING NONCORPORATE RECEIPTS IN NONCENSUS YEARS, CONFECTIONERY PRODUCTS INDUSTRY

Item[a]	1938	1939	1940	1941	1942	1943	1944	1945	1946	1947
Census ratio $= r$		.0605								.0823
Statistics of Income										
ratio $= s$[b]	.0330	.0330	(.0334)	.0338	(.0358)	.0379	(.0493)	.0607	(.0488)	.0369
Ratio, r to s	1.7834	1.8327	1.882	1.9314	1.9807	2.0301	2.0794	2.1288	2.1781	2.2274
r, estimated, $= s \times \left(\frac{r}{s}\right)$	.0589		.0629	.0653	.0710	.0769	.1025	.1292	.1064	

[a] Items are defined in the accompanying text.
[b] Numbers in parentheses are linear interpolations.

SOURCE: *Statistics of Income* and *Census of Manufactures* for each year.

We may illustrate the procedure with the calculation of the noncorporate shares of the confectionery products industry. Define the ratios:

r = ratio of value added of noncorporate enterprises to that of corporate enterprises (three-digit level)

s = ratio of business receipts in individual tax returns to those in corporate returns (two-digit level)

The ratio of r to s is known for the census years, and we interpolate linearly the ratio in the intercensal years and apply the interpolated ratio to s to obtain an estimated r. Illustrative computations are shown in Table A-4. Since the receipts of individual businesses were reported only in the odd-numbered years from 1939 to 1947, we use linear interpolation for the even-numbered years, and also assume that the 1939 ratio held in 1938.

There remains the problem of estimating the capital assets of noncorporate enterprises, once we have annual data on their receipts. It would be undesirable simply to use the ratio of receipts to capital that is found in the corporate sector because of a combination of two facts. First, most noncorporate enterprises are small; and small corporate enterprises have relatively low ratios of capital to receipts or sales. The second fact is documented in Table A-5 where it is shown that the ratio of assets to sales is almost twice as large in the asset class over $100 million as it is in the asset class under $50,000. A similar pattern is found within two-digit industries.

It is not possible to be equally precise in measuring the size of

TABLE A-5

RATIO OF ASSETS TO SALES IN MANUFACTURING CORPORATIONS, 1947

Asset Class ($000's)	Ratio, Assets to Sales
Under 50	.357
50–100	.394
100–250	.411
250–500	.432
500–1,000	.447
1,000–5,000	.508
5,000–10,000	.592
10,000–50,000	.647
50,000–100,000	.642
100,000 and over	.625
All	.625

SOURCE: *Statistics of Income*, for 1947.

noncorporate enterprises, but their general magnitude is tolerably clear. In 1947, for example, individual proprietorship tax returns showed average receipts of $34,800 and partnerships showed average receipts of $106,200; the two combined averaged $58,300. In the same year, manufacturing corporations with assets under $50,000 had average receipts of $60,800—almost identical with that for noncorporate enterprises. The same relationship held in 1939. We therefore use the average for 1942 and 1950 of the assets-to-sales ratios of the smallest asset class of corporations in converting the sales of noncorporate into assets.[7]

The procedure for estimating noncorporate assets will probably be less reliable, the larger the noncorporate sector of the industry. That is, the assets-to-sales ratio of the smallest asset-size class of corporations will probably be less representative of the corresponding ratio of noncorporate business if only a relatively few enterprises are incorporated. Nevertheless most noncorporate shares are small (see Table A-6). That for fur gar-

TABLE A-6
NONCORPORATE SHARE OF VALUE OF PRODUCTS, 1947
(per cent)

Number of Industries	Noncorporate Share of Value of Products
56	0–4
23	4–8
10	8–12
9	12–16
4	16–20
3	20–32
1	32–48
Total 106	

SOURCE: See text footnote 6.

ments, however, is so large (almost 50 per cent) that the industry is excluded in almost all our statistical analyses.

The noncorporate assets in 1958 are calculated, by the foregoing procedure, from the 1958 census data. As a result of extensive industry reclassification in 1958, it was necessary to weight four-digit industry ratios by the per cent of value added of each new four-digit Census industry in the old-basis three-digit Internal Revenue Service industries. These weights are based on information in Appendix C of Volume II of *1958 Census of Manufactures*. For the conversion from noncorporate value added

[7] When the noncorporate share of value added was under 2 per cent in 1947, for computational simplicity we used the value-added ratio directly to estimate total assets.

to noncorporate assets ratios, 1957 assets-to-receipts ratios of small corporations were computed wherever the 1947 or 1954 estimated share of assets was 4 per cent or more. For other industries, the assets-to-receipts ratios for 1958 are the same as those for prior years. The noncorporate shares for 1955–57 are linearly interpolated.

The sum of the book value assets of three-digit industries does not equal the corresponding two-digit book value assets. The discrepancies, which are minor, arise because the adjustments for corporations not reporting balance sheets and for noncorporate enterprises were performed independently at the two-digit level, in order to have book values comparable to the deflated (1947 price) assets. In addition, large-company reclassification adjustments were not carried to the two-digit level. The all-manufacturing assets (book value and deflated) are the sum of the corresponding two-digit assets. The all-manufacturing rate of return is the weighted average of two-digit rates of return.

CAPITAL IN CONSTANT DOLLARS

The figures on total assets of an industry, which are constructed by the foregoing procedures, are book values and are based upon price levels at various points in time. Some components of capital, such as inventories of raw materials and finished goods, may be valued in almost current prices. This is especially likely if a "first-in first-out" method of valuation is used, or if the older and more common basis of the "lower of cost or market" valuation is used in a period of stable or falling prices. Most durable assets will be valued at their historical or original cost, and may therefore be based upon market prices six months or twenty-five years ago.

This miscellany of valuation bases is not well suited to a study of the mobility of capital among industries. A 1950 increase in assets may be larger in current dollars than the increase in assets in 1940, whereas the increase in "real" assets (somehow defined) is larger in the earlier year. A nominally high rate of return on undervalued assets is no inducement to expand investment in one industry, while in another industry a nominally low rate of return on overvalued assets may conceal the attractiveness of additional investment.

A proper revaluation of assets would rest upon a reappraisal of a detailed and comprehensive inventory of assets of each industry in terms of constant prices. The constant prices could be either those of used assets in a given year or the replacement prices in the given year, less accumulated depreciation. The two sets of prices would be equivalent in the absence of improvements in the production of capital goods. If given capital goods were now produced more efficiently than when they were purchased, or if they were improved in quality without a corresponding rise in price, the depreciation charges would include also an obsolescence charge.

No such inventory exists, and the best available procedure in deflating fixed capital is as follows:

1. Average life of assets is estimated, chiefly from the tables of useful lives published by the Internal Revenue Service.[8]
2. The assets of an industry at a given date are assumed to be produced throughout the past period of useful life in the same time pattern as the national output of those assets during that period. For example, the assets of ages 5 and 7 years will be assumed to be in proportion to the national outputs of all manufacturing assets 5 and 7 years earlier.
3. The surviving values of the assets are calculated on the assumption of straight-line depreciation.
4. A constant-dollar price is used to calculate the sum of surviving asset values in the given year, and a historical price series is used to calculate the sum in historical prices. The ratio between the two values is the implicit "deflator."

This procedure is carried out separately for structures and for equipment. In addition, inventories are deflated by a procedure essentially identical with that employed in calculating inventory investment in the national income accounts,[9] and other working capital is deflated by the Department of Commerce implicit price deflator for gross national product.

The second step in the procedure is especially dubious, but there are weaknesses and uncertainties in each of the other steps: Average lives are not known very precisely and in any case assets of any type have a frequency distribution of lives. Not all enterprises used straight-line depreciation even before the 1954 liberalization of the Internal Revenue Code, and this method of depreciation is known to underestimate

[8] In our deflations of capital in two-digit industries, we use the estimates of Creamer *et al.*, (based upon Bulletin F, *Income Tax, Depreciation and Obsolescence, Estimated Useful Lives, and Depreciation Rates,* revised Jan. 1942, Internal Revenue Service) in Daniel Creamer, Sergei Dobrovolsky, and Israel Borenstein, *Capital in Manufacturing and Mining: Its Formation and Financing,* Princeton for National Bureau of Economic Research, 1960, p. 223.

[9] The inventories are revalued in end-of-current-year prices and then shifted to 1947 prices by an index for all inventories. We are indebted to the National Income Unit of the Department of Commerce for the data on inventories in end-of-current-year prices.

depreciation in early years and overstate it in later years of an asset's life.[10] The price indexes required for the last step are not impeccable.

These weaknesses do not destroy, although they certainly impair, the value of calculations of capital in constant dollars at the two-digit industry level. We therefore carry them out at this level, and will recur in a moment to the details of the procedure. But the weaknesses become more prominent when the procedure is applied to the finer (three-digit) industry classes, and it would be a bold man who would affirm that at this finer level a series on capital in constant dollars would have even two digits in which the user could put confidence. But this is equivalent to saying that annual investment—the first differences in the total capital series—would be affected at least as much by the vicissitudes of the statistical deflation process as by the investment history of the industry.

We have therefore chosen, or rather have been driven, to calculate a capital series in constant prices at the two-digit level, but not at the three-digit level. The comparison of capital in book values and in constant dollars for the broader industry groups should help to isolate the major effects of price movements, and further than this we cannot go.

Our basic capital concept embraces all the resources an enterprise requires for the conduct of its activities—cash and accounts receivable as well as inventory, plant, and land. Indeed the only category of assets we exclude is investments in other companies, because their inclusion would involve much duplication (as when Standard Oil of Indiana holds a large block of Standard Oil of New Jersey stock) and obscure the industry categories. In "real" terms we want this capital to represent general purchasing power of the industry: we want to reckon in the capital of the industry the increase in its assets due to the fact that prices have risen relatively more than those of other industries, for example. Correspondingly, our deflated income should include capital gains and differential inventory profits that are customarily excluded from social income accounting. These price fluctuations contribute to both the differences in profitability and the differences in volatility of profits of different industries and therefore should not be eliminated in the process of "deflating" the data.

The method of calculating capital values in 1947 prices for the various two-digit industries may be summarized as follows:

1. *Machinery and equipment* (fixed assets other than plant and land). We take the average life of equipment from Creamer *et al.*, whose

[10] See G. Terborgh, *Realistic Depreciation Policy*, University of Chicago Press, 1954, especially Chaps. 4–7.

estimates are based upon the Internal Revenue Service schedules of useful lives; they are given in Table A-7. The surviving value of

TABLE A-7

AVERAGE LIFE OF EQUIPMENT IN MANUFACTURING INDUSTRIES

Major Industry Groups	Length of Life (years)
Food and kindred products	15
Textiles and products	22
Leather and products	15
Rubber products	12
Lumber and wood products	20
Paper, and allied products	18
Printing and publishing	14
Chemicals	19
Petroleum refining and related industries	15
Stone, clay, and glass products	15
Iron and steel and products	17
Nonferrous metals and products	22
Machinery, except transportation equipment	18
Transportation equipment	15
Miscellaneous manufactures	18

SOURCE: Creamer, Dobrovolsky, and Borenstein, *Capital in Manufacturing*, p. 223.

equipment of an industry in each year is assumed to be the surviving fraction (with straight-line depreciation) of equipment purchased by all manufacturing industries in the past *n*-years, where *n* is the average life of equipment in this industry. The surviving book value is thus calculated in both 1947 prices and current prices, and the ratio of the latter to the former is the price index for that year for the industry. An illustrative calculation is given in Table A-8.[11]

2. *Buildings.* A parallel procedure was used in constructing a price index to deflate plant, except that a single average life (40 years) was used for all industries.[12]

[11] The series on output of manufacturing equipment is from L. J. Chawner, "Capital Expenditures for Manufacturing Plant and Equipment—1915 to 1940," *Survey of Current Business*, Mar. 1941, p. 11, which is spliced to the purchases of producer durable goods in *National Income Supplement* for 1954, p. 210, and the 1958 supplement, *U.S. Income and Output*, p. 192; the sum of lines 2, 3, 4, 5, 10, 11, 12, 15, 21, and 22 is taken as the output of equipment used in manufacturing through 1954. From 1955 on, the manufacturing equipment series is extrapolated by changes in total private purchases of producer durable equipment, *Survey of Current Business*, July 1960, p. 8. The price index to 1940 is implicit in Chawner's estimates; it is linked at 1940 to the price index used to deflate producer durables in *National Income Supplement* for 1954, pp. 216–17, and *Survey of Current Business*, July 1960, p. 8.

[12] The volume of manufacturing construction since 1915 is from *Construction Volume and Costs*, 1915–54, p. 2; *Business Statistics* (1959 Supplement to *Survey of Current Business*), p. 37; and *Survey of Current Business*, July 1960, p. 25. The earlier period was taken from

TABLE A-8

ILLUSTRATIVE CALCULATION OF PRICE INDEX OF BOOK VALUE OF MACHINERY AND EQUIPMENT, SEVENTEEN-YEAR LIFE, IRON AND STEEL PRODUCTS
(purchases in millions of dollars)

Year	Per Cent in Use, 1947 (1)	*Purchases of Producers' Durable Machinery and Equipment* (1947 prices): All Manufacturing Industries (2)	*Purchases of Producers' Durable Machinery and Equipment* (1947 prices): Weighted by Per Cent in Use, 1947 (1) × (2) (3)	Price Index 1947 = 100 (4)	*Purchases of Producers' Durable Machinery and Equipment in Current Prices* Weighted by Per Cent in Use, 1947 (3) × (4) (5)
1931	5.9	1,438	84.8	54.3	46.07
1932	11.8	894	105.5	51.0	53.80
1933	17.6	967	170.2	51.0	86.80
1934	23.5	1,225	287.9	58.2	167.54
1935	28.4	1,617	475.4	57.5	273.35
1936	35.3	2,038	719.4	57.5	413.66
1937	41.2	2,423	998.3	63.3	631.91
1938	47.0	1,725	810.8	63.9	518.07
1939	52.9	1,904	1,007.2	64.6	650.66
1940	58.8	2,453	1,442.4	66.0	951.96
1941	64.7	2,759	1,785.1	70.6	1,260.26
1942	70.6	1,986	1,402.1	76.4	1,071.22
1943	76.4	1,970	1,505.1	77.2	1,161.92
1944	82.3	2,575	2,119.2	78.3	1,659.35
1945	88.2	3,330	2,937.1	79.3	2,329.09
1946	94.1	3,991	3,755.5	87.4	3,282.33
1947	100.0	5,100	5,100.0	100.0	5,100.00
			Σ24,706.0		Σ19,651.99

NOTE: 1947 index of book values in 1947 prices = 79.6

SOURCE: See text footnote 11.

3. *Fixed capital.* Equipment and plant are combined in *Statistics of Income*, so it is necessary to deflate the total by a weighted index of equipment and plant prices. There is no comprehensive information on the relative investment in equipment and plant by industry so the relative weights for all manufacturing were employed. These weights were constructed by taking the Department of Commerce series for the two components in constant prices (*Survey of Current Business*, Nov. 1956 and July 1960; and 1958 Supplement, *U.S.*

Raymond W. Goldsmith, *A Study of Saving in the United States* (Vol. I, Princeton University Press, 1955), Table R-27, and linked at 1915 to the later series. The early price index is from Goldsmith, *ibid.* Vol. I, Table R-20; at 1915 it is linked to the Turner Construction Company index reported in *Construction Volume and Costs*, p. 29, and in *Engineering News Record*, Oct. 17, 1957, p. 84, and June 23, 1960, p. 73.

Income and Output, p. 197) and shifting them back to book value prices by use of our price indexes, to obtain book value investments in equipment and plant.

4. *Land.* In book value prices the investment in land was relatively stable, so any deflation would yield a declining value of land in 1947 prices, which is obviously unreasonable. Since there is no price series on industrial land, we assumed that the ratio of book value of land to that of buildings was at the same level in each year as it was in 1938, and this series of book values is deflated by the plant price index—in effect holding the value of land constant relative to plant, at the 1938 level.
5. *Inventories.* Inventories at end-of-year constant prices and the appropriate price indexes were supplied by the Department of Commerce, and they permitted calculation of inventories at end-of-year current prices. These in turn were deflated by the price index for all manufacturing industries, so differential inventory gains and losses of individual (two-digit) industries were not eliminated.
6. *Other working capital.* This category includes cash, accounts receivable, government securities, and other assets. These liquid items should be deflated by an index of the prices of materials, labor, and similar categories of business outlay; in the absence of such an index we used the deflator of gross national product.

2. *Rate of Return on Capital*

Determination of the rate of return on capital was our second large statistical task. The main problems in the calculation of this rate are three: (1) On what base—for what category of investment—is the rate to be calculated? (2) How are small companies, in which income may be withdrawn as salary, to be treated? (3) What adjustments should be made for price changes? After discussing these problems we turn to a variety of problems peculiar to certain industries.

THE INVESTMENT BASE

The rate of return as a guide to investment among industries is one of the oldest and most basic elements in the theory of a competitive, private enterprise economy. Despite its importance and antiquity, however, the precise concept of return has received remarkably little explicit discussion.

The main tradition of economic theory asserts that the entrepreneur seeks to maximize the present value of his net worth, and that this usually implies, under competition, that the rate of return on the entrepreneur's net worth guides the allocation of new investment.[13] Under competition one would therefore expect the rate of return on entrepreneur's net worth to be equal in all industries.

The main limitation of this line of analysis is that it leaves the characteristics of the capital lenders (among whom we may wish to include the preferred stockholders) unexplained. Lenders also wish to maximize the present value of their future income, and differ from entrepreneurs only in placing a higher value on security relative to earnings. Aside from this difference in tastes there is no difference in general between lenders and entrepreneurs. Both classes will abandon lending for entrepreneurship if the return to equity sufficiently outweighs the added risk, and both will abandon entrepreneurship for lending, if the rewards of risk-taking fall low enough.[14]

If lenders correctly estimate future risks on average, therefore, we should expect them to demand a nominally higher rate when they are asked to assume larger risks. If the rate is higher only by the actuarial value of future risks, we would say there is no risk aversion. In this case we would expect the net realized rate of return to be independent of the relative amounts of borrowed funds and entrepreneurial equity in an industry. If there is positive risk aversion on the part of lenders, we should expect the realized rate of return on all capital to be larger the higher the ratio of borrowed funds to entrepreneurial equity, but with a partially offsetting reduction in risk aversion premium demanded by entrepreneurs.

We omit at this point discussion of proper methods of isolating the effects of attitudes toward risk and uncertainty on the net earnings of various industries, for the problem is better discussed when we are armed with data. We do argue that the essential symmetry in the theory of interindustry allocation of loan funds and equity funds supports the view that they should be combined in calculating the rate of return. That is, we propose to make our investment base coterminous with the total assets of a firm or industry (excluding investments in other companies) and to make the return on this capital the sum of interest payments, dividends on

[13] Qualifications that have been made of this proposition because of the differences between lending and borrowing, and average and marginal rates are analyzed by F. and V. Lutz (*The Theory of Investment of the Firm*, Princeton University Press, 1951) and by J. Herschleifer ("On the Theory of Optimal Investment Decision," *Journal of Political Economy*, Aug. 1958, pp. 329–52).

[14] In large companies, the only difference between common stockholders (entrepreneurs) and bondholders is in their attitude toward risk, but in small companies, the entrepreneur must also be willing to undertake managerial duties. The difference in rates earned by lenders and entrepreneurs in an industry like farming or barbering, therefore, depends upon the distribution of tastes with respect to both risk and managerial responsibilities.

all types of stock, and undisturbed profits, less income taxes (and dividends received from other corporations).[15] This decision leaves open all questions of substance with respect to the influence of the capital structure of an industry on its realized rate of return.

The accounts payable and receivable (and the short-term noninterest bearing notes which are their equivalent) both contain implicit interest payments: higher prices are charged when credit is extended (accounts receivable) and higher prices are paid when credit is obtained (accounts payable). An enterprise would have the same amount of capital if it replaced accounts payable with a bank loan, and then interest payments to the bank would approximately equal the reduction in buying prices because of prompt payment; so operating income would not be affected. Yet our procedure would display a rise in income since we include explicit interest payments in the return to capital. Conversely, a supplier thus paid promptly would have cash instead of accounts receivable. He would experience a reduction in sales receipts because of his lower prices, which might be offset by the return on other forms of investment of the cash, or the cash might be used to reduce his own short-term debt; in either case his rate of return would not be much affected.[16]

The magnitude of this possible understatement of rates of return is not large in the aggregate. In 1950, accounts payable were $13 billion in all manufacturing industries. Interest payments on notes, bonds, etc. (amounting to more than $16 billion) were $600 million, or about 6 per cent of income after taxes. Hence the average rate of return is understated by something like one-twentieth (13/16 times .06), at the most. The effect on individual industries varies considerably, but is especially strong in industries such as apparel, where small firms make extensive use of trade credit. A portion of the differences in returns among industries may therefore be caught in our correction for excessive withdrawals by entrepreneurs.

SALARIES OF EXECUTIVES IN SMALL COMPANIES

In small companies, especially those with assets under $250,000, salaries of officers may contain not only a return for labor services performed but also a portion of the return on capital (or the net profits) of the enterprise. In 1942, for example, more than half the corporations with assets under

[15] We add 5 per cent of dividends received as an adjustment for the corporate tax on 15 per cent of dividends received. The tax need not be paid, if a consolidated return is made and there are credits for foreign taxes paid.

[16] I am indebted to Victor Fuchs for calling this problem to my attention.

$250,000 were wholly owned by one to three corporation officers.[17] These officers could set their own salaries within fairly wide (legal and economic) limits, and any subsequent disallowances of salaries by the IRS would not be reflected in the published returns.

McConnell added to the reported net income an estimate of excessive salary withdrawals, which he calculated by comparing average salaries in corporations of given size that had a substantial share (15 per cent or more) of stock held by nonofficers with salaries in officer-owned corporations. The average number of officers in three corporate-size classes was also calculated, as shown below.

Asset-size Class ($000's)	Average Number of Officers	*Average "True" Salary* 1941 (dollars)	1942
Under 50	1.1	2,000	2,500
50–100	1.4	4,000	5,000
100–250	1.7	6,000	7,000

Reported salaries were reduced to these levels. We may illustrate the procedure with the apparel industry (Table A-9). There were 1,400

TABLE A-9

Officers' Compensation and Profits in Apparel Corporations, 1941
(dollar amounts in thousands)

	Asset-size Class ($000's) Under 50	50–100	100–250
1. Number of returns	4,685	1,400	1,228
2. Reported officer compensation	26,146	17,271	23,790
3. Number of officers, estimated	5,154	1,960	2,088
4. Adjusted compensation	10,308	7,840	12,528
5. Net profit before taxes, reported	952	6,104	15,150
6. Net profit before taxes, adjusted	16,790	15,535	26,412

Source: Procedure based on McConnell, "1942 Corporate Profits."

corporations in 1941 with assets of $50,000 to $100,000, and they reported aggregate officers' salaries of $17,271,000. This salary total was reduced to 1.4 times 1,400 times $4,000, or $7,840,000, and profits before taxes were increased by $17,271,000 — $7,840,000 = $9,431,000. Similar adjustments were made for the other classes. The effect of the adjustment is very substantial: net profits before taxes were increased by $36.5 million

[17] Joseph L. McConnell, "1942 Corporate Profits by Size of Firms," *Survey of Current Business*, Jan. 1946, p. 11.

or 32 per cent of reported net income in the industry. The rate of return on investment in the industry was increased from 7.06 per cent to 9.32 per cent, although this calculation ignores the personal income tax on the excessive withdrawals.

McConnell's procedure rests upon the assumption that, among companies of a given size, any difference in income is due to differences in productivity of capital—hired officers and owner-officers on average perform the same quality and quantity of work. This assumption does not seem plausible; it would be more reasonable to assume, on the contrary, that capital yields the same product in both types of company and any differences in total income are due to entrepreneurial services. Conceivably, the reported salaries understate the wage income of owner-officers.

It would be possible to test these alternative assumptions, and perhaps find a better one than either, by examining the performance over time of the two types of company. If owner-officer corporations, for example, grew more rapidly, had a smaller portion of companies taking losses, etc., McConnell's assumption would have to be rejected. Since we cannot make such a study, which requires access to the individual tax returns over a period of years, it has seemed unwise to make his adjustments in the data on the score of salary overstatements or understatements.[18] We are not concerned in this study with differences in rate of return, by company size, so the problem is less important for us. Nevertheless, we make independent estimates of the effects of entrepreneurial withdrawals by a regression analysis described in Chapter 3.

PRICE CHANGES

Since it was impossible to construct a capital series in constant dollars at the three-digit level of industry classification, no adjustments for price changes were made in income in calculating the rates of return. At the broader two-digit level, however, capital in constant dollars was calculated and a parallel income series is necessary.

The chief point at which historical costs enter the profit calculations of a firm is through the depreciation charges, which (in the period we study) were usually uniform proration of the historical cost over the life of the assets. The only adjustment we can make is to apply the index of

[18] McConnell's technique would in any event be inapplicable to the postwar period unless a new set of average officer and average salary data were collected: it would be unreasonable to assume that after a substantial inflation these parameters remained fixed in companies of given dollar asset size.

the rates of depreciation in current dollars relative to book prices, which have been constructed for all manufacturing industries,[19] to the depreciation charges of each industry. This correction affects the various industries differently, to the extent that the ratio of depreciation to net income varies. In fact it varies widely among industries (see Table A-10). Income after

TABLE A-10

DEPRECIATION CHARGES AS PER CENT OF NET PROFIT AFTER TAXES IN MANUFACTURING INDUSTRIES, 1947

Industry	Regular Depreciation as Per Cent of Net Profits
Petroleum and coal products	45.5[a]
Rubber products	31.5
Primary metals products	28.5
Stone, glass, and clay products	25.5
Food and kindred products	25.1
Electrical machinery	21.3
Machinery, except electrical	20.3
Beverages	20.1
Furniture and fixtures	20.1
Chemicals and allied products	19.3
Motor vehicles and parts	19.0
Nonferrous metals	18.9
Textile mill products	16.2
Lumber and products	16.2
Paper and allied products	15.2
Printing and publishing	14.9
Leather and products	13.0
Apparel and fabric products	10.4
Cotton manufactures	8.7
Tobacco products	7.0
Other transportation equipment	[b]
All manufactures	22.8

[a] Before adjustment for overdepletion.
[b] Net loss in 1947.

SOURCE: *Statistics of Income* for 1947.

taxes in current prices was converted to 1947 prices by use of the deflator of gross national product.

The other point at which historical costs can affect current income estimates is in the withdrawal of materials from inventory. If a company uses first-in, first-out accounting, for example, raw materials will be billed at less than their current market price during a period of inflation. No adjustment of income for this effect (which became less important as companies shifted to last-in, first-out) seemed feasible.

[19] *Survey of Current Business,* Nov. 1956, p. 11; and July 1959, p. 31.

Our method of calculating the rate of return is consistent with the measure of real capital, but it deviates in principle from a measure of return on assets in current dollars. The difference may be stated in algebraic terms. Let assets be divided into three groups:

W = working capital, in book (and current price) values
I = inventories, in book (and hence historical) values
F = fixed assets, in book (and hence historical) values

The assets of an enterprise in current values would be

$$W + IP_I + FP_F,$$

where P_I is a price index which converts historical into current values for inventories, for this industry, P_F is a similar index for fixed assets. Then, since earnings, E, are already in current values, the true rate of return is

$$r = \frac{E}{W + IP_I + FP_F}.$$

Our concept of total assets in constant (say, 1947) prices is

$$\frac{W}{P_{GNP}} + \frac{IP_I}{P_{AI}} + \frac{FP_F}{P_C},$$

where P_{GNP} is the gross national product deflator, P_{AI} is the price index of all manufacturing inventories, P_C is the index of plant and equipment costs, in each case with 1947 = 100. Earnings are also deflated by P_{GNP}, so our rate of return is

$$\frac{E/P_{GNP}}{\frac{W}{P_{GNP}} + \frac{IP_I}{P_{AI}} + \frac{FP_F}{P_C}}$$

or

$$\frac{E}{W + IP_I\left(\frac{P_{GNP}}{P_{AI}}\right) + FP_F\left(\frac{P_{GNP}}{P_C}\right)}.$$

The last formulation ignores certain details such as the correction of historical depreciation in earnings. To the extent that the price movements of all inventories (P_{AI}) and construction costs (P_C) differ from the gross national product deflator (P_{GNP}), our deflated rates of return differ from the true rates.[20]

To determine the difference between the two rates of return, the true rate was calculated for each two-digit industry for 1948–57 (Table A-11). The industrial pattern is essentially identical with that in our basic tables: the correlation coefficient does not fall below .998 in any year.

[20] I am indebted to Gary S. Becker for calling this problem to my attention.

TABLE A-11

Rates of Return in Current Prices, Manufacturing Industries, 1948–57

Industry	1948	1949	1950	1951	1952	1953	1954	1955	1956	1957
Food and kindred products	6.96	6.92	7.10	5.62	5.26	5.82	5.73	6.54	6.45	6.29
Beverages	9.29	8.77	8.16	6.56	6.09	5.96	5.26	6.43	6.17	6.46
Tobacco products	7.44	7.62	7.33	5.66	5.51	5.68	6.39	7.55	7.70	8.05
Textile mill products	12.07	5.83	8.78	5.57	3.54	3.59	2.55	4.12	4.74	4.37
Apparel and fabric products	6.35	3.60	5.85	3.18	3.25	3.02	3.06	4.04	4.41	3.80
Lumber and wood products	11.23	6.35	11.47	8.52	6.56	5.75	6.18	8.42	5.72	4.14
Furniture and fixtures	9.00	6.68	9.39	6.57	5.95	5.11	4.67	7.19	7.22	6.04
Paper and allied products	11.15	7.84	10.58	8.81	7.22	7.25	7.06	8.06	8.74	6.94
Printing and publishing	8.83	7.75	7.54	6.73	6.43	6.35	6.11	7.90	8.21	7.79
Chemicals and allied products	9.78	9.06	11.29	8.19	6.76	6.70	7.32	9.08	8.80	8.44
Petroleum and coal products	10.63	6.99	8.49	8.31	6.86	7.26	6.10	7.41	7.35	7.04
Rubber products	7.73	5.39	10.31	6.93	5.33	5.89	5.59	7.11	7.13	6.84
Leather and products	6.19	4.52	7.07	3.55	4.82	4.32	4.63	6.24	5.53	5.93
Stone, clay, and glass products	10.30	9.61	11.54	8.30	7.00	7.23	7.94	9.84	8.75	7.20
Primary metals products	9.07	7.16	9.32	7.46	5.20	6.00	4.94	7.49	7.27	6.37
Fabricated metal products	10.87	7.35	9.97	8.17	6.54	6.28	5.83	6.89	6.91	6.27
Machinery, except transportation and electrical	10.70	8.42	9.91	8.28	7.23	6.52	6.27	6.78	7.82	7.10
Electrical machinery and equipment	10.57	8.34	11.87	7.92	7.16	6.90	6.65	6.67	6.46	7.50
Transportation equipment, except motor vehicles	5.12	4.56	6.89	4.44	4.16	4.57	5.85	6.00	5.36	5.70
Motor vehicles	13.50	15.00	15.69	9.18	8.07	7.83	8.09	13.68	8.63	9.44
Ordnance and accessories	8.72	5.42	10.19	8.02	7.97	7.75	7.30	9.02	7.74	5.50
Professional and scientific instruments	9.57	7.58	8.59	7.65	7.03	6.93	8.11	8.00	8.10	7.22
Miscellaneous manufactures	7.70	5.83	8.83	6.80	5.54	4.83	4.82	5.80	5.91	5.33
Total manufactures	9.81	7.78	9.69	7.41	6.22	6.28	6.04	7.66	7.26	6.89

Note: Method of computation is described in this section of the text, "Price Changes."

These true rates average slightly less than those in 1947 prices, ranging from 0.15 per cent (1954) to 0.46 (1956).[21]

ACCELERATED DEPRECIATION

From 1940 through 1945, a firm receiving a certificate from one or more of the national defense departments was permitted to depreciate plant and equipment over a period of sixty months and, if the emergency ended in a shorter period (it ended in September 1945), the firm was allowed to

TABLE A-12
AMORTIZATION (ACCELERATED DEPRECIATION) IN MANUFACTURING CORPORATIONS, 1940–57

Year	Amount (millions of dollars)
1940	6.0
1941	88.6
1942	309.5
1943	533.7
1944	740.7
1945	1,284.6
1946	33.9
1947	24.7
1948	10.1
1949	6.7
1950	16.9
1951	158.9
1952	521.3
1953	981.6
1954	[a]
1955	1,553.4
1956	1,521.8
1957	1,308.4

[a] Amortization was not reported separately in 1954.
SOURCE: *Statistics of Income,* for 1940 to 1957.

redistribute the investment over the shorter period and recalculate taxes for earlier years. Again in 1950, a similar policy was instituted, but this time only a fraction (on average, about two-thirds) of the value of the facilities could be depreciated at accelerated rates. In 1954, the amortization over a five-year period of capitalized research expenditures was authorized. The very large sums involved in these programs are summarized in Table A-12.

[21] The differences are not due exclusively to the difference in procedure, and are therefore to some extent exaggerated. For example, where later revisions of the price series have been issued these have been employed to get the best possible true rates of return.

These certificates were concentrated chiefly in the metal, chemical (including rubber and petroleum refining), machinery, and transportation equipment industries. Accelerated depreciation was granted on the assumption that capital expenditures of the desired industrial type, location, and volume would otherwise not be forthcoming, because those facilities had small or at least highly uncertain postwar usefulness. Many of them doubtless had small postwar value, while some probably depreciated at only normal rates.

It is, of course, quite impossible to estimate the extent to which the accelerated depreciation exaggerated the "true" depreciation of the emergency facilities. The maximum effect upon the reported assets and rates of return can be estimated by assuming that *all* facilities were subject to only normal depreciation, and we carry out an illustrative calculation on this basis for the metals and metal products industry, in Table A-13.[22]

The effect of the program on reported assets was not large; even on the present assumptions, assets were written down by less than 5 per cent compared with their hypothetical true value in 1945. The effect on the rates of return was of course more substantial: in 1945, in which year the effect was largest, the rate of return was reduced by almost one-third as compared with the true rate, and thereafter the direction of the difference was reversed. Hence the reported rate shows a large rise from 1945 to 1946 while the adjusted rate fell slightly. But if averages are taken for a period of years the differences are not very great,[23] and they would presumably be smaller, if, in fact, a substantial fraction of the assets had reduced postwar usefulness. Since any adjustment would be highly arbitrary, we make none in our basic tables.

Internal Revenue Code of 1954 permitted the use of more rapid depreciation formulas, such as the sum-of-digits and declining balance methods. Both methods are now being used extensively, and an increasing downward bias relative to earlier years is present in our capital data after 1954. As yet the magnitude is not very large: Creamer estimates that, for all manufacturing industries, fixed assets were understated 0.8 per

[22] The calculations rest upon the arbitrary assumption that the true period of expected life was 15 years and that all the emergency investment during World War II was made before 1945. Various refinements in our procedure are omitted here.

[23] For metals and metal products the average rates of return are:

	1941–47	1947–54
Reported	7.03	7.92
Adjusted	7.39	7.80

TABLE A-13

HYPOTHETICAL ADJUSTMENTS FOR ACCELERATED DEPRECIATION, METALS AND METAL PRODUCTS

(millions of dollars)

Procedure (by line number)	1941	1942	1943	1944	1945	1946	1947	1948	1949	1950	1951	1952	1953	1954
1. Accelerated depreciation	26.5	103.2	173.6	233.1	333.6	2.8	2.0	1.6	0.9	7.3	59.3	200.6	428.9	534.8
2. Normal depreciation	8.8	34.4	57.9	74.3	74.4	74.4	74.4	74.4	74.4	74.7	94.5	141.6	217.7	252.7
3. Overdepreciation: 1 − 2	17.7	68.8	115.7	148.8	259.2	−71.5	−72.4	−72.8	−73.8	−67.5	−35.2	59.0	211.2	282.2
a. Cumulative	17.7	86.5	202.2	351.0	610.2	538.7	466.3	393.5	319.7	252.2	217.0	276.0	487.2	769.4
4. Reported assets	9,617	12,119	13,821	13,766	12,589	13,072	14,572	16,353	16,149	18,901	22,043	23,071	24,685	24,564
5. Adjusted assets: 4 + 3a	9,635	12,206	14,023	14,117	13,199	13,610	15,039	16,746	16,468	19,153	22,260	23,347	25,172	25,333
6. Net profit after taxes	932	895	893	759	496	807	1,468	1,728	1,227	1,938	1,781	1,292	1,533	1,226
7. Adjusted net profits: 6 + 3	949	964	1,009	907	755	735	1,396	1,655	1,153	1,871	1,746	1,351	1,744	1,508
8. Reported rate of return: 6 ÷ 4	9.69	7.38	6.46	5.51	3.94	6.17	10.08	10.56	7.60	10.26	8.08	5.60	6.21	4.99
9. Adjusted rate of return: 7 ÷ 5	7.85	7.89	7.19	6.43	5.72	5.40	9.28	9.88	7.00	9.77	7.84	5.79	6.93	5.95

NOTE: Assumptions underlying these calculations are presented in the accompanying text.

cent by 1955, 1.4 per cent by 1956, 2.3 per cent by 1957, and 3.9 per cent by 1959.[24]

DEPLETION

Depletion allowances to mineral industries are very generous, and reported deductions strongly affect the income of the petroleum industry, since the larger companies are usually integrated back into the production of crude petroleum.[25] In 1950, reported net profits of the petroleum and coal production industry were $810 million (after taxes, and excluding dividends received), compared with depletion charges of $762 million. The nominal rates of return in petroleum refining are understated.

The Treasury analyzed the depletion charges of the larger petroleum companies for the years 1946–49.[26] Their allowable depletion was $3,142 million in those years, whereas the "adjusted basis depletion" (essentially depletion on a historical cost basis) was $167 million, or about 5 per cent of allowable depletion, but this estimate seems extreme. A small study we made of the ratio of depletion to receipts as reported by large petroleum companies to their stockholders indicates that this ratio is about 2/11 of the corresponding ratio in the tax returns. We accordingly exclude four-fifths of the reported depletion. The remainder is treated in the same manner as depreciation in calculating income, i.e., it is adjusted for price changes.

OTHER INCOME ADJUSTMENTS

Among numerous other sources of differences between reported and actual income, two merit at least brief mention.

The data in *Statistics of Income* are based upon unaudited tax returns. Additional assessments are reported each year but they are not allocated in the statistics to year or industry. It may be estimated, very roughly and indirectly, that additional assessments less refunds for the tax years from 1947 through 1956 amounted to $4.9 billion or 2.0 per cent of net income after taxes during that period. To the unknown extent that IRS disallowed depreciation or other capital charges, assets would be increased. The underestimate of average rates of return in the unaudited returns was therefore of the order of 0.15 per cent a year. Carrybacks of losses also affect the after-tax income of earlier years, and the data available to

[24] Daniel Creamer, *Capital Expansion and Capacity in Postwar Manufacturing*, National Industrial Conference Board, 1961, Appendix B.

[25] See D. H. Eldridge, "Tax Incentives for Mineral Enterprise," *Journal of Political Economy*, Apr. 1950, pp. 222–240.

[26] W. F. Hellmuth, Jr., "Erosion of the Federal Corporation Income Tax Base," *National Tax Association Proceedings*, 1955, p. 328.

estimate their effect is even more sketchy. As a rough estimate, carrybacks increased rates of return by about 0.06 per cent a year.

The rates of return for World War II were also considerably affected by renegotiation of profits. For the period 1942–45, net income after taxes was reduced by roughly 8 per cent (so average rates of return were reduced by about 0.5 per cent), the heaviest impact being on the transportation (aircraft), iron and steel, and machinery industries.

Basic Tables, Data on Capital and Rates of Return, All Manufacturing Industries, 1938–47 and 1947–57

TABLE A-14

BEVERAGES, 1938–47

(assets in thousands of dollars)

	1938	1939	1940	1941	1942	1943	1944	1945	1946	1947
TOTAL ASSETS, EXCLUDING OTHER INVESTMENTS										
Total beverages (1947 prices)	2,552,000	2,495,000	2,558,000	2,631,000	2,762,000	2,617,000	2,770,000	2,882,000	3,066,000	3,252,000
Total beverages (book values)	1,297,043	1,296,512	1,370,242	1,513,310	1,638,926	1,739,499	1,984,463	2,192,096	2,549,366	2,778,180
Breweries	602,371	610,248	603,989	632,771	679,978	755,811	833,571	913,111	1,003,580	1,106,917
Distilled and rectified	386,959	374,335	414,783	476,368	524,160	500,174	596,425	686,030	873,218	981,276
Wines[a]	41,232	35,674	43,548	53,005	47,448	77,282	101,199	113,102	147,947	101,317
Nonalcoholic	240,179	252,064	290,376	336,605	372,635	394,197	439,953	451,498	504,886	580,046
CORPORATE ASSETS, EXCLUDING OTHER INVESTMENTS										
Total beverages (1947 prices)	2,381,000	2,333,000	2,395,000	2,467,000	2,586,000	2,448,000	2,549,000	2,614,000	2,841,000	3,076,000
Total beverages (book values)	1,210,253	1,212,329	1,283,064	1,419,085	1,534,658	1,626,909	1,826,174	1,988,152	2,362,366	2,627,446
Breweries	596,209	603,808	597,345	625,522	671,486	745,562	818,523	892,364	984,682	1,090,670
Distilled and rectified	381,875	370,255	410,044	471,313	518,791	495,292	589,691	677,674	865,838	976,010
Wines[a]	35,922	31,130	38,008	46,272	41,178	66,692	84,061	90,650	123,653	88,362
Nonalcoholic	197,816	207,350	239,242	277,106	303,913	318,580	336,671	328,314	388,463	473,416
RATE OF RETURN ON CORPORATE ASSETS (per cent)										
Total beverages (1947 prices)	7.46	9.05	7.96	9.07	8.78	9.43	8.55	8.36	13.13	10.52
Total beverages (book values)	8.20	9.77	8.26	9.27	9.58	10.00	8.60	8.17	13.14	10.70
Breweries	7.49	9.86	6.77	8.45	8.93	10.10	8.97	8.81	14.99	13.81
Distilled and rectified	5.92	5.34	6.22	7.39	8.24	8.14	6.48	7.27	12.87	10.18
Wines[a]	0.82	4.21	5.46	5.44	7.80	8.51	8.17	1.38	7.82	–8.16
Nonalcoholic	15.99	18.21	15.89	14.91	13.50	12.98	11.45	10.14	10.75	8.13

[a] Data unreliable because of year-to-year differences in classification of large companies.

TABLE A-15

FOOD AND KINDRED PRODUCTS, 1938–47

(assets in thousands of dollars)

	1938	1939	1940	1941	1942	1943	1944	1945	1946	1947
TOTAL ASSETS, EXCLUDING OTHER INVESTMENTS										
Total food and kindred products (1947 prices)	10,716,000	10,522,000	10,534,000	10,891,000	11,081,000	11,181,000	11,534,000	11,514,000	12,119,000	11,965,000
Total food and kindred products (book values)	5,481,586	5,577,899	5,669,609	6,368,235	6,858,031	7,220,899	7,656,799	7,893,971	9,133,122	9,937,541
Bakery products	634,491	641,194	650,395	663,249	707,028	746,783	769,620	799,775	861,628	909,466
Confectionery	276,568	271,706	283,101	306,163	346,440	413,928	465,436	456,211	525,732	615,827
Canning	650,618	643,162	655,037	775,616	822,106	897,528	950,188	981,036	1,366,279	1,420,447
Meat products	979,406	990,664	1,039,997	1,218,497	1,306,009	1,349,398	1,398,627	1,368,041	1,595,623	1,822,013
Grain mill products, excluding cereals	489,396	528,588	500,648	592,281	668,869	747,088	774,144	829,229	1,006,309	1,192,232
Cereal preparations[a]	111,260	114,935	118,046	110,321	138,851	109,342	199,939	165,317	179,883	148,580
Dairy products	590,497	587,779	596,286	689,298	842,311	895,758	1,016,773	1,106,403	1,228,242	1,212,281
Sugar	664,245	717,059	712,733	784,065	775,907	727,610	688,039	751,089	753,947	951,897
Miscellaneous foods	915,939	935,007	951,128	1,066,796	1,150,846	1,166,293	1,216,740	1,221,847	1,452,830	1,594,059
CORPORATE ASSETS, EXCLUDING OTHER INVESTMENTS										
Total food and kindred products (1947 prices)	9,625,000	9,480,000	9,510,000	9,853,000	10,001,000	10,072,000	10,135,000	9,894,000	10,757,000	10,957,000
Total food and kindred products (book values)	4,923,694	5,025,756	5,118,590	5,761,238	6,189,656	6,504,257	6,726,780	6,782,053	8,105,417	9,099,386
Bakery products	541,355	551,617	563,352	578,547	617,614	653,955	657,604	670,920	755,665	830,310
Confectionery	267,459	262,509	273,151	294,999	332,736	396,236	439,270	424,320	495,086	587,653
Canning	612,949	606,277	617,425	731,034	772,659	841,223	874,790	887,800	1,260,909	1,336,816
Meat products	914,795	925,674	971,419	1,137,745	1,215,113	1,251,085	1,269,580	1,216,666	1,451,273	1,695,191
Grain mill products, excluding cereals	450,086	484,323	456,564	537,553	601,308	665,022	663,556	683,777	854,896	1,047,112
Cereal preparations[a]	110,566	114,250	117,366	109,709	138,074	108,729	198,562	163,999	178,798	147,945
Dairy products	516,222	515,688	524,308	607,485	739,925	784,674	863,026	912,945	1,054,808	1,082,514
Sugar	657,277	708,713	703,518	772,896	763,240	714,122	670,385	725,976	732,298	929,869
Miscellaneous foods	865,247	884,067	899,573	1,009,289	1,033,303	1,098,575	1,127,882	1,115,581	1,351,221	1,509,762

TABLE A-15 (concluded)

	1938	1939	1940	1941	1942	1943	1944	1945	1946	1947
RATE OF RETURN ON CORPORATE ASSETS (per cent)										
Total food and kindred products (1947 prices)	3.65	6.04	5.79	6.88	7.23	6.88	6.31	6.08	10.51	8.89
Total food and kindred products (book values)	3.82	6.33	5.93	6.90	7.62	7.54	6.90	6.57	11.68	9.42
Bakery products	7.19	6.68	5.70	5.32	7.41	8.08	7.65	7.77	14.37	10.36
Confectionery	8.67	10.08	9.41	9.43	11.30	10.90	10.00	9.84	16.05	16.55
Canning	0.43	7.44	7.84	10.56	8.98	7.43	7.34	7.23	12.36	7.19
Meat products	0.42	4.41	4.80	4.11	5.63	5.57	5.54	3.03	10.86	7.15
Grain mill products, excluding cereals	3.97	5.42	4.89	6.50	6.66	8.63	5.98	7.99	14.36	11.50
Cereal preparations[a]	6.30	9.04	8.87	10.29	11.09	12.43	6.46	10.01	12.25	12.10
Dairy products	4.94	6.29	5.40	6.45	8.29	8.22	6.88	6.92	10.51	8.26
Sugar	0.15	3.40	3.21	5.57	5.02	4.26	4.32	3.91	5.22	6.17
Miscellaneous foods	7.90	8.54	7.44	8.60	9.26	8.80	8.39	7.91	11.17	11.34

[a] Data unreliable because of year-to-year differences in classification of large companies.

TABLE A-16

TOBACCO AND PRODUCTS, 1938–47
(assets in thousands of dollars)

	1938	1939	1940	1941	1942	1943	1944	1945	1946	1947
TOTAL ASSETS, EXCLUDING OTHER INVESTMENTS										
Total tobacco (1947 prices)	1,805,000	1,860,000	1,693,000	1,712,000	2,107,000	2,263,000	2,436,000	2,548,000	2,444,000	2,211,000
Total tobacco (book values)	1,006,269	1,052,837	1,077,573	1,177,168	1,311,889	1,413,049	1,554,357	1,753,136	1,913,513	2,116,086
CORPORATE ASSETS, EXCLUDING OTHER INVESTMENTS										
Total tobacco (1947 prices)	1,769,000	1,825,000	1,662,000	1,683,000	2,074,000	2,231,000	2,396,000	2,503,000	2,408,000	2,184,000
Total tobacco (book values)	986,313	1,032,993	1,058,302	1,157,255	1,291,451	1,392,867	1,529,092	1,721,936	1,885,202	2,090,578
RATE OF RETURN ON CORPORATE ASSETS (per cent)										
Total tobacco (1947 prices)	9.88	10.27	11.01	9.89	6.68	5.73	4.96	4.60	5.74	6.34
Total tobacco (book values)	10.27	10.44	10.04	8.99	7.48	6.95	6.01	5.33	6.42	6.40

TABLE A-17

TEXTILE MILL PRODUCTS, 1938–47
(assets in thousands of dollars)

	1938	1939	1940	1941	1942	1943	1944	1945	1946	1947
TOTAL ASSETS, EXCLUDING OTHER INVESTMENTS										
Total textile mill products (1947 prices)	5,744,000	5,744,000	6,011,000	6,335,000	6,668,000	6,402,000	6,399,000	6,383,000	7,453,000	7,654,000
Total textile mill products (book values)	2,998,804	3,099,042	3,243,317	3,729,761	4,167,759	4,226,540	4,355,064	4,452,523	5,692,962	6,431,464
Cotton manufactures	1,007,167	1,094,398	1,092,635	1,276,678	1,514,711	1,526,987	1,541,003	1,590,135	2,000,500	2,242,811
Woolen and worsted	417,502	468,962	516,603	639,283	688,473	695,412	727,506	730,013	857,558	942,028
Rayon and silk	245,633	264,870	282,918	376,891	428,384	452,267	466,584	502,546	650,726	836,405
Knit goods	408,465	430,430	433,149	471,219	519,599	530,873	569,211	572,591	795,542	866,858
Hats, except cloth and millinery	51,623	54,077	62,882	79,052	71,334	73,777	77,005	77,355	100,021	87,683
Carpets	184,146	194,342	210,092	242,199	227,776	233,198	248,277	243,636	293,897	352,323
Dyeing and finishing	161,122	170,760	171,848	198,905	222,541	231,001	248,531	262,788	321,113	351,612
Miscellaneous	532,482	480,394	481,739	458,924	504,483	491,625	487,802	485,682	692,454	770,043
CORPORATE ASSETS, EXCLUDING OTHER INVESTMENTS										
Total textile mill products (1947 prices)	5,621,000	5,621,000	5,882,000	6,200,000	6,529,000	6,272,000	6,241,000	6,198,000	7,259,000	7,477,000
Total textile mill products (book values)	2,934,434	3,032,657	3,173,894	3,649,986	4,080,711	4,140,385	4,247,182	4,322,950	5,543,850	6,281,750
Cotton manufactures	989,997	1,026,998	1,074,831	1,256,344	1,491,684	1,504,856	1,514,469	1,558,707	1,965,837	2,209,200
Woolen and worsted	408,033	458,673	505,638	626,172	675,159	682,758	712,010	712,442	839,745	925,391
Rayon and silk	239,256	258,247	276,107	368,171	419,092	443,094	455,587	489,267	636,007	820,463
Knit goods	386,050	406,992	409,593	445,625	492,047	503,380	533,654	530,876	743,171	815,939
Hats, except cloth and millinery	51,123	53,457	62,071	77,906	70,212	72,530	75,279	75,147	97,254	85,372
Carpets	184,146	193,392	207,923	238,392	223,087	227,328	239,177	231,456	278,789	334,203
Dyeing and finishing	160,055	169,326	170,097	196,524	219,550	227,576	243,531	255,933	312,872	342,905
Miscellaneous	514,369	464,641	466,514	444,968	490,080	478,480	472,644	468,757	671,742	750,582

(continued)

TABLE A-17 (concluded)

	1938	1939	1940	1941	1942	1943	1944	1945	1946	1947
RATE OF RETURN ON CORPORATE ASSETS (per cent)										
Total textile mill products (1947 prices)	−0.25	4.37	4.77	8.95	7.98	6.81	6.35	6.13	13.79	13.62
Total textile mill products (book values)	−0.62	4.42	4.82	9.09	8.42	7.27	6.75	6.56	15.46	15.17
Cotton manufactures	−0.21	3.34	5.45	10.01	9.26	7.28	6.35	6.23	17.16	19.73
Woolen and worsted	−2.92	5.10	5.34	8.72	7.72	7.45	7.23	6.83	16.21	10.21
Rayon and silk	0.96	6.36	4.92	8.38	9.04	7.39	6.94	6.40	11.94	15.93
Knit goods	1.13	3.60	2.32	8.48	8.51	7.99	7.81	8.05	16.66	11.51
Hats, except cloth and millinery	−1.03	4.57	4.94	6.62	5.07	6.89	7.30	6.20	10.86	6.52
Carpets	−2.06	8.36	6.22	8.16	5.17	3.67	4.27	3.99	10.03	12.43
Dyeing and finishing	0.35	4.94	3.67	9.74	9.99	9.65	8.90	9.09	20.00	13.78
Miscellaneous	−1.38	3.95	4.71	8.79	7.45	6.79	6.06	5.64	12.30	13.82

TABLE A-[illegible]

APPAREL AND PRODUCTS MADE FROM FABRICS, 1938–47
(assets in thousands of dollars)

	1938	1939	1940	1941	1942	1943	1944	1945	1946	1947
TOTAL ASSETS, EXCLUDING OTHER INVESTMENTS										
Total apparel (1947 prices)	1,790,000	1,842,000	2,033,000	2,437,000	2,539,000	2,427,000	2,509,000	2,812,000	3,410,000	3,293,000
Total apparel (book values)	967,303	1,030,341	1,127,444	1,501,237	1,670,498	1,695,444	1,817,689	2,095,551	2,900,509	3,112,525
Men's clothing	403,620	452,838	473,988	589,884	603,583	625,500	648,273	682,539	959,765	1,117,530
Women's clothing	284,369	291,395	319,569	431,036	515,885	518,357	561,845	677,711	1,091,661	1,191,467
Furs[b]	48,073	45,995	62,293	68,391	96,928	95,038	98,679	150,157	133,214	120,768
Millinery	16,237	17,178	14,241	16,939	19,284	23,868	26,757	32,704	37,418	34,681
Miscellaneous	213,639	218,265	256,941	393,706	446,250	437,362	492,306	592,112	714,352	667,718
CORPORATE ASSETS, EXCLUDING OTHER INVESTMENTS										
Total apparel (1947 prices)	1,464,000	1,498,000	1,633,000	1,933,000	1,967,000	1,835,000	1,766,000	1,845,000	2,485,000	2,716,000
Total apparel (book values)	790,951	837,960	905,587	1,190,623	1,293,906	1,282,057	1,279,179	1,374,972	2,113,615	2,566,763
Men's clothing	355,877	398,771	415,012	513,507	518,900	531,020	527,596	533,018	802,195	1,006,215
Women's clothing	220,931	224,520	242,087	320,937	372,459	362,720	359,401	397,521	726,237	924,543
Furs[b]	30,123	28,069	36,498	38,465	51,154	47,059	41,705	54,761	58,800	69,486
Millinery	13,057	13,394	10,679	12,209	13,152	15,376	15,156	16,308	21,385	23,959
Miscellaneous	168,472	171,476	199,496	302,062	334,256	319,804	333,659	373,188	505,495	541,088
RATE OF RETURN ON CORPORATE ASSETS (per cent)										
Total apparel (1947 prices)	0.65	6.31	5.73	7.08	7.31	7.74	7.57	7.43	14.10	10.82
Total apparel (book values)	0.23	3.67	4.14	7.06	7.61	8.24	7.95	7.81	14.47	10.86
Men's clothing	0.51	4.40	4.59	7.52	8.10	7.77	7.21	6.96	14.54	11.64
Women's clothing	0.17	2.76	3.05	6.25	7.50	8.95	9.48	9.39	16.13	10.87
Furs[b]	−2.15	1.36	3.57	3.40	2.65	7.71	3.81	5.15	3.23	3.61
Millinery	−3.79	−1.93	−1.78	2.54	4.62	10.52	11.01	9.81	11.27	4.47
Miscellaneous	0.47	4.02	5.00	7.88	7.94	8.35	7.88	7.66	13.40	10.65

[b] Data unreliable because of large proportion of noncorporate firms.

TABLE A-19

BASIC LUMBER, 1938–47

(assets in thousands of dollars)

	1938	1939	1940	1941	1942	1943	1944	1945	1946	1947
TOTAL ASSETS, EXCLUDING OTHER INVESTMENTS										
Total lumber (1947 prices)	2,984,000	2,883,000	2,888,000	2,883,000	2,814,000	2,710,000	2,697,000	2,603,000	2,905,000	3,174,000
Total lumber (book values)	1,535,547	1,488,442	1,510,570	1,634,310	1,702,537	1,720,628	1,739,588	1,736,972	2,097,969	2,545,011
Logging camps and miscellaneous	1,210,607	1,183,461	1,183,084	1,260,112	1,323,259	1,320,164	1,305,697	1,281,394	1,536,040	1,829,025
Planing mills	175,409	173,370	175,382	223,877	221,846	230,701	262,833	277,260	370,928	505,887
Wooden containers	134,957	117,761	132,015	130,441	138,305	148,573	149,525	156,994	168,120	183,639
CORPORATE ASSETS, EXCLUDING OTHER INVESTMENTS										
Total lumber (1947 prices)	2,632,000	2,557,000	2,515,000	2,472,000	2,385,000	2,276,000	2,222,000	2,112,000	2,427,000	2,725,000
Total lumber (book values)	1,354,211	1,320,309	1,315,424	1,401,200	1,443,014	1,445,272	1,433,079	1,409,558	1,752,607	2,185,090
Logging camps and miscellaneous	1,082,154	1,063,186	1,045,032	1,097,148	1,139,712	1,127,215	1,094,569	1,058,665	1,302,418	1,589,330
Planing mills	150,966	150,418	149,138	187,328	183,616	189,516	211,994	220,878	306,184	431,740
Wooden containers	121,537	106,420	118,735	116,838	121,425	128,147	126,976	131,533	146,212	165,519
RATE OF RETURN ON CORPORATE ASSETS (per cent)										
Total lumber (1947 prices)	−0.20	1.69	3.78	7.05	6.16	5.17	5.29	4.80	9.53	13.52
Total lumber (book values)	−0.46	1.69	3.93	7.35	6.56	5.58	5.81	5.21	10.96	15.49
Logging camps and miscellaneous	−0.70	1.26	3.50	6.91	6.30	5.24	5.55	4.87	10.41	15.88
Planing mills	0.57	3.76	7.05	9.17	7.20	6.21	5.88	6.41	13.55	16.37
Wooden containers	0.39	3.02	3.91	8.57	7.94	7.65	7.90	5.83	10.28	9.30

TABLE A-20

FURNITURE AND FINISHED LUMBER, 1938–47

(assets in thousands of dollars)

	1938	1939	1940	1941	1942	1943	1944	1945	1946	1947
TOTAL ASSETS, EXCLUDING OTHER INVESTMENTS										
Total furniture (1947 prices)	1,514,000	1,585,000	1,689,000	1,648,000	1,483,000	1,404,000	1,435,000	1,445,000	1,764,000	1,824,000
Total furniture (book values)	794,032	844,975	901,336	976,333	948,467	942,242	999,124	1,034,183	1,365,568	1,759,224
Furniture	426,046	440,320	466,472	532,833	504,323	482,715	497,715	528,928	764,827	908,689
Partitions and fixtures	42,707	38,130	52,091	57,542	52,277	58,077	61 681	65,791	89,744	113,070
Miscellaneous	324,745	365,496	382,910	387,600	391,116	401,272	441,022	439,537	509,931	555,399
CORPORATE ASSETS, EXCLUDING OTHER INVESTMENTS										
Total furniture (1947 prices)	1,372,000	1,442,000	1,531,000	1,465,000	1,301,000	1,214,000	1,232,000	1,226,000	1,543,000	1,649,000
Total furniture (book values)	719,572	768,727	816,928	882,204	842,126	824,065	862,736	883,677	1,208,316	1,608,484
Furniture	391,711	406,712	429,066	488,917	455,971	430,959	439,069	463,279	690,366	843,466
Partitions and fixtures	37,283	33,403	45,307	49,722	43,947	47,621	49,451	51,691	73,932	97,604
Miscellaneous	290,573	328,498	342,736	345,788	342,200	345,289	374,229	368,742	444,794	502,512
RATE OF RETURN ON CORPORATE ASSETS (per cent)										
Total furniture (1947 prices)	0.99	4.02	5.06	8.01	6.40	5.73	6.02	5.65	9.82	10.05
Total furniture (book values)	0.85	4.16	5.26	7.97	6.48	5.93	6.29	5.82	10.53	9.33
Furniture	0.75	4.61	6.26	8.98	7.19	6.47	6.83	6.37	11.99	10.99
Partitions and fixtures	−0.49	1.84	3.60	5.95	4.90	6.53	7.38	5.14	10.88	12.34
Miscellaneous	1.14	3.84	4.23	6.79	5.74	5.19	5.52	5.23	8.18	9.02

TABLE A-21

PAPER AND ALLIED PRODUCTS, 1938–47
(assets in thousands of dollars)

	1938	1939	1940	1941	1942	1943	1944	1945	1946	1947
TOTAL ASSETS, EXCLUDING OTHER INVESTMENTS										
Total paper (1947 prices)	3,467,000	3,453,000	3,628,000	4,047,000	3,738,000	3,705,000	3,704,000	3,665,000	3,943,000	4,403,000
Total paper (book values)	1,756,455	1,823,155	1,935,686	2,270,311	2,239,853	2,368,969	2,453,230	2,505,764	2,920,717	3,571,515
Pulp, paper, and paperboard	1,064,113	1,116,374	1,182,278	1,437,676	1,484,430	1,622,180	1,651,336	1,693,196	1,936,246	2,361,919
Miscellaneous	695,338	709,552	757,128	841,016	758,258	747,674	806,375	819,049	997,483	1,222,461
CORPORATE ASSETS, EXCLUDING OTHER INVESTMENTS										
Total paper (1947 prices)	3,410,000	3,398,000	3,572,000	3,986,000	3,685,000	3,655,000	3,645,000	3,599,000	3,881,000	4,344,000
Total paper (book values)	1,726,986	1,793,939	1,906,085	2,237,264	2,209,616	2,339,417	2,418,069	2,466,019	2,881,744	3,532,137
Pulp, paper, and paperboard	1,059,997	1,111,628	1,176,792	1,430,444	1,476,569	1,613,195	1,639,412	1,677,866	1,919,549	2,342,820
Miscellaneous	668,775	683,502	730,427	812,581	734,283	725,631	778,898	787,935	965,144	1,189,193
RATE OF RETURN ON CORPORATE ASSETS (per cent)										
Total paper (1947 prices)	2.91	5.26	7.31	8.18	6.78	6.43	6.23	5.82	11.03	14.33
Total paper (book values)	2.97	5.44	7.57	8.55	7.15	6.87	6.62	6.07	12.30	16.28
Pulp, paper, and paperboard	2.65	4.60	7.64	7.71	6.73	6.16	5.78	5.32	11.16	16.65
Miscellaneous	3.46	6.79	7.45	9.98	7.99	8.43	8.38	7.68	14.52	15.57

TABLE A-22

Printing and Publishing, 1938–47

(assets in thousands of dollars)

	1938	1939	1940	1941	1942	1943	1944	1945	1946	1947
TOTAL ASSETS, EXCLUDING OTHER INVESTMENTS										
Total printing and publishing (1947 prices)	3,964,000	3,988,000	4,067,000	3,951,000	3,916,000	3,885,000	4,107,000	4,233,000	4,200,000	4,454,000
Total printing and publishing (book values)	2,076,032	2,107,787	2,189,881	2,255,675	2,361,163	2,533,262	2,809,805	3,019,931	3,287,360	3,801,580
Newspapers	948,645	935,177	986,935	989,976	1,107,908	1,129,652	1,199,937	1,282,608	1,322,780	1,528,336
Periodicals	215,930	250,483	284,724	289,827	283,506	343,774	434,349	483,384	491,469	537,893
Books	147,487	146,871	163,837	192,726	215,626	243,770	282,331	292,727	329,650	387,476
Commercial printing and lithographing	358,079	347,295	402,478	445,317	450,459	487,335	502,650	566,109	699,584	822,210
Miscellaneous	420,892	441,548	363,199	350,686	312,837	338,378	396,657	403,753	462,885	549,315
CORPORATE ASSETS, EXCLUDING OTHER INVESTMENTS										
Total printing and publishing (1947 prices)	3,684,000	3,712,000	3,784,000	3,674,000	3,641,000	3,611,000	3,800,000	3,900,000	3,884,000	4,134,000
Total printing and publishing (book values)	1,929,685	1,962,054	2,037,177	2,097,239	2,194,552	2,353,887	2,598,482	2,780,468	3,037,921	3,525,894
Newspapers	893,480	881,962	930,408	932,984	1,043,978	1,064,397	1,126,438	1,199,931	1,241,474	1,438,884
Periodicals	210,216	244,011	277,328	282,271	276,109	334,811	422,338	469,318	477,884	523,791
Books	140,567	140,049	156,083	183,441	205,076	231,667	267,250	276,024	311,448	366,788
Commercial printing and lithographing	310,795	302,380	350,159	387,208	391,609	423,670	433,417	484,492	603,140	713,992
Miscellaneous	374,645	393,646	323,234	311,587	277,577	299,856	348,500	351,844	405,380	483,431

(continued)

TABLE A-22 (concluded)

	1938	1939	1940	1941	1942	1943	1944	1945	1946	1947
RATE OF RETURN ON CORPORATE ASSETS (per cent)										
Total printing and publishing (1947 prices)	3.19	5.12	5.17	5.53	5.20	7.36	7.81	7.64	12.05	10.11
Total printing and publishing (book values)	3.29	5.16	5.34	5.67	5.57	8.16	8.56	8.27	13.20	10.95
Newspapers	4.13	6.15	5.69	5.89	5.80	8.65	8.69	7.95	14.04	11.77
Periodicals	1.37	4.68	5.05	5.08	5.32	10.44	9.08	9.05	10.52	8.24
Books	3.82	3.47	3.45	4.82	5.57	5.97	7.63	7.05	9.37	6.68
Commercial printing and lithographing	2.98	4.79	5.76	6.76	5.83	7.38	8.86	8.93	15.00	12.68
Miscellaneous	2.45	4.12	5.02	4.71	4.59	6.66	7.84	8.31	13.97	12.09

TABLE A-23

Chemicals and Allied Products, 1938–47

(assets in thousands of dollars)

	1938	1939	1940	1941	1942	1943	1944	1945	1946	1947
TOTAL ASSETS, EXCLUDING OTHER INVESTMENTS										
Total chemicals (1947 prices)	7,232,000	7,751,000	8,189,000	8,953,000	9,349,000	9,595,000	9,593,000	9,209,000	9,899,000	10,758,000
Total chemicals (book values)	3,813,828	4,134,391	4,431,829	5,224,647	5,800,532	6,373,512	6,597,148	6,561,749	7,630,473	9,062,837
Paints and varnishes	311,097	430,737	433,535	508,642	495,944	524,862	574,937	591,062	695,243	782,058
Industrial chemicals	1,461,910	1,593,333	1,803,187	2,136,875	2,621,087	2,837,785	2,795,969	2,795,297	3,107,737	3,857,248
Soap and glycerin	291,575	303,789	325,130	403,727	338,878	396,901	399,036	361,021	429,146	548,032
Drugs and toilet preparations	591,926	619,285	650,948	749,582	798,654	904,213	1,025,734	1,022,380	1,178,964	1,267,528
Oils	249,142	234,638	223,002	297,315	299,232	332,033	332,436	351,185	500,335	616,842
Rayon	175,227	188,511	198,475	210,465	226,996	231,907	255,470	231,246	289,247	313,761
Plastic materials	48,575	51,802	58,684	87,651	86,856	105,657	108,994	107,600	112,692	134,140
Fertilizers	191,690	183,612	181,909	198,890	196,668	199,173	216,278	224,323	246,694	292,888
Miscellaneous chemicals	526,245	562,390	586,092	666,433	766,348	882,383	936,449	931,335	1,139,148	1,354,334
CORPORATE ASSETS, EXCLUDING OTHER INVESTMENTS										
Total chemicals (1947 prices)	7,136,000	7,645,000	8,074,000	8,823,000	9,213,000	9,455,000	9,418,000	9,006,000	9,698,000	10,559,000
Total chemicals (book values)	3,763,320	4,077,947	4,369,433	5,148,854	5,715,885	6,280,069	6,476,083	6,416,174	7,474,063	8,893,433
Paints and varnishes	305,275	422,568	425,194	498,715	486,352	514,808	561,355	574,421	677,376	763,945
Industrial chemicals	1,448,957	1,579,936	1,787,597	2,117,890	2,497,725	2,812,439	2,764,743	2,757,586	3,069,112	3,813,656
Soap and glycerin	289,194	301,275	322,401	400,290	336,020	393,588	394,918	356,571	424,325	542,494
Drugs and toilet preparations	579,470	606,564	637,885	734,897	783,738	888,133	1,004,110	997,694	1,154,037	1,244,379
Oils	237,658	223,894	212,846	283,849	286,053	317,821	315,312	330,136	473,391	587,373
Rayon	175,227	188,511	196,931	207,212	221,886	225,149	244,259	217,106	270,747	293,414
Plastic materials	48,575	51,802	58,679	87,637	86,836	105,625	108,944	107,530	112,616	134,048
Fertilizers	185,350	177,793	176,389	193,124	191,358	194,180	210,036	217,137	239,993	286,259
Miscellaneous chemicals	497,156	531,146	553,326	628,942	723,920	834,330	874,514	859,019	1,058,593	1,268,198

(continued)

TABLE A-23 (concluded)

	1938	1939	1940	1941	1942	1943	1944	1945	1946	1947
RATE OF RETURN ON CORPORATE ASSETS (per cent)										
Total chemicals (1947 prices)	5.77	9.12	9.32	9.24	7.84	7.35	6.81	6.20	10.61	11.00
Total chemicals (book values)	6.04	9.63	9.70	9.45	8.24	7.77	7.12	6.37	11.42	11.72
Paints and varnishes	2.47	6.77	6.45	8.24	6.29	5.44	5.68	5.10	10.18	12.90
Industrial chemicals	6.41	10.68	10.90	10.35	8.30	7.49	7.17	6.30	9.94	9.98
Soap and glycerin	11.57	13.85	12.16	7.98	9.30	9.83	9.09	8.71	17.26	17.34
Drugs and toilet preparations	10.58	12.23	11.35	10.54	10.20	10.51	8.79	8.69	13.47	9.96
Oils	3.05	5.55	6.60	7.04	6.20	6.14	4.76	5.27	13.01	16.88
Rayon	0.94	5.14	8.07	7.69	7.39	6.31	5.12	−2.23	10.85	15.30
Plastic materials	0.71	8.47	8.45	11.10	7.56	7.99	6.41	6.43	10.46	8.16
Fertilizers	3.12	3.56	3.92	6.13	6.66	5.49	4.97	5.66	10.33	10.73
Miscellaneous chemicals	3.46	8.79	8.69	9.42	8.26	7.73	7.09	6.51	11.64	12.59

TABLE A-24

PETROLEUM AND COAL PRODUCTS, 1938–47
(assets in thousands of dollars)

	1938	1939	1940	1941	1942	1943	1944	1945	1946	1947
TOTAL ASSETS, EXCLUDING OTHER INVESTMENTS										
Total petroleum and coal products (1947 prices)	12,186,000	12,651,000	12,767,000	14,456,000	16,511,000	16,118,000	16,759,000	16,073,000	16,032,000	16,857,000
Total petroleum and coal products (book values)	6,177,360	6,594,961	6,797,031	8,022,653	9,616,333	9,766,446	10,491,802	10,459,715	11,333,187	13,130,160
Petroleum refining	5,908,533	6,349,902	6,515,052	7,661,821	9,163,174	9,310,058	9,921,347	10,002,439	10,822,626	12,497,503
Miscellaneous petroleum and coal products	264,001	238,953	273,951	355,806	444,707	440,172	536,261	414,881	465,286	570,501
CORPORATE ASSETS, EXCLUDING OTHER INVESTMENTS										
Total petroleum and coal products (1947 prices)	12,077,000	12,529,000	12,635,000	14,297,000	16,323,000	15,928,000	16,505,000	15,771,000	15,748,000	16,579,000
Total petroleum and coal products (book values)	6,123,009	6,531,392	6,725,714	7,931,626	9,501,700	9,644,779	10,322,149	10,248,358	11,115,171	12,893,363
Petroleum refining	5,860,340	6,294,968	6,455,389	7,587,770	9,072,102	9,215,180	9,792,237	9,842,116	10,659,783	12,323,464
Miscellaneous petroleum and coal products	262,661	237,525	272,066	353,034	440,928	436,138	529,702	408,386	458,213	562,228
RATE OF RETURN ON CORPORATE ASSETS (per cent)										
Total petroleum and coal products (1947 prices)	1.68	3.22	3.96	5.22	5.02	6.01	5.31	4.40	6.32	8.86
Total petroleum and coal products (book values)	1.42	3.17	3.78	5.11	5.22	6.55	5.70	4.41	6.52	9.23
Petroleum refining	1.29	3.08	3.68	5.06	5.21	6.65	5.84	4.45	6.50	9.17
Miscellaneous petroleum and coal products	4.28	5.57	5.96	6.04	5.37	4.43	3.17	3.28	7.00	10.71

TABLE A-25

RUBBER AND PRODUCTS, 1938–47
(assets in thousands of dollars)

	1938	1939	1940	1941	1942	1943	1944	1945	1946	1947
TOTAL ASSETS, EXCLUDING OTHER INVESTMENTS										
Total rubber (1947 prices)	1,431,000	1,585,000	1,672,000	1,757,000	1,929,000	2,109,000	2,215,000	1,993,000	2,013,000	2,066,000
Total rubber (book values)	753,116	864,617	904,676	1,040,795	1,254,700	1,460,746	1,547,771	1,448,437	1,579,961	1,801,014
Tires and tubes	561,800	691,825	702,815	810,932	1,033,704	1,209,914	1,273,568	1,173,783	1,244,367	1,421,340
Miscellaneous rubber	186,738	168,298	195,140	222,322	211,803	240,703	261,588	261,351	324,197	368,610
CORPORATE ASSETS, EXCLUDING OTHER INVESTMENTS										
Total rubber (1947 prices)	1,414,000	1,567,000	1,653,000	1,738,000	1,910,000	2,089,000	2,191,000	1,968,000	1,992,000	2,048,000
Total rubber (book values)	744,162	854,674	894,611	1,029,607	1,241,986	1,446,819	1,530,465	1,430,104	1,562,722	1,784,322
Tires and tubes	561,128	691,069	702,119	810,213	1,032,913	1,209,130	1,272,714	1,173,021	1,243,802	1,420,931
Miscellaneous rubber	183,605	165,592	192,135	219,051	208,906	237,639	257,742	257,072	319,700	364,351
RATE OF RETURN ON CORPORATE ASSETS (per cent)										
Total rubber (1947 prices)	2.83	6.00	5.47	8.02	5.62	7.26	6.21	5.44	10.98	7.39
Total rubber (book values)	2.83	6.07	5.52	7.98	5.46	7.45	6.43	5.43	11.65	7.06
Tires and tubes	3.24	5.97	5.22	7.52	4.95	7.38	6.05	4.97	11.30	6.20
Miscellaneous rubber	1.57	6.46	6.66	9.70	7.99	7.83	8.32	7.53	12.98	10.41

TABLE A-26

LEATHER AND PRODUCTS, 1938–47
(assets in thousands of dollars)

	1938	1939	1940	1941	1942	1943	1944	1945	1946	1947
TOTAL ASSETS, EXCLUDING OTHER INVESTMENTS										
Total leather (1947 prices)	1,260,000	1,250,000	1,298,000	1,412,000	1,416,000	1,352,000	1,381,000	1,428,000	1,500,000	1,474,000
Total leather (book values)	688,295	698,798	723,121	862,793	935,640	946,475	978,867	1,059,179	1,254,836	1,341,926
Tanning, currying, and finishing	196,075	208,248	221,617	266,289	296,283	290,450	289,655	304,840	362,067	407,336
Footwear, except rubber	415,477	420,339	405,107	481,596	515,450	519,008	539,066	575,936	685,782	741,305
Miscellaneous	78,243	69,751	99,423	118,447	126,825	142,336	158,490	192,780	221,642	201,620
CORPORATE ASSETS, EXCLUDING OTHER INVESTMENTS										
Total leather (1947 prices)	1,211,000	1,197,000	1,236,000	1,337,000	1,329,000	1,257,000	1,252,000	1,261,000	1.367,000	1,394,000
Total leather (book values)	661,691	669,217	688,691	816,977	878,066	879,790	887,561	935,097	1,143,465	1,269,164
Tanning, currying, and finishing	192,555	203,930	216,278	258,792	286,308	278,945	274,001	283,570	342,895	394,185
Footwear, except rubber	403,234	407,174	391,188	463,530	493,430	493,990	504,926	530,358	645,596	715,407
Miscellaneous	65,794	57,350	80,800	94,269	97,723	106,049	108,411	121,015	154,622	160,760
RATE OF RETURN ON CORPORATE ASSETS (per cent)										
Total leather (1947 prices)	0.96	4.68	4.42	7.52	7.22	6.83	6.34	6.14	11.92	10.03
Total leather (book values)	0.83	4.69	4.43	7.49	7.40	7.17	6.74	6.41	12.32	10.30
Tanning, currying, and finishing	−1.05	5.20	3.95	8.58	7.09	6.90	6.65	5.97	16.02	13.53
Footwear, except rubber	2.10	4.75	4.77	6.83	7.44	6.99	6.41	6.26	10.59	9.22
Miscellaneous	−1.43	2.51	4.11	7.77	8.23	8.73	8.48	8.06	11.32	7.08

TABLE A-27

STONE, CLAY, AND GLASS PRODUCTS, 1938–47

(assets in thousands of dollars)

	1938	1939	1940	1941	1942	1943	1944	1945	1946	1947
TOTAL ASSETS, EXCLUDING OTHER INVESTMENTS										
Total stone, clay, and glass (1947 prices)	3,401,000	3,500,000	3,575,000	3,659,000	3,328,000	3,135,000	2,964,000	2,988,000	3,181,000	3,416,000
Total stone, clay, and glass (book values)	1,755,503	1,808,068	1,890,686	2,058,207	2,039,764	2,030,580	1,975,002	2,061,172	2,361,574	2,783,490
Pottery and porcelain	87,271	88,040	94,281	101,707	109,293	112,757	115,312	124,102	145,551	172,361
Concrete	215,294	233,828	273,022	292,436	290,407	245,692	237,756	280,622	380,176	507,607
Cut stone[a]	84,228	86,637	85,559	78,260	76,350	43,096	52,732	63,308	70,211	84,451
Structural clay	328,812	323,358	305,779	314,012	315,660	292,245	271,649	287,776	337,166	351,428
Glass	455,497	459,134	480,233	519,163	411,312	473,041	474,043	504,497	539,737	636,421
Cement	406,516	401,709	404,165	432,177	407,714	365,710	343,021	345,390	382,327	417,787
Miscellaneous stone, clay, and glass	188,294	226,726	260,293	332,396	440,899	499,888	488,484	468,666	521,919	642,380
CORPORATE ASSETS, EXCLUDING OTHER INVESTMENTS										
Total stone, clay, and glass (1947 prices)	3,297,000	3,389,000	3,458,000	3,535,000	3,214,000	3,027,000	2,836,000	2,833,000	3,028,000	3,265,000
Total stone, clay, and glass (book values)	1,701,926	1,750,822	1,828,591	1,988,177	1,969,564	1,960,003	1,889,095	1,952,862	2,246,139	2,658,581
Pottery and porcelain	85,735	86,152	91,897	98,746	105,776	108,804	109,912	116,676	137,025	162,654
Concrete	197,114	212,679	246,678	262,470	259,585	218,785	205,156	234,260	320,292	432,370
Cut stone[a]	72,310	73,303	71,343	64,324	62,141	34,758	40,146	45,401	51,026	62,427
Structural clay	305,374	301,039	285,342	293,716	296,387	275,427	253,490	266,191	315,207	331,858
Glass	448,285	451,755	472,391	510,552	404,542	465,319	464,481	492,344	527,859	623,788
Cement	406,516	401,709	404,026	431,880	407,304	365,230	342,334	344,409	381,187	416,523
Miscellaneous stone, clay, and glass	186,402	224,272	257,269	328,271	435,211	493,211	480,086	458,673	511,393	630,305

(continued)

TABLE A-27 (concluded)

	1938	1939	1940	1941	1942	1943	1944	1945	1946	1947
RATE OF RETURN ON CORPORATE ASSETS (per cent)										
Total stone, clay, and glass (1947 prices)	2.94	6.45	5.99	8.32	6.67	5.29	4.62	4.61	9.06	9.53
Total stone, clay, and glass (book values)	2.94	6.91	7.30	8.70	6.96	5.52	4.75	4.72	9.97	10.26
Pottery and porcelain	1.57	5.17	5.97	8.60	6.76	4.16	5.33	6.23	13.48	12.89
Concrete	4.29	7.55	5.92	8.39	7.57	4.89	4.17	4.47	11.21	10.63
Cut stone[a]	−2.17	−0.57	−0.86	−0.27	0.87	4.47	3.25	4.44	8.43	7.36
Structural clay	0.15	3.57	3.68	5.75	3.67	1.90	1.66	3.14	9.26	11.70
Glass	5.19	9.35	10.13	10.27	8.85	7.88	8.05	6.98	11.29	9.58
Cement	3.30	6.59	5.64	7.89	6.03	3.01	0.74	2.26	8.54	10.29
Miscellaneous stone, clay, and glass	2.48	9.55	10.27	11.93	8.85	7.81	6.24	4.77	8.60	9.49

[a] Data unreliable because of year-to-year differences in classification of large companies.

TABLE A-28

METALS AND METAL PRODUCTS, 1938–47

(assets in thousands of dollars)

	1938	1939	1940	1941	1942	1943	1944	1945	1946	1947
TOTAL ASSETS, EXCLUDING OTHER INVESTMENTS										
Total metals and metal products (1947 prices)	14,505,000	14,891,000	15,578,000	17,213,000	20,228,000	22,194,000	21,441,000	18,991,000	18,219,000	18,335,000
Total metals and metal products (book values)	7,326,630	7,743,299	8,304,908	9,801,548	12,356,262	14,095,854	14,114,237	12,980,083	13,450,652	14,961,006
Blast furnaces and rolling mills	3,540,756	3,616,046	3,726,639	4,021,709	5,482,664	5,896,324	5,983,878	5,582,119	5,336,921	5,804,865
Structural steel	187,010	170,780	213,500	275,443	365,953	341,666	341,115	338,469	411,041	575,097
Tin cans	344,501	370,461	388,262	431,600	387,394	419,529	428,994	436,083	447,549	502,743
Hand tools, cutlery, etc.	378,550	351,057	360,471	428,704	503,663	485,397	484,742	489,719	580,384	643,160
Heating apparatus	567,101	640,194	717,411	871,054	1,061,153	1,030,472	994,657	887,310	1,132,012	1,298,007
Miscellaneous iron and steel	1,160,559	1,427,865	1,653,460	2,227,011	2,614,255	3,170,582	3,185,738	2,809,245	2,794,022	3,084,512
Nonferrous metals, basic	575,820	673,413	689,131	699,126	976,814	919,407	1,078,068	1,036,729	1,611,440	1,726,587
Miscellaneous nonferrous metals[a]	558,711	469,478	533,136	832,025	928,801	1,822,759	1,643,488	1,341,788	1,042,946	1,244,845
CORPORATE ASSETS, EXCLUDING OTHER INVESTMENTS										
Total metals and metal products (1947 prices)	14,266,000	14,635,000	15,297,000	16,889,000	19,841,000	21,762,000	20,913,000	18,421,000	17,709,000	17,862,000
Total metals and metal products (book values)	7,206,924	7,610,570	8,155,702	9,617,360	12,119,383	13,820,874	13,765,687	12,588,662	13,071,619	14,572,387
Blast furnaces and rolling mills	3,540,756	3,616,046	3,726,396	4,021,185	5,481,615	5,894,854	5,981,597	5,579,099	5,333,892	5,801,522
Structural steel	178,399	162,845	203,478	262,381	348,811	325,867	321,852	315,909	386,028	543,544
Tin cans	342,413	368,372	386,235	429,527	385,735	417,943	427,226	434,216	446,062	501,497
Hand tools, cutlery, etc.	360,474	334,802	344,283	410,053	482,934	466,534	462,720	464,599	554,523	618,633
Heating apparatus	551,997	623,179	698,359	847,940	1,033,654	1,004,408	964,118	855,341	1,095,277	1,260,548
Miscellaneous iron and steel	1,129,482	1,388,563	1,606,654	2,162,223	2,537,914	3,077,750	3,069,635	2,686,159	2,680,910	2,970,617
Nonferrous metals, basic	575,112	672,156	687,404	696,926	973,199	915,522	1,071,702	1,028,592	1,598,792	1,713,338
Miscellaneous nonferrous metals[a]	526,358	441,955	501,459	781,929	873,380	1,715,041	1,524,880	1,227,504	961,475	1,156,767

(continued)

TABLE A-28 (concluded)

	1938	1939	1940	1941	1942	1943	1944	1945	1946	1947
RATE OF RETURN ON CORPORATE ASSETS (per cent)										
Total metals and metal products (1947 prices)	0.88	4.84	7.12	9.28	6.97	5.91	5.15	3.89	5.86	9.38
Total metals and metal products (book values)	0.69	5.11	7.42	9.69	7.38	6.46	5.51	3.94	6.17	10.08
Blast furnaces and rolling mills	−0.30	3.28	6.18	8.59	6.42	4.93	3.80	2.24	3.98	7.70
Structural steel	1.66	4.86	6.44	11.42	9.24	8.18	8.42	6.99	9.31	14.60
Tin cans	5.90	7.69	7.53	6.67	5.00	3.65	4.28	5.24	2.93	7.27
Hand tools, cutlery, etc.	1.21	6.54	9.81	10.11	9.55	8.75	7.49	5.40	10.56	10.72
Heating apparatus	0.30	4.45	6.57	9.12	7.24	7.71	6.67	5.65	9.20	13.34
Miscellaneous iron and steel	−0.01	5.82	8.29	11.95	9.51	8.87	7.67	5.83	7.79	12.96
Nonferrous metals, basic	3.12	7.34	7.78	9.06	5.83	5.78	5.83	4.73	6.06	10.13
Miscellaneous nonferrous metals[a]	2.60	12.26	13.23	11.17	8.26	6.80	5.83	3.83	8.38	9.71

[a] Data unreliable because of year-to-year differences in classification of large companies.

TABLE A-29

MACHINERY AND EQUIPMENT, EXCEPT TRANSPORTATION AND ELECTRICAL, 1938–47
(assets in thousands of dollars)

	1938	1939	1940	1941	1942	1943	1944	1945	1946	1947
TOTAL ASSETS, EXCLUDING OTHER INVESTMENTS										
Total machinery and equipment (1947 prices)	6,856,000	7,197,000	8,034,000	9,834,000	11,576,000	10,745,000	10,038,000	8,790,000	9,892,000	10,524,000
Total machinery and equipment (book values)	3,618,469	3,857,684	4,403,929	5,808,699	7,566,470	7,505,887	7,156,677	6,416,708	7,761,500	9,267,679
Engines and turbines[a]	119,443	129,562	170,841	254,962	432,001	613,488	535,630	373,529	257,159	276,541
Agricultural machinery	763,107	775,430	831,589	954,431	1,163,685	1,197,103	1,273,240	1,263,136	1,277,924	1,492,238
Special industry machinery	548,424	551,106	604,478	686,011	791,914	699,045	666,372	671,484	1,003,824	1,246,074
General industry machinery	663,544	719,128	775,958	1,078,956	1,454,836	1,564,123	1,491,011	1,316,351	1,503,523	1,767,346
Metalworking machinery[a]	333,857	409,629	632,063	1,023,890	1,774,300	1,665,539	1,415,270	1,150,128	1,156,990	1,276,240
Construction and mining machinery	405,457	407,077	450,982	574,109	708,302	707,405	689,873	625,909	734,541	838,119
Office and store machines[a]	288,221	292,167	322,321	445,064	495,673	303,452	296,952	342,718	566,174	740,090
Household and service industry machinery[a]	309,141	336,263	370,994	438,771	323,391	188,562	198,624	243,773	625,385	839,988
Miscellaneous machinery	184,640	236,411	243,589	355,494	435,771	588,601	612,390	479,254	650,360	806,891
CORPORATE ASSETS, EXCLUDING OTHER INVESTMENTS										
Total machinery and equipment (1947 prices)	6,690,000	7,016,000	7,825,000	9,568,000	11,260,000	10,448,000	9,690,000	8,421,000	9,506,000	10,147,000
Total machinery and equipment (book values)	3,531,082	3,760,923	4,289,219	5,651,792	7,359,563	7,298,445	6,908,533	6,147,250	7,458,384	8,935,507
Engines and turbines[a]	119,247	129,340	170,534	254,484	431,176	612,297	534,310	372,401	256,436	275,827
Agricultural machinery	759,189	769,886	823,963	943,753	1,148,674	1,179,723	1,247,766	1,203,669	1,244,567	1,454,337
Special industry machinery	524,290	526,356	576,749	653,882	754,901	666,468	628,086	625,533	940,530	1,174,593
General industry machinery	644,413	697,219	751,022	1,042,482	1,404,388	1,508,637	1,424,043	1,244,168	1,426,036	1,682,909
Metalworking machinery[a]	324,460	396,567	609,533	983,564	1,699,522	1,591,040	1,332,718	1,066,154	1,075,481	1,190,852
Construction and mining machinery	394,924	396,864	440,055	560,694	692,727	692,800	673,250	608,920	717,380	821,519
Office and store machines[a]	286,834	290,636	320,491	442,343	492,500	301,429	294,385	339,018	560,372	732,998
Household and service industry machinery[a]	305,897	332,828	367,303	434,523	320,417	186,917	196,574	240,897	618,960	832,576
Miscellaneous machinery	171,552	220,440	227,930	333,816	411,203	558,062	576,402	448,528	615,397	771,262

TABLE A-29 (concluded)

	1938	1939	1940	1941	1942	1943	1944	1945	1946	1947
RATE OF RETURN ON CORPORATE ASSETS per (cent)										
Total machinery and equipment (1947 prices)	4.09	6.29	9.54	10.55	9.15	8.73	7.17	5.43	5.14	9.92
Total machinery and equipment (book values)	4.23	6.57	9.89	10.90	9.54	9.25	7.52	5.54	5.15	10.16
Engines and turbines[a]	1.23	6.82	9.82	10.98	8.41	8.17	8.10	6.78	−6.25	3.90
Agricultural machinery	4.95	3.48	7.40	8.58	6.34	5.77	5.58	4.69	1.46	7.51
Special industry machinery	3.24	5.62	7.28	8.88	8.69	7.81	6.22	4.10	6.26	10.88
General industry machinery	2.76	7.58	10.56	11.75	10.18	10.49	9.24	5.81	6.96	11.66
Metalworking machinery[a]	5.89	10.54	16.57	16.29	12.69	11.90	7.72	5.83	5.38	7.70
Construction and mining machinery	5.17	6.66	8.61	11.02	8.73	9.44	7.73	6.74	7.10	13.10
Office and store machinery[a]	6.89	8.42	9.66	9.31	8.70	8.44	7.51	5.85	9.20	13.23
Household and service industry machinery[a]	3.66	7.71	10.13	6.28	7.79	6.10	6.47	6.38	4.94	11.47
Miscellaneous machinery	2.98	4.82	7.94	10.79	9.82	9.81	7.95	5.07	5.37	9.32

[a] Data unreliable because of year-to-year differences in classification of large companies.

TABLE A-30

ELECTRICAL MACHINERY AND EQUIPMENT, 1938–47

(assets in thousands of dollars)

	1938	1939	1940	1941	1942	1943	1944	1945	1946	1947
TOTAL ASSETS, EXCLUDING OTHER INVESTMENTS										
Total electrical machinery (1947 prices)	2,540,000	2,674,000	2,970,000	3,854,000	4,980,000	5,866,000	5,938,000	5,055,000	5,159,000	5,571,000
Total electrical machinery (book values)	1,381,398	1,435,575	1,636,237	2,315,999	3,308,326	4,168,656	4,326,759	3,797,926	4,100,102	4,991,687
Electrical equipment for public utility, etc.	549,713	576,806	678,522	1,017,620	1,547,268	1,962,192	1,858,629	1,741,550	1,509,888	1,926,156
Automotive equipment	65,489	64,072	76,634	84,893	110,377	129,516	127,167	121,511	134,621	158,624
Communications equipment	272,703	277,238	392,785	558,060	857,688	1,227,749	1,374,174	1,089,992	1,394,260	1,554,862
Electrical appliances[a]	91,842	82,638	92,317	105,500	92,863	42,255	51,266	58,933	168,855	250,031
Miscellaneous equipment	404,098	436,688	398,462	551,458	693,476	810,424	921,969	784,009	894,821	1,098,207
CORPORATE ASSETS, EXCLUDING OTHER INVESTMENTS										
Total electrical machinery (1947 prices)	2,526,000	2,654,000	2,942,000	3,809,000	4,913,000	5,777,000	5,814,000	4,917,000	5,019,000	5,424,000
Total electrical machinery (book values)	1,373,941	1,424,827	1,620,562	2,288,973	3,263,862	4,105,651	4,236,712	3,694,236	3,988,892	4,859,980
Electrical equipment for public utility, etc.	543,575	570,135	670,393	1,005,006	1,527,900	1,937,426	1,829,150	1,708,032	1,482,962	1,894,750
Automotive equipment	64,740	63,372	75,835	84,051	109,362	128,416	125,926	120,198	133,398	157,435
Communications equipment	272,220	275,344	388,128	548,660	839,421	1,196,442	1,323,873	1,036,105	1,323,912	1,476,830
Electrical appliances[a]	91,618	82,391	91,989	105,067	92,439	42,044	50,920	58,419	167,414	247,982
Miscellaneous equipment	400,343	432,365	394,269	545,312	685,502	800,840	908,016	679,366	879,094	1,080,302

(continued)

TABLE A-30 (concluded)

	1938	1939	1940	1941	1942	1943	1944	1945	1946	1947
RATE OF RETURN ON CORPORATE ASSETS (per cent)										
Total electrical machinery (1947 prices)	4.49	9.93	12.29	12.32	7.63	8.08	7.25	5.42	1.88	9.73
Total electrical machinery (book values)	4.43	9.76	12.66	12.45	7.66	8.32	7.43	5.39	1.40	9.74
Electrical equipment for public utility, etc.	6.14	12.75	15.46	15.34	8.86	8.59	7.10	5.88	4.95	12.91
Automotive equipment	5.90	15.53	12.62	13.82	12.06	12.55	10.70	7.62	4.89	11.18
Communications equipment	2.44	6.25	11.79	10.51	6.17	8.22	8.33	4.45	0.30	5.75
Electrical appliances[a]	6.18	11.51	12.78	11.32	6.13	10.96	8.05	8.57	11.31	13.55
Miscellaneous equipment	2.82	6.89	8.75	9.13	6.39	7.01	6.30	4.97	−5.34	8.59

[a] Data unreliable because of year-to-year differences in classification of large companies.

TABLE A-31

TRANSPORTATION EQUIPMENT, EXCEPT VEHICLES, 1938–47

(assets in thousands of dollars)

	1938	1939	1940	1941	1942	1943	1944	1945	1946	1947
TOTAL ASSETS, EXCLUDING OTHER INVESTMENTS										
Total transportation equipment (1947 prices)	1,940,000	2,397,000	3,779,000	5,716,000	12,444,000	16,346,000	14,035,000	10,684,000	3,619,000	3,095,000
Total transportation equipment (book values)	991,358	1,260,842	2,056,411	3,394,158	8,204,594	11,666,887	10,305,221	8,030,886	2,912,329	2,815,426
Railroad and railway equipment	487,163	604,084	695,376	790,110	966,924	934,317	842,386	829,263	660,982	918,782
Aircraft and parts[a]	238,148	368,435	1,043,306	1,868,430	5,472,673	8,231,184	7,875,887	6,015,313	1,444,873	1,240,404
Ship and boat building	226,269	261,051	285,662	721,093	1,722,531	2,454,426	1,599,076	1,129,654	745,145	606,970
Motorcycles and bicycles	16,052	16,671	19,256	24,977	31,438	28,940	24,529	23,366	29,374	38,401
Miscellaneous equipment[a]	5,522	4,839	4,686	4,899	5,924	5,204	4,911	4,410	6,645	9,633
CORPORATE ASSETS, EXCLUDING OTHER INVESTMENTS										
Total transportation equipment (1947 prices)	1,919,000	2,369,000	3,734,000	5,645,000	12,287,000	16,138,000	13,810,000	10,476,000	3,553,000	3,044,000
Total transportation equipment (book values)	980,383	1,246,327	2,031,827	3,351,979	8,101,303	11,518,340	10,139,883	7,874,127	2,859,525	2,768,642
Railroad and railway equipment	487,163	604,084	694,973	789,194	965,280	932,247	839,536	825,287	657,658	914,093
Aircraft and parts[a]	236,791	366,251	1,036,877	1,856,476	5,437,207	8,177,241	7,810,752	5,954,695	1,431,360	1,229,781
Ship and boat building[a]	219,916	253,232	276,561	696,745	1,662,468	2,366,341	1,526,029	1,066,353	705,721	577,073
Motorcycles and bicycles	15,884	16,498	19,057	24,719	31,122	28,657	24,238	23,041	29,007	37,977
Miscellaneous equipment[a]	5,402	4,660	4,443	4,574	5,458	4,735	4,307	3,711	5,586	8,120

(continued)

TABLE A-31 (concluded)

	1938	1939	1940	1941	1942	1943	1944	1945	1946	1947
RATE OF RETURN ON CORPORATE ASSETS (per cent)										
Total transportation equipment (1947 prices)	0.93	4.43	7.36	8.41	6.26	6.27	6.60	4.75	−1.98	−1.18
Total transportation equipment (book values)	0.81	4.67	7.71	8.74	6.46	6.51	6.80	4.75	−2.65	−2.09
Railroad and railway equipment	−2.56	1.86	5.92	7.54	5.53	4.97	5.34	4.02	4.51	5.18
Aircraft and parts[a]	7.61	8.70	8.07	9.59	7.06	7.27	6.86	4.95	−8.83	−9.88
Ship and boat building[a]	0.77	5.32	10.57	7.46	4.97	4.49	7.10	4.24	2.70	1.96
Motorcycles and bicycles	4.40	8.89	12.70	12.78	10.37	7.87	3.70	3.12	5.39	12.10
Miscellaneous equipment	−0.07	2.27	3.60	7.39	5.53	5.01	6.01	6.39	8.23	6.76

[a] Data unreliable because of year-to-year differences in classification of large companies.

TABLE A-32

Motor Vehicles and Parts, 1938–47

(assets in thousands of dollars)

	1938	1939	1940	1941	1942	1943	1944	1945	1946	1947
TOTAL ASSETS, EXCLUDING OTHER INVESTMENTS										
Total motor vehicles and parts (1947 prices)	5,034,000	5,258,000	5,907,000	6,231,000	3,742,000	3,080,000	2,734,000	2,416,000	6,400,000	7,083,000
Total motor vehicles and parts (book values)	2,684,468	2,806,152	3,271,458	3,664,612	2,473,473	2,098,285	1,976,623	1,794,156	4,972,373	6,192,890
Motor vehicles, including trucks, bodies, and industrial trailers[a]	2,276,666	2,395,104	2,811,913	3,068,325	2,020,375	1,708,901	1,575,918	1,304,170	4,112,742	5,046,050
Motor vehicle parts and accessories	426,904	427,206	475,945	621,814	473,080	412,678	418,048	524,286	894,423	1,191,988
CORPORATE ASSETS, EXCLUDING OTHER INVESTMENTS										
Total motor vehicles and parts (1947 prices)	4,999,000	5,218,000	5,859,000	6,176,000	3,708,000	3,051,000	2,701,000	2,379,000	6,308,000	6,988,000
Total motor vehicles and parts (book values)	2,665,680	2,784,890	3,244,746	3,632,531	2,450,892	2,078,397	1,952,425	1,766,824	4,900,614	6,109,480
Motor vehicles, including trucks, bodies, and industrial trailers[a]	2,276,666	2,395,104	2,809,803	3,063,717	2,015,927	1,704,000	1,569,018	1,296,082	4,085,989	5,012,742
Motor vehicle parts and accessories	388,792	389,840	435,131	569,562	434,980	380,862	380,169	470,294	812,723	1,096,731
RATE OF RETURN ON CORPORATE ASSETS (per cent)										
Total motor vehicles and parts (1947 prices)	1.06	8.07	9.72	10.16	6.48	7.00	5.60	3.12	1.24	11.68
Total motor vehicles and parts (book values)	0.90	8.57	9.92	10.22	6.48	7.49	5.67	2.86	0.62	12.05
Motor vehicles, including trucks, bodies, and industrial trailers[a]	0.83	8.34	9.55	9.48	5.28	6.55	4.58	1.51	−0.44	12.04
Motor vehicle parts and accessories	1.28	10.01	12.29	14.21	12.06	11.55	10.24	6.57	5.91	12.11

Residual Manufacturing, 1938–47
(assets in thousands of dollars)

	1938	1939	1940	1941	1942	1943	1944	1945	1946	1947
TOTAL ASSETS, EXCLUDING OTHER INVESTMENTS										
Residual manufacturing (1947 prices)	3,268,000	2,669,000	2,947,000	3,491,000	3,900,000	4,374,000	4,488,000	4,242,000	4,693,000	4,279,000
Residual manufacturing (book values)	1,742,141	1,429,320	1,602,768	2,052,754	2,508,147	3,031,249	3,184,733	3,083,597	3,720,813	3,740,089
Clocks and watches	79,512	94,816	106,632	114,378	120,264	116,674	117,285	112,620	153,899	180,323
Jewelry, except costume	109,005	100,903	128,999	176,188	164,774	153,214	175,326	197,482	301,482	306,859
Matches	42,473	39,121	42,919	37,994	46,083	44,880	46,998	44,835	51,608	74,498[c]
Miscellaneous manufacturing	1,510,371	1,192,449	1,322,937	1,726,642	2,176,817	2,717,336	2,847,509	2,732,749	3,216,354	3,171,195
CORPORATE ASSETS, EXCLUDING OTHER INVESTMENTS										
Residual manufacturing (1947 prices)	3,055,000	2,497,000	2,758,000	3,269,000	3,659,000	4,111,000	4,165,000	3,889,000	4,342,000	3,995,000
Residual manufacturing (book values)	1,628,786	1,337,040	1,499,969	1,921,968	2,352,881	2,849,035	2,955,501	2,826,604	3,441,873	3,491,078
Clocks and watches	78,254	93,264	104,826	112,376	118,141	114,599	114,670	109,579	150,050	176,200
Jewelry, except costume	97,234	90,264	115,713	158,475	148,957	139,193	156,614	173,709	269,401	278,405
Matches	41,750	38,504	42,242	37,404	45,282	44,049	46,108	44,000	50,949	73,903[c]
Miscellaneous manufacturing	1,411,313	1,114,672	1,237,019	1,614,989	2,039,721	2,550,749	2,638,029	2,499,473	2,968,719	2,953,755
RATE OF RETURN ON CORPORATE ASSETS (per cent)										
Residual manufacturing (1947 prices)	3.60	7.25	7.29	8.72	7.32	7.74	7.08	6.02	6.75	8.14
Residual manufacturing (book values)	3.65	7.62	7.56	8.98	7.62	8.14	7.45	6.24	6.97	8.12
Clocks and watches	3.14	7.92	3.89	8.75	7.08	7.46	7.02	7.95	5.48	10.97
Jewelry, except costume	2.45	8.06	6.58	7.50	7.11	8.20	8.63	8.21	14.69	11.07
Matches	5.25	7.72	4.12	8.01	7.11	7.39	8.04	7.86	7.47	8.65
Miscellaneous manufacturing	3.71	7.56	7.66	9.15	7.71	8.18	7.39	6.00	6.34	7.65

[c] Adjusted for variability of assets due to shifts of large companies between industries.

TABLE A-34

ORDNANCE EQUIPMENT, 1938–47

	1938	1939	1940	1941	1942	1943	1944	1945	1946	1947
CORPORATE ASSETS, EXCLUDING OTHER INVESTMENTS (thousands of dollars)										
Total ordnance equipment (1947 prices)	—	—	—	355,000	2,038,000	3,774,000	3,446,000	2,760,000	275,000	223,000
Total ordnance equipment (book values)	—	—	—	218,791	1,339,872	2,669,485	2,485,682	2,067,085	217,285	197,878
Firearms	—	—	—	68,528	403,108	695,384	597,461	336,638	46,609	43,270
Ammunition	—	—	—	81,064	614,124	1,208,619	1,229,964	1,001,657	140,334	134,268
Tanks	—	—	—	38,283	170,600	340,695	338,622	300,579	792	271
Sighting and fire control equipment	—	—	—	21,268	125,105	349,370	260,248	386,687	14,465	15,441
Ordnance, n.e.c.	—	—	—	9,605	26,787	76,329	59,038	43,273	15,086	4,628
RATE OF RETURN ON CORPORATE ASSETS (per cent)										
Total ordnance equipment (1947 prices)	—	—	—	8.20	8.06	8.04	6.52	5.48	2.03	7.31
Total ordnance equipment (book values)	—	—	—	8.22	8.45	8.46	6.81	5.59	1.80	7.47
Firearms	—	—	—	7.78	7.78	6.89	4.83	4.21	−2.44	5.76
Ammunition	—	—	—	9.84	9.84	9.45	7.52	6.37	5.14	9.12
Tanks	—	—	—	6.16	6.16	8.77	6.72	5.83	−0.13	11.14
Sighting and fire control equipment	—	—	—	6.72	6.72	8.62	8.61	4.55	−13.56	−2.47
Ordnance, n.e.c.	—	—	—	9.23	9.23	4.92	4.90	5.63	−1.40	8.64

NOTE: Noncorporate sector negligible; ordnance industries excluded from analysis.

TABLE A-35

TOTAL MANUFACTURING, 1938–47

(assets in thousands of dollars)

	1938	1939	1940	1941	1942	1943	1944	1945	1946	1947
TOTAL ASSETS, EXCLUDING OTHER INVESTMENTS										
Total manufacturing assets (1947 prices)	94,189,000	96,195,000	101,817,000	113,466,000	128,549,000	135,282,000	132,623,000	122,714,000	122,186,000	125,911,000
Total manufacturing assets (book values)	48,846,000	50,955,000	55,049,000	65,892,000	80,303,000	89,675,000	90,511,000	86,445,000	93,156,000	106,339,000
CORPORATE ASSETS, EXCLUDING OTHER INVESTMENTS										
Total manufacturing assets (1947 prices)	90,548,000	92,582,000	97,355,000	109,198,000	123,880,000	130,445,000	126,734,000	116,002,000	116,048,000	120,809,000
Total manufacturing assets (book values)	46,957,000	49,035,000	52,964,000	63,395,000	77,374,000	86,461,000	86,471,000	81,677,000	88,371,000	101,951,000
RATE OF RETURN ON CORPORATE ASSETS (per cent)										
Total manufacturing assets (1947 prices)	2.63	5.77	6.95	8.36	6.95	6.80	6.20	5.26	7.65	9.84
Total manufacturing assets (book values)	2.62	6.00	7.12	8.56	7.30	7.30	6.59	5.43	8.13	10.34

TABLE A-36

BEVERAGES, 1947–57

(assets in thousands of dollars)

	1947	1948	1949	1950	1951*	1953*	1954	1955	1956	1957
TOTAL ASSETS, EXCLUDING OTHER INVESTMENTS										
Total beverages (1947 prices)	3,252,000	3,520,000	3,463,000	3,632,000	3,781,000[d]	3,559,000	3,691,000	3,567,000	3,352,000	3,389,000
Total beverages (book values)	2,778,180	3,152,686	3,153,861	3,407,284	3,885,944[e]	3,890,174	4,030,710	3,982,589	3,907,418	4,114,854
Nonalcoholic	580,046	757,597	697,517	691,164	698,611	721,229	769,120	865,914	905,899	965,092
Malt	1,106,917	1,203,351	1,261,589	1,356,055	1,422,918	1,452,674	1,605,375	1,515,965	1,533,664	1,624,493
Wine	101,317	120,951	115,744	121,665	130,776	119,010[c]	112,579[c]	133,074	138,645	149,004
Distilled	981,276	1,083,992	1,071,894	1,217,521	1,592,692	1,491,907	1,493,049	1,428,673	1,294,314	1,336,965
CORPORATE ASSETS, EXCLUDING OTHER INVESTMENTS										
Total beverages (1947 prices)	3,076,000	3,335,000	3,287,000	3,466,000	3,628,000[f]	3,397,000	3,527,000	3,411,000	3,207,000	3,245,000
Total beverages (book values)	2,627,446	2,966,514	2,993,496	3,251,985	3,728,769[g]	3,638,121	3,851,609	3,808,247	3,738,870	3,940,035
Nonalcoholic	473,416	624,915	581,432	589,281	608,596	623,959	671,124	758,815	797,264	853,014
Malt	1,090,670	1,188,076	1,247,415	1,344,073	1,413,383	1,445,587	1,600,018	1,511,551	1,529,839	1,621,121
Wine	88,362	105,618	101,199	107,538	116,873	104,223[c]	98,565[c]	117,218	122,874	132,870
Distilled	976,010	1,078,026	1,065,852	1,211,038	1,584,763	1,482,515	1,483,360	1,421,296	1,289,363	1,333,644
RATE OF RETURN ON CORPORATE ASSETS (per cent)										
Total beverages (1947 prices)	10.52	9.54	8.94	8.45	6.92[h]	6.21	5.44	6.60	6.47	6.84
Total beverages (book values)	10.70	9.81	9.02	8.38	6.20[i]	5.58	4.67	5.86	5.26	5.49
Nonalcoholic	8.13	6.03	6.46	6.21	6.48	6.13	5.66	6.57	6.09	6.30
Malt	13.81	12.55	12.59	9.28	6.98	6.30	5.38	6.53	5.13	5.47
Wine	−8.16	0.33	3.53	5.21	−1.30	2.73	3.60	5.60	4.32	4.37
Distilled	10.18	9.89	6.76	8.71	5.96	4.81	3.53	4.80	5.00	5.10

NOTES: [c] Adjusted for variability of assets due to shifts of large companies between industries.

* 1952 minor industry data not available. Major industry data appear below:

[e] 1952 = 3,947,694.

[f] 1952 = 3,560,000.

[g] 1952 = 3,777,652.

[h] 1952 = 6.26 per cent.

FOOD AND KINDRED PRODUCTS, 1947–57
(assets in thousands of dollars)

	1947	1948	1949	1950	1951*	1953*	1954	1955	1956	1957
TOTAL ASSETS, EXCLUDING OTHER INVESTMENTS										
Total food and kindred products (1947 prices)	11,966,000	12,068,000	11,913,000	13,074,000	12,665,000[d]	12,360,000	12,566,000	12,875,000	12,816,000	12,280,000
Total food and kindred products (book values)	9,937,541	10,293,301	10,485,863	12,065,667	12,630,147[e]	12,924,025	13,317,432	14,118,433	14,740,209	14,658,836
Meat	1,822,013	1,999,704	1,962,391	2,234,428	2,338,336	2,314,205	2,340,700	2,496,523	2,624,319	2,546,387
Dairy	1,212,281	1,327,522	1,355,093	1,603,808	1,787,238	1,614,734	1,654,911	1,844,112	2,076,705	1,909,916
Canning	1,420,447	1,600,755	1,590,845	1,762,508	1,923,813	2,017,750	2,069,584	2,230,086	2,519,942	2,530,453
Grain mill	1,192,232	1,121,321	1,215,471	1,450,097	1,476,769	1,453,923	1,565,373	1,613,595	1,691,876	1,750,907
Bakery	909,466	978,163	1,030,768	1,121,789	1,164,242	1,245,673	1,247,932	1,394,020	1,387,154	1,456,133
Sugar	951,897	830,013	790,986	942,997	957,503	977,448	987,624	986,492	988,821	1,001,055
Confectionery	615,827	600,376	605,595	675,288	706,915	699,306	684,347	708,268	718,076	739,590
Cereal	148,580	153,279	148,234	152,601	191,090	205,814	208,534	257,662	292,418	302,977
Miscellaneous food and kindred products	1,594,059	1,551,427	1,733,195	1,881,876	1,852,528	2,034,188	2,165,691	2,295,733	2,355,038	2,390,246
CORPORATE ASSETS, EXCLUDING OTHER INVESTMENTS										
Total food and kindred products (1947 prices)	10,957,000	11,037,000	10,832,000	12,010,000	11,705,000[f]	11,215,000	11,378,000	11,680,000	11,648,000	11,182,000
Total food and kindred products (book values)	9,099,386	9,413,706	9,578,712	11,083,997	11,672,908[g]	11,726,911	12,058,170	12,807,694	13,396,780	13,347,814
Meat	1,695,191	1,858,826	1,822,565	2,085,015	2,192,994	2,138,178	2,159,045	2,288,121	2,390,068	2,304,548
Dairy	1,082,514	1,182,836	1,204,878	1,435,551	1,611,479	1,420,137	1,450,683	1,553,604	1,683,983	1,492,787
Canning	1,336,816	1,507,726	1,499,601	1,669,995	1,832,260	1,905,105	1,954,239	2,097,680	2,361,243	2,362,040
Grain mill	1,047,112	988,854	1,076,209	1,300,133	1,340,317	1,303,787	1,407,352	1,444,010	1,507,132	1,552,608
Bakery	830,310	897,706	950,368	1,045,932	1,096,463	1,170,105	1,177,107	1,313,119	1,304,881	1,367,916
Sugar	929,869	811,494	773,985	924,953	941,358	959,001	969,523	968,982	971,833	984,428
Confectionery	587,653	574,239	580,673	650,957	684,878	676,038	662,791	682,339	688,155	705,070
Cereal	147,945	152,711	147,767	152,234	190,755	205,591	208,413	257,484	292,187	302,708
Miscellaneous food and kindred products	1,509,762	1,473,236	1,650,089	1,802,474	1,784,535	1,953,690	2,084,035	2,202,607	2,252,849	2,279,812

(continued)

TABLE A-37 (concluded)

	1947	1948	1949	1950	1951*	1953*	1954	1955	1956	1957
RATE OF RETURN ON CORPORATE ASSETS (per cent)										
Total food and kindred products (1947 prices)	8.89	7.14	7.04	7.34	5.92[h]	6.05	5.93	6.80	6.84	6.74
Total food and kindred products (book values)	9.42	7.25	6.94	7.15	5.14[i]	5.41	5.26	6.13	5.84	5.50
Meat	7.15	5.32	3.78	3.64	3.49	4.43	2.60	5.13	4.16	2.89
Dairy	8.26	7.17	9.11	7.21	5.49	5.58	6.32	5.77	5.12	5.32
Canning	7.19	5.26	4.65	8.32	4.08	4.28	3.92	5.95	5.19	3.71
Grain mill	11.50	6.16	6.28	6.54	5.25	5.98	6.65	5.33	5.21	5.65
Bakery	10.36	11.35	10.94	9.34	7.16	6.49	6.36	7.29	6.99	7.12
Sugar	6.17	4.66	5.58	7.05	5.93	3.84	3.99	4.14	5.32	5.60
Confectionery	16.55	9.83	8.56	9.12	5.06	6.35	6.52	7.60	8.67	8.15
Cereal	12.10	12.60	14.72	10.72	7.67	8.10	8.96	9.02	8.88	9.57
Miscellaneous food and kindred products	11.34	9.73	7.87	8.37	5.96	6.59	6.75	7.53	7.39	7.62

NOTES: * 1952 minor industry data not available. Major industry data appear below:
[d] 1952 = 12,803,000.
[e] 1952 = 12,929,204.
[f] 1952 = 11,726,000.
[g] 1952 = 11,841,466.
[h] 1952 = 5.48 per cent.
[i] 1952 = 4.81 per cent.

TABLE A-38

TOBACCO PRODUCTS, 1947–57
(assets in thousands of dollars)

	1947	1948	1949	1950	1951*	1953*	1954	1955	1956	1957
TOTAL ASSETS, EXCLUDING OTHER INVESTMENTS										
Total tobacco (1947 prices)	2,211,000	2,216,000	2,338,000	2,310,000	2,324,000[d]	2,564,000	2,400,000	2,343,000	2,325,000	2,333,000
Total tobacco (book values)	2,116,086	2,329,781	2,375,238	2,480,758	2,677,202[e]	3,098,996	2,874,542	2,870,037	2,952,391	3,028,524
Cigars	209,572	230,720	215,385	223,369	224,267	218,434	246,960	237,953	239,089	238,314
Other products	1,923,050	2,097,501	2,157,617	2,255,164	2,449,125	2,877,648	2,623,169	2,629,066	2,710,853	2,788,068
CORPORATE ASSETS, EXCLUDING OTHER INVESTMENTS										
Total tobacco (1947 prices)	2,184,000	2,192,000	2,315,000	2,290,000	2,306,000[f]	2,550,000	2,387,000	2,331,000	2,314,000	2,323,000
Total tobacco (book values)	2,090,578	2,304,508	2,352,744	2,459,545	2,656,668[g]	3,081,598	2,858,404	2,855,730	2,938,931	3,016,008
Cigars	200,323	221,404	207,441	215,562	216,851	211,802	239,663	231,272	232,724	232,318
Other products	1,907,740	2,083,342	2,145,464	2,244,302	2,439,232	2,869,918	2,617,723	2,624,002	2,706,090	2,783,642
RATE OF RETURN ON CORPORATE ASSETS (per cent)										
Total tobacco (1947 prices)	6.34	7.63	7.62	7.50	5.94[h]	5.78	6.50	7.74	8.00	8.37
Total tobacco (book values)	6.40	7.40	7.74	7.28	5.69[i]	5.47	6.27	7.44	7.58	8.01
Cigars	4.34	5.32	4.87	5.23	4.32	4.79	2.61	4.04	4.95	5.16
Other products	6.54	7.62	8.02	7.48	5.82	5.53	6.60	7.74	7.81	8.25

NOTES: * 1952 minor industry data not available. Major industry data appear below:
[d] 1952 = 2,370,000.
[e] 1952 = 2,746,438.
[f] 1952 = 2,354,000.
[g] 1952 = 2,727,399.
[h] 1952 = 5.62 per cent.
[i] 1952 = 5.45 per cent.

TABLE A-39

TEXTILE MILL PRODUCTS, 1947–57
(assets in thousands of dollars)

	1947	1948	1949	1950	1951*	1953*	1954	1955	1956	1957
TOTAL ASSETS, EXCLUDING OTHER INVESTMENTS										
Total textile mill products (1947 prices)	7,655,000	7,993,000	7,955,000	8,477,000	9,096,000[d]	7,878,000	7,645,000	8,042,000	7,706,000	7,210,000
Total textile mill products (book values)	6,431,464	7,038,474	6,970,425	8,086,568	8,731,883[e]	8,183,901	8,221,208	8,854,871	8,850,222	8,500,370
Yarn and thread	894,989	987,832	981,748	1,143,526	1,246,959	1,205,450	1,192,432	1,350,660	1,325,959	1,421,980
Broad wool	713,133	734,096	693,448	842,213	857,448	647,410	593,823	518,065	514,477	514,478
Broad cotton	1,713,669	1,815,672	1,730,468	1,915,409	2,113,503	1,822,091	1,963,264	2,130,019	2,107,701	1,980,959
Narrow woven	134,564	153,507	140,720	174,421	186,960	168,638	177,549	198,330	174,025	185,008
Knit goods	866,862	940,173	962,534	1,120,027	1,154,463	1,151,866	1,141,341	1,289,974	1,251,104	1,023,199
Dyeing and finishing	352,196	348,713	352,267	387,480	389,627	388,741	368,970	450,418	397,016	361,320
Carpets	440,316[c]	536,567	534,524	640,070	688,768	647,261	679,088	729,676	856,957	709,335
Hats	87,683	89,120	88,401	94,534	84,456	77,633	74,608	78,062	91,831	56,696
Miscellaneous textile mill	1,253,555	1,468,352	1,485,924	1,773,773	2,014,288	2,067,352	2,017,267	2,101,950	2,128,415	2,237,404
CORPORATE ASSETS, EXCLUDING OTHER INVESTMENTS										
Total textile mill products (1947 prices)	7,477,000	7,848,000	7,789,000	8,304,000	8,914,000[f]	7,723,000	7,493,000	7,885,000	7,559,000	7,076,000
Total textile mill products (book values)	6,281,750	6,910,370	6,825,276	7,921,495	8,557,332[g]	8,022,603	8,057,615	8,682,523	8,681,710	8,342,120
Yarn and thread	876,348	969,910	966,402	1,127,640	1,231,715	1,194,111	1,182,659	1,339,754	1,315,409	1,410,834
Broad wool	706,979	728,367	688,584	836,701	852,226	643,916	590,764	514,020	509,091	507,729
Broad cotton	1,700,831	1,804,015	1,721,074	1,906,370	2,104,958	1,816,845	1,958,622	2,125,110	2,102,948	1,976,591
Narrow woven	121,305	139,536	128,952	160,544	172,831	156,857	165,445	186,238	164,689	176,459
Knit goods	815,939	886,597	909,608	1,058,426	1,091,064	1,087,229	1,075,619	1,216,647	1,180,911	966,550
Dyeing and finishing	342,905	340,234	344,411	379,249	381,755	381,443	362,184	442,510	390,380	355,584
Carpets	417,671[c]	513,142	515,067	620,235	671,006	636,537	670,717	720,248	845,375	699,328
Hats	85,372	86,857	86,249	92,243	82,422	75,737	72,744	75,083	87,146	53,094
Miscellaneous textile mill	1,229,119	1,440,174	1,458,041	1,740,022	1,975,534	2,025,738	1,975,126	2,059,968	2,087,848	2,196,807

(continued)

TABLE A-39 (concluded)

	1947	1948	1949	1950	1951*	1953*	1954	1955	1956	1957
				RATE OF RETURN ON CORPORATE ASSETS (per cent)						
Total textile mill products (1947 prices)	13.62	12.37	5.93	9.07	5.86[h]	3.74	2.64	4.30	5.05	4.69
Total textile mill products (book values)	15.17	13.58	5.92	9.09	5.69[i]	2.99	1.65	3.53	3.99	3.42
Yarn and thread	13.65	12.84	5.59	9.92	7.25	3.57	1.58	4.10	4.27	3.35
Broad wool	10.81	10.25	2.53	5.72	4.96	−1.97	−3.89	−1.51	4.40	1.78
Broad cotton	21.32	17.81	6.31	9.52	8.65	5.18	2.59	3.73	4.61	4.10
Narrow woven	9.72	9.07	4.41	7.63	5.31	4.05	3.60	3.29	4.30	4.22
Knit goods	11.51	9.36	5.10	8.73	3.96	2.97	2.32	3.26	3.37	3.29
Dyeing and finishing	13.78	11.02	8.79	8.74	3.47	3.50	3.81	5.85	2.60	−0.62
Carpets	12.43	12.89	6.80	10.04	2.49	2.46	2.53	4.09	4.91	3.01
Hats	6.52	2.28	2.74	5.54	0.42	1.98	0.35	3.41	3.68	0.25
Miscellaneous textile mill	15.69	15.04	6.68	9.97	4.58	2.32	1.24	3.72	3.33	4.08

NOTES: [c] Adjusted for variability of assets due to shifts of large companies between industries.

* 1952 minor industry data not available. Major industry data appear below:

[d] 1952 = 8,189,000.

[e] 1952 = 8,205,960.

[f] 1952 = 8,026,000.

[g] 1952 = 8,043,047.

[h] 1952 = 3.68 per cent.

[i] 1952 = 2.97 per cent.

TABLE A-40

APPAREL AND PRODUCTS MADE FROM FABRICS, 1947–57

(assets in thousands of dollars)

	1947	1948	1949	1950	1951*	1953*	1954	1955	1956	1957
TOTAL ASSETS, EXCLUDING OTHER INVESTMENTS										
Total apparel (1947 prices)	3,293,000	3,325,000	3,196,000	3,505,000	3,363,000[d]	3,284,000	3,256,000	3,468,000	3,169,000	2,984,000
Total apparel (book values)	3,112,525	3,271,568	3,146,213	3,762,239	3,649,116[e]	3,606,453	3,719,047	4,130,818	3,916,739	3,669,986
Men's clothing	1,117,530	1,152,734	1,092,046	1,369,983	1,332,504	1,353,265	1,356,348	1,477,085	1,412,776	1,393,821
Women's clothing	1,191,467	1,288,954	1,259,906	1,475,340	1,395,369	1,362,188	1,426,376	1,621,655	1,504,852	1,326,096
Millinery	34,681	32,400	35,420	40,569	40,427	45,413	39,764	38,669	35,327	34,741
Furs[b]	120,768	110,434	104,075	114,509	110,704	95,256	88,020	90,128	87,285	85,100
Miscellaneous apparel	667,718	707,555	675,254	778,301	786,897	755,890	821,807	927,751	907,377	855,307
CORPORATE ASSETS, EXCLUDING OTHER INVESTMENTS										
Total apparel (1947 prices)	2,716,000	2,761,000	2,672,000	2,951,000	2,852,000[f]	2,808,000	2,806,000	2,994,000	2,740,000	2,584,000
Total apparel (book values)	2,566,763	2,716,332	2,630,274	3,167,809	3,094,759[g]	3,083,796	3,204,892	3,565,815	3,386,571	3,178,440
Men's clothing	1,006,215	1,043,246	993,447	1,252,937	1,225,205	1,253,778	1,263,876	1,375,876	1,315,483	1,297,350
Women's clothing	924,543	1,009,508	996,074	1,177,837	1,125,044	1,111,531	1,176,453	1,338,960	1,243,844	1,097,262
Millinery	23,959	22,825	25,457	29,771	30,305	35,227	31,588	30,825	28,259	27,888
Furs[b]	69,486	64,636	61,987	69,462	68,420	60,197	56,787	58,170	56,357	54,968
Miscellaneous apparel	541,088	574,865	550,062	635,818	644,687	619,828	673,880	760,184	742,942	699,792
RATE OF RETURN ON CORPORATE ASSETS (per cent)										
Total apparel (1947 prices)	10.82	6.47	3.62	5.97	3.30[h]	3.09	3.10	4.13	4.57	3.95
Total apparel (book values)	10.86	6.21	3.15	5.36	2.68[i]	2.60	2.54	3.55	3.80	3.20
Men's clothing	11.64	7.06	4.16	6.36	3.87	3.70	3.29	4.52	4.93	3.97
Women's clothing	10.87	6.74	2.58	4.04	1.08	1.90	2.36	2.94	2.85	2.83
Millinery	4.47	2.08	1.01	1.03	0.07	−5.30	−1.86	0.38	0.85	1.52
Furs[b]	3.61	−3.06	−6.53	2.30	−3.30	−3.60	1.41	0.70	1.01	1.68
Miscellaneous apparel	10.65	4.94	3.58	6.38	3.94	2.70	1.77	3.20	3.71	2.55

NOTES: [b] Data unreliable because of large proportion of non-corporate firms.

* 1952 minor industry data not available. Major industry data appear below:

[e] 1952 = 3,709,229.

[f] 1952 = 2,821,000.

[g] 1952 = 3,158,105.

[h] 1952 = 3.31 per cent

TABLE A-41

BASIC LUMBER, 1947–57

(assets in thousands of dollars)

	1947	1948	1949	1950	1951*	1953*	1954	1955	1956	1957
				TOTAL ASSETS, EXCLUDING OTHER INVESTMENTS						
Total basic lumber (1947 prices)	3,482,000	3,704,000	3,531,000	3,953,000	4,148,000[d]	3,962,000	3,940,000	4,299,000	4,858,000	4,433,000
Total basic lumber (book values)	2,815,975	3,136,594	3,068,176	3,662,428	4,064,526[e]	4,000,266	4,135,592	4,726,085	5,473,763	5,095,664
Wooden containers	212,786	223,514	218,927	239,510	263,030[c]	265,132[c]	217,874	247,511	214,969	204,511
Miscellaneous lumber	2,627,284	2,910,370	2,850,637	3,424,693	3,750,803	3,755,159	3,909,039	4,431,210	5,159,785	4,761,565
				CORPORATE ASSETS, EXCLUDING OTHER INVESTMENTS						
Total basic lumber (1947 prices)	2,997,000	3,232,000	3,128,000	3,475,000	3,618,000[f]	3,369,000	3,336,000	3,634,000	4,100,000	3,735,000
Total basic lumber (book values)	2,424,042	2,737,029	2,717,845	3,219,632	3,545,348[g]	3,401,576	3,501,925	3,995,135	4,619,716	4,293,689
Wooden containers	165,519	200,260	194,959	211,968	231,314[c]	234,144[c]	191,699	217,902	189,446	180,256
Miscellaneous lumber	2,257,682	2,536,786	2,522,869	3,008,527	3,270,095	3,193,149	3,310,805	3,777,930	4,429,600	4,114,232
				RATE OF RETURN ON CORPORATE ASSETS (per cent)						
Total basic lumber (1947 prices)	13.21	11.51	6.49	11.88	8.96[h]	6.00	6.41	8.78	6.13	4.49
Total basic lumber (book values)	14.92	12.71	5.31	12.38	8.76[i]	5.47	5.89	8.29	5.26	3.27
Wooden containers	9.30	6.45	3.89	7.86	5.72	4.96	2.04	5.03	4.45	3.85
Miscellaneous lumber	15.33	13.20	5.50	12.69	9.02	5.51	6.11	8.48	5.30	3.24

NOTES: [c] Adjusted for variability of assets due to shifts of large companies between industries.

* 1952 minor industry data not available. Major industry data appear below:

[d] 1952 = 4,105,000.

[e] 1952 = 4,137,605.

[f] 1952 = 3,536,000.

[g] 1952 = 3,564,048.

[h] 1952 = 6.84 per cent.

[i] 1952 = 6.28 per cent.

TABLE A-42

FURNITURE AND FINISHED LUMBER, 1947–57

(assets in thousands of dollars)

	1947	1948	1949	1950	1951*	1953*	1954	1955	1956	1957
TOTAL ASSETS, EXCLUDING OTHER INVESTMENTS										
Total furniture (1947 prices)	1,385,000	1,368,000	1,389,000	1,604,000	1,615,000[d]	1,628,000	1,695,000	1,847,000	1,835,000	1,778,000
Total furniture (book values)	1,192,768	1,241,808	1,258,938	1,556,464	1,659,199[e]	1,719,531	1,845,236	2,101,547	2,156,294	2,179,750
Furniture[a]	908,689	985,165	1,016,755	1,274,201	1,334,240	1,393,146	1,470,303	1,663,866	1,748,108	1,728,663
Partitions, etc.	113,070	114,262	109,850	125,784	146,705	142,496	171,967	200,627	197,361	226,730
Miscellaneous furniture	169,965	131,724	119,650	139,204	162,471	169,561	190,360	227,567	201,138	221,968
CORPORATE ASSETS, EXCLUDING OTHER INVESTMENTS										
Total furniture (1947 prices)	1,255,000	1,237,000	1,253,000	1,444,000	1,451,000[f]	1,477,000	1,537,000	1,683,000	1,679,000	1,635,000
Total furniture (book values)	1,080,546	1,122,653	1,135,793	1,401,320	1,490,734[g]	1,559,793	1,673,634	1,914,954	1,973,399	2,004,147
Furniture[a]	843,466	914,396	942,069	1,178,531	1,231,886	1,295,100	1,366,452	1,547,235	1,626,495	1,609,316
Partitions, etc.	97,604	98,669	94,905	108,739	126,920	125,676	152,145	178,069	175,735	202,539
Miscellaneous furniture	142,531	109,603	98,770	113,990	131,961	139,063	155,465	189,571	170,976	192,615
RATE OF RETURN ON CORPORATE ASSETS (per cent)										
Total furniture (1947 prices)	10.14	9.20	6.77	9.63	6.87[h]	5.34	4.80	7.42	7.57	6.37
Total furniture (book values)	10.82	9.49	6.76	9.67	6.43[i]	4.89	4.14	6.93	6.90	5.36
Furniture[a]	10.99	10.07	6.93	10.25	6.58	5.12	4.06	6.94	6.87	5.05
Partitions, etc.	12.34	8.10	8.22	5.62	5.52	3.34	4.60	6.50	7.49	7.48
Miscellaneous furniture	8.53	5.84	3.72	7.57	5.91	4.16	4.41	7.29	6.61	5.70

NOTES: [a] Data unreliable because of year-to-year differences in classification of large companies.

* 1952 minor industry data not available. Major industry data appear below:

[d] 1952 = 1,662,000.

[e] 1952 = 1,753,253.

[f] 1952 = 1,500,000.

[g] 1952 = 1,582,765.

[h] 1952 = 6.14 per cent.

[i] 1952 = 5.65 per cent.

TABLE A-43

PAPER AND ALLIED PRODUCTS, 1947–57
(assets in thousands of dollars)

	1947	1948	1949	1950	1951*	1953*	1954	1955	1956	1957
TOTAL ASSETS, EXCLUDING OTHER INVESTMENTS										
Total paper and allied products (1947 prices)	4,392,000	4,606,000	4,690,000	5,228,000	5,839,000[d]	5,802,000	6,111,000	6,740,000	7,171,000	7,188,000
Total paper and allied products (book values)	3,571,515	3,934,389	4,052,333	4,840,574	5,753,808[e]	6,031,970	6,468,150	7,385,676	8,093,000	8,461,143
Pulp, paper, etc.	2,361,919	2,671,875	2,778,286	3,310,953	3,913,478	4,052,935	4,414,950	5,011,849	5,596,937	5,791,768
Miscellaneous paper	1,222,461	1,277,711	1,282,228	1,559,506	1,853,716	1,987,047	2,056,170	2,359,770	2,525,901	2,653,234
CORPORATE ASSETS, EXCLUDING OTHER INVESTMENTS										
Total Paper and allied products (1947 prices)	4,344,000	4,560,000	4,647,000	5,183,000	5,792,000[f]	5,760,000	6,068,000	6,692,000	7,120,000	7,136,000
Total paper and allied products (book values)	3,532,137	3,894,896	4,015,502	4,799,209	5,707,671[g]	5,988,307	6,422,988	7,333,316	8,034,987	8,399,991
Pulp, paper, etc.	2,342,820	2,653,393	2,762,074	3,294,206	3,896,582	4,040,615	4,404,034	5,000,797	5,586,100	5,782,112
Miscellaneous paper	1,189,193	1,245,943	1,253,258	1,526,274	1,816,529	1,950,825	2,019,892	2,317,726	2,480,435	2,604,990
RATE OF RETURN ON CORPORATE ASSETS (per cent)										
Total paper and allied products (1947 prices)	14.33	11.44	8.03	10.95	9.27[h]	7.60	7.37	8.46	9.41	7.61
Total paper and allied products (book values)	16.28	12.52	8.28	11.32	9.32[i]	7.34	7.05	8.12	8.90	6.53
Pulp, paper, etc.	16.65	13.23	8.59	11.03	9.26	7.49	7.27	8.30	9.06	6.51
Miscellaneous paper	15.57	10.98	7.60	11.79	9.42	7.02	6.56	7.77	8.42	6.62

NOTES: * 1952 minor industry data not available. Major industry data appear below:

[d] 1952 = 5,768,000.
[e] 1952 = 5,830,950.
[f] 1952 = 5,724,000.
[g] 1952 = 5,786,494.
[h] 1952 = 7.56 per cent.
[i] 1952 = 7.31 per cent.

TABLE A-44

PRINTING AND PUBLISHING, 1947–57

(assets in thousands of dollars)

	1947	1948	1949	1950	1951*	1953*	1954	1955	1956	1957
TOTAL ASSETS, EXCLUDING OTHER INVESTMENTS										
Total printing and publishing (1947 prices)	4,457,000	4,527,000	4,673,000	4,787,000	4,722,000[d]	4,820,000	4,882,000	5,177,000	5,288,000	5,274,000
Total printing and publishing (book values)	3,801,580	4,086,326	4,265,330	4,569,777	4,889,844[e]	5,294,584	5,525,389	6,022,293	6,395,679	6,632,554
Newspapers	1,528,336	1,619,277	1,716,452	1,830,031	1,975,025	2,151,629	2,126,630	2,296,614	2,391,568	2,451,335
Periodicals	537,893	568,501	577,343	605,951	639,916	625,898	660,939	715,575	736,341	715,663
Books	337,769	375,416	408,634	442,451	455,272	545,894	599,896	671,687	758,437	807,251
Commercial	822,210	975,583	1,082,683	1,211,304	1,349,640	1,486,883	1,544,454	1,809,634	1,964,414	2,099,455
Miscellaneous printing	601,452	578,565	511,923	511,536	502,747	522,301	636,914	568,784	577,282	588,904
CORPORATE ASSETS, EXCLUDING OTHER INVESTMENTS										
Total printing and publishing (1947 prices)	4,134,000	4,203,000	4,342,000	4,476,000	4,442,000[f]	4,505,000	4,571,000	4,836,000	4,928,000	4,903,000
Total printing and publishing (book values)	3,525,894	3,793,477	3,963,424	4,272,676	4,599,484[g]	4,948,604	5,172,990	5,625,262	5,959,836	6,165,917
Newspapers	1,438,884	1,526,115	1,619,463	1,735,712	1,882,734	2,042,287	2,021,948	2,180,668	2,267,835	2,321,450
Periodicals	523,791	554,095	563,234	592,738	627,560	613,328	648,436	701,847	722,030	701,575
Books	321,892	357,754	389,397	423,091	436,849	520,789	572,552	642,615	727,364	776,054
Commercial	712,028	848,344	942,821	1,066,521	1,201,213	1,307,027	1,361,375	1,592,161	1,725,153	1,840,352
Miscellaneous printing	526,883	507,792	450,180	454,761	451,702	464,538	568,300	507,979	516,043	526,917

(continued)

TABLE A-44 (concluded)

	1947	1948	1949	1950	1951*	1953*	1954	1955	1956	1957
RATE OF RETURN ON CORPORATE ASSETS (per cent)										
Total printing and publishing (1947 prices)	10.11	9.02	7.92	7.77	7.02[h]	6.59	6.30	8.17	8.63	8.26
Total printing and publishing (book values)	10.95	9.40	8.08	7.63	6.45[i]	5.96	5.50	7.40	7.55	6.95
Newspapers	11.77	9.88	9.18	8.36	6.92	6.66	6.43	8.61	8.72	7.73
Periodicals	8.24	7.00	5.95	5.86	5.34	4.36	1.56	6.16	6.94	5.90
Books	6.69	6.65	7.00	6.50	4.98	4.65	5.45	6.86	6.18	6.33
Commercial	12.68	10.58	8.07	7.98	6.77	5.83	5.65	6.60	6.86	6.69
Miscellaneous printing	11.70	10.54	7.74	7.34	6.59	6.82	6.34	7.07	7.46	6.77

NOTES: * 1952 minor industry data not available. Major industry data appear below:

[d] 1952 = 4,794,000.

[e] 1952 = 5,105,792.

[f] 1952 = 4,494,000.

[g] 1952 = 4,786,763.

[h] 1952 = 6.70 per cent.

[i] 1952 = 6.10 per cent.

TABLE A-45

Chemicals and Allied Products, 1947–57

(assets in thousands of dollars)

	1947	1948	1949	1950	1951*	1953*	1954	1955	1956	1957
TOTAL ASSETS, EXCLUDING OTHER INVESTMENTS										
Total chemicals and allied products (1947 prices)	10,760,000	10,898,000	11,440,000	12,344,000	13,427,000[d]	14,043,000	13,962,000	14,857,000	14,927,000	15,141,000
Total chemicals and allied products (book values)	9,062,837	9,471,346	10,174,899	11,795,854	13,496,950[e]	14,734,253	15,011,380	16,521,662	17,371,596	18,267,787
Drugs	1,043,692	1,149,891	1,250,551	1,340,081	1,605,320	1,565,169	1,608,600	1,799,687	1,836,614	1,960,597
Soaps	624,107	598,305	648,611	724,265	801,222	864,308	883,390	890,328	935,377	999,384
Paints	782,058	858,880	846,108	1,009,735	1,103,490	1,159,208	1,115,612	1,255,559	1,373,866	1,400,595
Perfume and cosmetics	122,262	136,941	175,645	212,664	246,206	291,427[c]	285,518	301,160	343,219	326,139
Fertilizers	270,700	338,787	374,253	438,631	547,832	697,187	651,165	732,914	673,052	744,653
Oils	698,257	716,572	710,789	860,723	838,646	724,624	714,477	736,521	660,725	666,028
Industrial and miscellaneous chemicals	5,274,990	5,738,582	6,224,349	7,302,659	8,412,307	9,511,309	9,847,406	10,930,695	11,650,410	12,264,771
CORPORATE ASSETS, EXCLUDING OTHER INVESTMENTS										
Total chemicals and allied products (1947 prices)	10,559,000	10,716,000	11,270,000	12,174,000	13,258,000[f]	13,891,000	13,820,000	14,717,000	14,797,000	15,020,000
Total chemicals and allied products (book values)	8,893,433	9,312,747	10,023,323	11,633,823	13,326,651[g]	14,574,496	14,858,811	16,365,535	17,220,059	18,121,726
Drugs	1,026,880	1,133,146	1,234,189	1,323,734	1,587,113	1,549,474	1,593,224	1,783,458	1,821,062	1,945,075
Soaps	609,541	584,768	634,463	708,456	783,753	845,024	863,139	870,881	915,968	979,740
Paints	763,945	839,717	828,017	988,252	1,080,165	1,134,379[c]	1,091,171	1,229,614	1,347,192	1,375,155
Perfume and cosmetics	119,014	133,669	171,896	208,460	241,715	286,810	281,251	297,084	339,052	322,635
Fertilizers	260,702	324,710	357,331	416,694	518,035	652,706	606,055	676,569	616,280	676,367
Oils	644,374	663,542	660,580	800,568	780,727	674,484	664,219	684,289	613,481	618,014
Industrial and miscellaneous chemicals	5,191,070	5,646,903	6,133,153	7,198,254	8,301,728	9,399,984	9,742,092	10,835,666	11,572,757	12,208,004

(continued)

TABLE A-45 (concluded)

	1947	1948	1949	1950	1951*	1953*	1954	1955	1956	1957
RATE OF RETURN ON CORPORATE ASSETS (per cent)										
Total chemicals and allied products (1947 prices)	11.00	10.03	9.25	11.66	8.61[h]	7.00	7.61	9.49	9.40	9.14
Total chemicals and allied products (book values)	11.72	10.47	9.42	11.63	8.20[i]	6.42	7.00	9.87	8.28	7.69
Drugs	10.82	12.65	12.24	12.65	9.42	7.21	8.05	10.32	11.31	12.51
Soaps	17.05	5.27	7.91	10.56	5.61	6.56	7.78	8.86	6.90	8.15
Paints	12.90	9.31	5.08	9.86	7.14	5.79	6.29	7.88	8.20	7.57
Perfumes and cosmetics	7.21	8.11	6.98	8.72	6.40	6.55	7.60	8.67	9.04	9.87
Fertilizers	10.61	9.08	7.98	7.12	6.06	3.89	4.05	3.77	2.77	1.99
Oils	16.25	9.05	8.24	8.19	6.45	5.00	5.62	4.16	4.09	3.26
Industrial and miscellaneous chemicals	11.85	11.03	9.38	12.51	8.74	6.11	7.11	9.36	8.41	7.38

NOTES: [c] Adjusted for variability of assets due to shifts of large companies between industries.

* 1952 minor industry data not available. Major industry data appear below:

[d] 1952 = 13,861,000.

[e] 1952 = 14,274,307.

[f] 1952 = 13,699,000.

[g] 1952 = 14,107,026.

[h] 1952 = 7.05 per cent.

[i] 1952 = 6.46 per cent.

TABLE A-46

PETROLEUM AND COAL PRODUCTS, 1947–57

(assets in thousands of dollars)

	1947	1948	1949	1950	1951*	1953*	1954	1955	1956	1957
TOTAL ASSETS, EXCLUDING OTHER INVESTMENTS										
Total petroleum and coal (1947 prices)	16,883,000	19,086,000	19,584,000	18,530,000	19,766,000[d]	21,290,000	24,046,000	24,173,000	25,675,000	26,344,000
Total petroleum and coal (book values)	13,130,160	15,558,867	16,327,196	16,401,786	18,850,118[e]	21,626,253	25,123,247	26,116,024	28,932,133	30,445,344
Petroleum refining	12,497,503	14,832,088	15,571,219	15,776,730	18,145,977	20,950,873	24,444,724	25,423,348	28,219,444	30,084,844
Miscellaneous petroleum and coal	610,150	674,683	714,957	585,592	669,038	652,918	667,668	676,016	692,703	654,491[c]
CORPORATE ASSETS, EXCLUDING OTHER INVESTMENTS										
Total petroleum and coal (1947 prices)	16,579,000	18,765,000	19,278,000	18,250,000	19,478,000[f]	20,993,000	23,713,000	23,838,000	25,319,000	26,053,000
Total petroleum and coal (book values)	12,893,363	15,296,950	16,071,812	16,154,076	18,575,514[g]	21,324,774	24,774,824	25,753,832	28,530,886	30,108,728
Petroleum refining	12,323,464	14,632,775	15,370,371	15,573,873	17,913,777	20,678,296	24,118,861	25,084,440	27,843,262	29,637,612
Miscellaneous petroleum and coal	599,421	664,044	704,915	577,998	661,056	646,200	661,214	669,481	686,007	646,373[c]
RATE OF RETURN ON CORPORATE ASSETS (per cent)										
Total petroleum and coal (1947 prices)	8.86	10.92	7.19	8.82	8.78[h]	7.64	6.40	7.80	7.94	7.70
Total petroleum and coal (book values)	9.23	11.73	7.03	8.63	8.25[i]	7.07	5.62	7.07	6.86	6.44
Petroleum refining	9.17	11.85	7.05	8.59	8.28	7.11	5.68	7.09	6.88	6.46
Miscellaneous petroleum and coal	11.08	9.16	6.45	9.67	7.51	5.97	3.64	6.11	5.97	5.35

NOTES: [c] Adjusted for variability of assets due to shifts of large companies between industries.

* 1952 minor industry data not available. Major industry data appear below:

[e] 1952 = 20,140,256.

[f] 1952 = 20,138,000.

[g] 1952 = 19,853,199.

[h] 1952 = 7.21 per cent

TABLE A-47

RUBBER PRODUCTS, 1947–57
(assets in thousands of dollars)

	1947	1948	1949	1950	1951*	1953*	1954	1955	1956	1957
TOTAL ASSETS, EXCLUDING OTHER INVESTMENTS										
Total rubber (1947 prices)	2,067,000	1,997,000	1,985,000	2,084,000	2,453,000[d]	2,547,000	2,419,000	2,748,000	2,808,000	2,733,000
Total rubber (book values)	1,801,014	1,863,643	1,862,632	2,149,268	2,579,307[e]	2,832,674	2,785,961	3,234,443	3,407,559	3,406,825
Tires and tubes	1,421,340	1,479,575	1,471,770	1,678,932	2,053,916	2,205,948	2,161,562	2,469,950	2,632,181	2,704,978
Miscellaneous rubber	368,610	371,196	377,158	454,916	505,647	603,250	598,391	737,044	744,843	691,069
CORPORATE ASSETS, EXCLUDING OTHER INVESTMENTS										
Total rubber (1947 prices)	2,048,000	1,978,000	1,966,000	2,064,000	2,428,000[f]	2,519,000	2,391,000	2,716,000	2,776,000	2,716,000
Total rubber (book values)	1,784,322	1,846,148	1,845,099	2,128,282	2,553,319[g]	2,801,743	2,753,900	3,197,221	3,368,345	3,385,200
Tires and tubes	1,420,931	1,479,217	1,471,476	1,678,649	2,053,630	2,205,755	2,161,424	2,469,792	2,632,013	2,702,168
Miscellaneous rubber	364,351	366,930	372,880	449,638	499,669	595,684	590,553	727,390	735,087	681,440
RATE OF RETURN ON CORPORATE ASSETS (per cent)										
Total rubber (1947 prices)	7.39	7.91	5.47	10.58	7.23[h]	6.07	5.75	7.35	7.49	7.26
Total rubber (book values)	7.06	7.27	4.58	9.70	6.50[i]	5.25	4.69	6.36	6.20	5.69
Tires and tubes	6.20	6.70	3.84	9.07	5.92	4.97	4.62	5.99	5.81	5.45
Miscellaneous rubber	10.41	9.58	7.51	12.04	8.89	6.30	4.96	7.63	7.60	6.66

NOTES: * 1952 minor industry data not available. Major industry data appear below:
[d] 1952 = 2,637,000.
[e] 1952 = 2,789,290.
[f] 1952 = 2,609,000.
[g] 1952 = 2,759,980.
[h] 1952 = 5.49 per cent.
[i] 1952 = 4.84 per cent.

TABLE A-48

LEATHER AND PRODUCTS, 1947–57
(assets in thousands of dollars)

	1947	1948	1949	1950	1951*	1953*	1954	1955	1956	1957
TOTAL ASSETS, EXCLUDING OTHER INVESTMENTS										
Total leather (1947 prices)	1,474,000	1,438,000	1,369,000	1,429,000	1,498,000[d]	1,318,000	1,311,000	1,279,000	1,289,000	1,202,000
Total leather (book values)	1,341,926	1,342,218	1,293,141	1,462,222	1,448,377[e]	1,408,454	1,400,923	1,506,032	1,539,298	1,521,683
Tanning, etc.	407,336	405,479	375,706	399,644	365,469	310,049	294,615	294,285	302,561	271,543
Footwear	679,251	698,512	695,113	790,741	802,930	813,508	822,441	880,128	943,974	914,415
Miscellaneous leather	243,277	226,683	212,373	267,416	280,374	301,651	293,027	345,514	299,598	346,301
CORPORATE ASSETS, EXCLUDING OTHER INVESTMENTS										
Total leather (1947 prices)	1,394,000	1,364,000	1,302,000	1,363,000	1,433,000[f]	1,266,000	1,263,000	1,234,000	1,245,000	1,162,000
Total leather (book values)	1,269,164	1,272,975	1,229,869	1,394,678	1,385,465[g]	1,352,776	1,349,689	1,452,549	1,486,311	1,470,964
Tanning, etc.	394,185	392,679	364,118	387,621	354,753	292,311	286,306	286,030	294,125	264,018
Footwear	676,923	694,777	690,063	783,487	794,036	800,066	808,047	865,842	929,868	901,932
Miscellaneous leather	196,626	185,184	175,386	223,332	236,827	259,155	254,876	301,806	262,812	305,079
RATE OF RETURN ON CORPORATE ASSETS (per cent)										
Total leather (1947 prices)	10.03	6.33	4.55	7.23	3.71[h]	4.43	4.72	6.39	5.74	6.18
Total leather (book values)	10.30	6.26	4.24	6.85	3.46[i]	4.10	4.51	5.86	5.09	5.25
Tanning, etc.	13.53	6.83	2.68	5.94	1.13	2.12	1.94	4.17	3.24	3.49
Footwear	9.43	6.63	5.57	7.32	5.07	5.28	5.74	6.65	5.89	6.23
Miscellaneous leather	6.87	3.65	2.28	6.80	4.91	2.71	3.48	5.19	4.31	3.89

NOTES: * 1952 minor industry data not available. Major industry data appear below:

[d] 1952 = 1,338,000.
[e] 1952 = 1,467,286.
[f] 1952 = 1,282,000.
[g] 1952 = 1,406,314.
[h] 1952 = 4.94 per cent.
[i] 1952 = 4.40 per cent.

TABLE A-49

STONE, CLAY, AND GLASS PRODUCTS, 1947–57

(assets in thousands of dollars)

	1947	1948	1949	1950	1951*	1953*	1954	1955	1956	1957
TOTAL ASSETS, EXCLUDING OTHER INVESTMENTS										
Total stone, clay, and glass (1947 prices)	3,418,000	3,533,000	3,544,000	3,999,000	4,194,000[d]	4,537,000	4,725,000	5,279,000	5,535,000	5,752,000
Total stone, clay, and glass (book values)	2,783,490	3,084,602	3,147,739	3,752,322	4,210,029[e]	4,914,982	5,214,732	5,911,322	6,402,725	6,986,766
Glass	636,421	693,597	680,189	835,167	902,373	1,163,857	1,208,562	1,395,767	1,509,870	1,528,407
Cement	417,787	463,132	517,244	587,119	685,791	738,950	806,329	1,028,851	1,200,305	1,451,238
Structural clay	351,428	395,488	407,824	475,391	537,668	548,763	607,553	606,031	656,549	780,023
Pottery	172,361	189,640	174,588	200,120	217,482	177,667	211,451	191,013	186,581[c]	186,372[c]
Concrete	507,607	586,176	596,299	722,464	801,864	1,031,326	1,149,893	1,310,495	1,454,561	1,586,103
Cut stone	84,451	80,291	91,411	86,475	91,255	84,586	93,932	107,889	90,108[c]	91,414[c]
Miscellaneous stone, clay, and glass	642,380	709,608	705,611	869,023	997,044	1,174,081	1,155,948	1,284,172	1,236,110	1,276,882
CORPORATE ASSETS, EXCLUDING OTHER INVESTMENTS										
Total stone, clay, and glass (1947 prices)	3,265,000	3,385,000	3,406,000	3,848,000	4,041,000[f]	4,379,000	4,561,000	5,096,000	5,344,000	5,554,000
Total stone, clay, and glass (book values)	2,658,581	2,955,151	3,024,762	3,610,650	4,056,569[g]	4,743,350	5,033,536	5,706,791	6,181,967	6,746,783
Glass	623,788	681,241	669,388	822,912	890,182	1,150,271	1,195,294	1,380,458	1,493,309	1,511,643
Cement	416,523	462,006	516,266	586,257	685,059	738,696	806,329	1,028,851	1,200,305	1,451,238
Structural clay	331,858	374,569	387,428	452,065	511,811	522,722	578,446	580,501	632,733	756,349
Pottery	162,654	178,858	164,658	188,358	204,335	166,111	197,016	179,331	176,514[c]	177,680[c]
Concrete	432,370	506,363	522,172	637,780	713,463	928,686	1,039,764	1,188,259	1,322,545	1,446,158
Cut stone	62,427	61,326	72,058	69,670	75,105	72,195	81,428	92,164	75,868[c]	75,877[c]
Miscellaneous stone, clay, and glass	630,305	696,633	693,133	853,597	979,316	1,152,603	1,134,166	1,261,825	1,216,380	1,258,347

(continued)

TABLE A-49 (concluded)

	1947	1948	1949	1950	1951*	1953*	1954	1955	1956	1957
RATE OF RETURN ON CORPORATE ASSETS (per cent)										
Total stone, clay, and glass (1947 prices)	9.53	10.57	9.84	11.93	8.74[h]	7.56	8.24	10.27	9.37	7.83
Total stone, clay, and glass (book values)	10.26	10.97	10.02	12.10	8.19[i]	6.73	7.53	9.70	8.42	6.33
Glass	9.58	8.01	11.03	13.62	8.97	8.08	9.41	12.33	9.77	9.65
Cement	10.29	14.05	14.50	13.79	8.91	8.61	10.61	11.26	9.88	5.07
Structural clay	11.70	12.47	9.16	12.36	7.80	5.30	4.50	8.10	7.18	4.92
Pottery	12.89	11.53	4.35	8.38	6.66	2.61	3.44	4.81	7.82	3.37
Concrete	10.63	12.43	10.29	11.98	7.95	6.84	8.44	9.48	7.92	6.78
Cut stone	7.36	8.55	8.00	7.40	4.36	2.45	−0.18	3.01	3.17	1.24
Miscellaneous stone, clay, and glass	9.49	9.93	7.53	10.63	7.93	5.69	5.34	7.73	6.91	4.99

NOTES: [c] Adjusted for variability of assets due to shifts of large companies between industries.
* 1952 minor industry data not available. Major industry data appear below:
[d] 1952 = 4,185,000.
[e] 1952 = 4,323,639.
[f] 1952 = 4,036,000.
[g] 1952 = 4,169,357.
[h] 1952 = 7.31 per cent.
[i] 1952 = 6.60 per cent.

TABLE A-30

PRIMARY METAL PRODUCTS, 1947–57

(assets in thousands of dollars)

	1947	1948	1949	1950	1951*	1953*	1954	1955	1956	1957
TOTAL ASSETS, EXCLUDING OTHER INVESTMENTS										
Total primary metals (1947 prices)	12,634,000	13,255,000	13,030,000	14,317,000	15,633,000[d]	17,138,000	16,633,000	18,104,000	18,219,000	18,735,000
Total primary metals (book values)	10,168,919	11,201,042	11,070,913	12,931,031	15,039,990[e]	17,115,195	16,926,300	19,324,140	20,128,376	21,451,540
Blast furnaces	6,297,273	7,221,828	6,920,820	8,060,759	9,507,784	10,322,988	10,327,396	11,486,694	11,852,651	12,660,625
Iron and steel foundries	795,128	848,349	749,633	909,419	1,093,743	1,106,548	1,068,448	1,212,030	1,316,408	1,242,266
Smelting etc., nonferrous	2,373,720	2,407,687	2,466,835	2,853,595	3,128,052	4,269,820	4,265,207	5,056,403	5,339,165	5,859,863
Nonferrous foundries	198,278	215,170	203,569	264,852	294,723	274,954	267,810	328,699	313,687	310,583
Miscellaneous primary metals	670,404	708,877	698,894	810,203	983,862	1,075,733	964,547	1,195,616	1,280,310	1,358,820
CORPORATE ASSETS, EXCLUDING OTHER INVESTMENTS										
Total primary metals (1947 prices)	12,512,000	13,137,000	12,924,000	14,205,000	15,517,000[f]	17,019,000	16,519,000	17,990,000	18,115,000	18,638,000
Total primary metals (book values)	10,071,049	11,101,494	10,980,491	12,830,163	14,928,082[g]	16,996,078	16,810,464	19,202,778	20,013,300	21,340,994
Blast furnaces	6,293,721	7,216,663	6,914,998	8,052,822	9,497,158	10,308,579	10,311,351	11,468,803	11,834,190	12,640,905
Iron and steel foundries	775,474	828,944	733,841	891,093	1,072,684	1,086,560	1,049,445	1,191,336	1,294,849	1,222,787
Smelting etc., nonferrous	2,358,252	2,394,086	2,454,891	2,841,381	3,116,342	4,257,715	4,254,787	5,045,303	5,328,721	5,849,801
Nonferrous foundries	180,200	196,238	186,368	242,592	270,120	251,744	244,734	302,002	289,777	288,480
Miscellaneous primary metals	660,301	698,629	689,250	799,118	970,534	1,061,057	951,124	1,178,051	1,260,495	1,336,724
RATE OF RETURN ON CORPORATE ASSETS (per cent)										
Total primary metals (1947 prices)	8.42	9.30	7.32	9.64	7.84[h]	6.30	5.16	7.83	7.78	6.93
Total primary metals (book values)	9.01	9.95	7.59	10.08	7.90[i]	6.23	4.75	7.85	7.52	6.33
Blast furnaces	7.50	9.23	8.62	10.24	7.84	6.78	4.86	8.35	7.59	7.49
Iron and steel foundries	12.01	12.08	6.73	9.53	8.84	6.27	4.92	7.74	8.83	6.69
Smelting etc., nonferrous	10.06	9.47	5.07	9.09	6.94	4.70	4.53	6.76	6.65	3.75
Nonferrous foundries	10.31	9.97	3.48	11.00	8.80	6.06	2.48	5.90	5.80	2.82
Miscellaneous primary metals	13.09	13.22	8.13	12.35	10.32	7.23	4.89	8.31	9.67	7.08

NOTES: * 1952 minor industry data not available. Major industry data appear below:

[d] 1952 = 16,346,000.
[e] 1952 = 15,890,000.
[f] 1952 = 16,228,000.
[g] 1952 = 15,775,708.
[h] 1952 = 5.45 per cent.
[i] 1952 = 5.21 per cent.

TABLE A-51

FABRICATED METAL PRODUCTS, 1947–57

(assets in thousands of dollars)

	1947	1948	1949	1950	1951*	1953*	1954	1955	1956	1957
TOTAL ASSETS, EXCLUDING OTHER INVESTMENTS										
Total fabricated metals (1947 prices)	6,082,000	6,262,000	6,169,000	6,838,000	7,440,000[d]	7,737,000	7,685,000	8,240,000	8,221,000	8,599,000
Total fabricated metals (book values)	5,040,739	5,546,780	5,437,183	6,389,017	7,493,782[e]	8,097,463	8,173,128	9,088,227	9,485,942	10,232,462
Tin cans	502,743	555,640	592,295	677,471	785,862	840,664	868,040	930,935	1,145,913	1,327,345
Hand tools	643,160	697,492	653,965	728,037	811,025	831,562	866,531	981,602	986,420	938,136
Heating apparatus	1,078,401	1,200,718	1,082,248	1,244,939	1,386,791	1,444,772	1,477,062	1,483,428	1,464,172	1,550,102
Fabricated structural	930,339	1,127,625	1,116,521	1,310,354	1,576,649	1,755,928	1,825,512	2,177,341	2,398,901	2,738,598
Metal stamping	636,633	675,266	720,281	896,042	1,091,078	1,324,969	1,136,736	1,205,740	1,222,703	1,243,183
Lighting fixtures	111,445	121,715	122,415	145,665	157,768	180,269	177,570	209,053	217,248	239,711
Fabricated wire	309,396	332,027	331,626	372,680	454,484	493,310	452,096	513,536	532,240	551,886
Miscellaneous fabricated metals	797,111	804,336	791,077	989,648	1,206,598	1,204,889	1,343,551	1,575,210	1,512,747	1,648,111
CORPORATE ASSETS, EXCLUDING OTHER INVESTMENTS										
Total fabricated metals (1947 prices)	5,750,000	5,932,000	5,857,000	6,493,000	7,066,000[f]	7,343,000	7,284,000	7,834,000	7,839,000	8,224,000
Total fabricated metals (book values)	4,765,798	5,254,542	5,161,888	6,066,632	7,117,535[g]	7,684,630	7,746,732	8,639,985	9,045,257	9,786,585
Tin cans	501,497	554,428	591,066	676,081	784,270	838,957	866,246	929,086	1,143,751	1,324,973
Hand tools	618,633	672,344	631,774	703,895	784,769	805,187	838,873	951,229	956,844	910,909
Heating apparatus	1,056,936	1,178,341	1,063,449	1,223,995	1,364,218	1,422,128	1,453,960	1,460,168	1,441,157	1,525,676
Fabricated structural	864,596	1,052,776	1,047,220	1,231,478	1,484,699	1,657,185	1,723,068	2,056,190	2,266,578	2,588,858
Metal stamping	581,673	618,938	662,513	824,468	1,004,406	1,218,283	1,043,199	1,106,986	1,122,993	1,142,243
Lighting fixtures	102,954	112,512	113,293	134,602	145,595	165,620	162,568	192,418	201,035	223,018
Fabricated wire	292,048	313,475	313,301	351,612	428,294	463,177	423,295	483,214	503,324	524,532
Miscellaneous fabricated metals	742,625	749,109	736,977	920,000	1,119,583	1,112,002	1,235,171	1,458,028	1,409,790	1,546,549

(continued)

TABLE A-51 (concluded)

	1947	1948	1949	1950	1951*	1953*	1954	1955	1956	1957
RATE OF RETURN ON CORPORATE ASSETS (per cent)										
Total fabricated metals (1947 prices)	11.60	11.13	7.47	10.26	8.57[h]	6.51	6.01	7.15	7.31	6.69
Total fabricated metals (book values)	12.74	11.85	7.64	10.64	8.44[i]	6.17	5.52	6.68	6.53	5.70
Tin cans	7.27	7.75	5.99	7.66	6.30	6.33	5.92	6.97	6.37	5.56
Hand tools	10.72	9.55	6.64	11.41	7.97	5.87	6.47	7.35	8.23	6.60
Heating apparatus	12.78	11.82	6.86	10.82	7.34	5.35	4.56	6.21	5.26	4.02
Fabricated structural	18.16	15.04	9.18	9.20	9.56	6.64	6.12	5.58	7.29	6.74
Metal stamping	12.75	12.77	7.48	11.73	8.55	6.29	5.34	7.23	6.26	4.92
Lighting fixtures	6.44	6.22	3.57	8.49	6.61	2.67	4.93	6.94	6.01	5.16
Fabricated wire	12.43	12.40	10.21	12.77	9.15	5.48	5.57	7.84	7.96	6.11
Miscellaneous fabricated metals	12.85	12.42	7.63	12.41	9.99	7.28	5.12	7.27	5.37	5.72

NOTES: * 1952 minor industry data not available. Major industry data appear below:

[d] 1952 = 7,485,000.

[e] 1952 = 7,663,136.

[f] 1952 = 7,106,000.

[g] 1952 = 7,275,256.

[h] 1952 = 6.78 per cent.

[i] 1952 = 6.47 per cent.

TABLE A-52

MACHINERY, EXCEPT TRANSPORTATION AND ELECTRICAL, 1947–57

(assets in thousands of dollars)

	1947	1948	1949	1950	1951*	1953*	1954	1955	1956	1957
TOTAL ASSETS, EXCLUDING OTHER INVESTMENTS										
Total machinery (1947 prices)	10,524,000	10,794,000	10,790,000	11,835,000	13,286,000[d]	14,297,000	13,898,000	15,046,000	15,876,000	15,926,000
Total machinery (book values)	9,267,679	10,172,682	10,096,615	11,657,753	14,204,912[e]	15,751,821	15,518,120	17,239,050	18,982,082	19,708,300
Engines and turbines	276,541	294,098	294,023	321,197	433,646	491,272	428,958	450,726	517,168	494,082
Agricultural	1,492,238	1,802,517	1,878,449	2,100,338	2,460,014	2,635,991	2,628,505	2,868,691	2,902,540	2,993,736
Construction	838,119	978,445	949,635	1,167,250	1,494,830	1,467,006	1,499,118	1,745,069	2,077,089	2,154,618
Metal working	1,247,569	1,307,772	1,251,068	1,456,375	2,013,550	2,297,493	2,121,018	2,391,355	2,703,381	2,806,153
Special industry	1,246,074	1,305,855	1,269,174	1,386,613	1,459,678	1,558,480	1,472,907	1,638,512	1,928,483	1,857,331
General industry	1,031,542	1,136,546	1,117,763	1,348,506	1,695,595	1,994,421	1,928,841	2,097,908	2,353,253	2,445,333
Office and store	740,090	858,225	891,197	994,072	1,221,546	1,497,647	1,567,806	1,639,727	1,870,816	2,282,550
House and service	945,758	1,058,489	1,067,262	1,383,253	1,487,367	1,790,494	1,707,706	1,985,894	1,920,709	1,890,711
Miscellaneous machinery	1,577,429	1,479,573	1,418,995	1,524,694	1,989,496	2,061,211	2,202,643	2,490,345	2,804,789	2,901,064
CORPORATE ASSETS, EXCLUDING OTHER INVESTMENTS										
Total machinery (1947 prices)	10,147,000	10,431,000	10,441,000	11,452,000	12,857,000[f]	13,826,000	13,429,000	14,543,000	15,351,000	15,405,000
Total machinery (book values)	8,935,507	9,830,294	9,769,692	11,280,627	13,746,607[g]	15,233,296	14,994,076	16,663,171	18,354,363	19,063,201
Engines and turbines	275,827	293,366	293,321	320,410	432,620	490,091	427,901	449,467	515,554	492,378
Agricultural	1,454,337	1,759,764	1,837,032	2,055,616	2,409,480	2,584,166	2,577,095	2,813,711	2,848,057	2,938,723
Construction	821,519	959,341	931,482	1,144,599	1,465,469	1,436,804	1,467,063	1,712,598	2,044,218	2,126,548
Metal working	1,164,099	1,224,800	1,176,222	1,371,109	1,898,298	2,168,388	2,001,007	2,236,165	2,505,845	2,578,569
Special industry	1,174,593	1,239,515	1,212,598	1,330,612	1,406,630	1,512,343	1,433,431	1,594,690	1,876,997	1,807,833
General industry	1,008,210	1,112,276	1,095,330	1,322,080	1,663,183	1,957,117	1,892,550	2,060,247	2,313,075	2,405,735
Office and store	732,998	850,811	884,497	987,368	1,214,165	1,490,392	1,560,993	1,630,450	1,857,774	2,263,649
House and service	931,267	1,042,570	1,051,608	1,362,728	1,465,099	1,762,551	1,680,090	1,956,045	1,894,004	1,866,558
Miscellaneous machinery	1,439,341	1,346,220	1,288,888	1,378,315	1,790,813	1,835,892	1,948,396	2,207,655	2,491,817	2,582,971

(continued)

TABLE A-52 (concluded)

	1947	1948	1949	1950	1951*	1953*	1954	1955	1956	1957
RATE OF RETURN ON CORPORATE ASSETS (per cent)										
Total machinery (1947 prices)	9.92	10.95	8.53	10.19	8.66[h]	6.73	6.46	7.02	8.23	7.53
Total machinery (book values)	10.16	10.94	8.36	9.90	8.04[i]	6.11	5.69	6.25	7.19	6.22
Engines and turbines	3.90	10.31	7.56	8.33	7.87	5.98	5.47	7.02	8.56	8.12
Agricultural	7.51	9.65	9.22	10.00	7.15	4.70	3.95	5.04	4.62	3.70
Construction	13.10	14.18	10.41	9.83	9.10	7.66	7.13	8.18	8.71	8.49
Metal working	7.78	8.13	5.30	9.48	8.97	8.66	7.86	5.24	8.40	6.63
Special industry	10.88	10.80	8.40	8.68	6.80	4.94	4.56	5.54	6.33	4.80
General industry	12.32	12.30	9.04	9.89	8.69	6.58	6.21	7.36	7.87	7.09
Office and store	13.23	12.03	10.91	10.87	8.32	6.18	6.44	7.43	7.24	6.72
House and service	12.03	11.97	8.37	11.95	6.57	3.71	4.47	5.17	6.05	4.69
Miscellaneous machinery	9.19	10.54	6.21	9.30	8.79	6.59	5.55	6.70	8.23	7.29

NOTES: * 1952 minor industry data not available. Major industry data appear below:

[d] 1952 = 14,204,000.
[e] 1952 = 15,402,395.
[f] 1952 = 13,741,000.
[g] 1952 = 14,900,183.
[h] 1952 = 7.46 per cent.
[i] 1952 = 6.89 per cent.

TABLE A-53

Electrical Machinery and Equipment, 1947–57

(assets in thousands of dollars)

	1947	1948	1949	1950	1951*	1953*	1954	1955	1956	1957
TOTAL ASSETS, EXCLUDING OTHER INVESTMENTS										
Total electrical (1947 prices)	5,571,000	5,414,000	5,510,000	6,168,000	7,119,000[d]	8,748,000	7,918,000	8,239,000	8,910,000	8,758,000
Total electrical (book values)	4,991,687	5,162,921	5,172,888	6,181,249	7,664,233[e]	9,622,666	8,600,391	9,092,332	10,130,271	10,293,775
Electrical generating	1,714,256	1,840,124	1,806,968	2,042,377	2,672,992	3,617,086	3,039,999	3,348,252	3,911,960	4,102,227
Appliances	189,975	189,695	213,095	245,500	258,068	313,093	315,118	337,248[c]	385,014[c]	410,635
Insulated wire	207,221	220,268	213,506	275,349	337,707	375,753[c]	370,957	449,981	471,131	438,722
Automotive electric	158,624	157,564	162,733	213,008	221,983	232,068[c]	271,480	335,796	334,768	323,240
Electric lamps[a]	57,310	66,693	73,320	15,427	15,564	18,375	16,594	17,939	25,650	23,063
Communications[j]	1,554,862	1,537,838	1,558,728	2,202,307	2,623,549	3,427,517[c]	3,438,657[c]	3,767,830[c]	3,961,834[c]	4,217,042[c]
Miscellaneous electrical	1,047,142	1,154,639	1,148,501	1,202,097	1,566,551	1,893,126	2,031,535	1,888,761	2,049,331	1,863,109
CORPORATE ASSETS, EXCLUDING OTHER INVESTMENTS										
Total electrical (1947 prices)	5,424,000	5,288,000	5,401,000	6,061,000	7,012,000[f]	8,652,000	7,846,000	8,171,000	8,843,000	8,699,000
Total electrical (book values)	4,859,980	5,042,728	5,070,364	6,073,979	7,549,319[g]	9,517,475	8,521,786	9,017,040	10,054,460	10,224,961
Electrical generating	1,687,737	1,812,597	1,780,970	2,013,030	2,634,701	3,564,233	2,994,421	3,301,275	3,860,804	4,052,503
Appliances	188,179	187,852	210,994	242,963	255,290	309,386	311,161	332,474[c]	378,966[c]	403,549
Insulated wire	202,980	216,160	209,898	270,971	332,666	370,686[c]	366,130	445,239	467,336	436,283
Automotive electric	157,435	156,372	161,503	211,343	220,197	230,054[c]	269,001	332,821	331,901	320,560
Electric lamps[a]	57,177	66,553	73,182	15,400	15,539	18,349	16,572	17,917	25,623	23,042
Communications[j]	1,476,830	1,443,350	1,505,328	2,139,793	2,563,868	3,384,310[c]	3,411,694[c]	3,741,639[c]	3,937,813[c]	4,195,227[c]
Miscellaneous electrical	1,022,378	1,129,249	1,125,127	1,178,575	1,537,110	1,859,382	1,995,678	1,856,130	2,014,718	1,832,362

(continued)

TABLE A-53 (concluded)

	1947	1948	1949	1950	1951*	1953*	1954	1955	1956	1957
RATE OF RETURN ON CORPORATE ASSETS (per cent)										
Total electrical (1947 prices)	9.73	10.80	8.44	12.16	8.27[h]	7.10	6.83	6.88	6.78	7.91
Total electrical (book values)	9.74	10.57	8.21	11.88	7.61[i]	6.66	6.48	6.48	6.12	7.16
Electric generating	13.20	13.21	9.50	13.38	9.25	6.74	8.23	8.03	8.15	9.52
Appliances	12.47	10.00	7.75	13.94	9.14	6.18	7.50	7.71	8.00	4.57
Insulated wire	10.47	10.53	3.04	10.97	9.75	7.73	5.30	8.00	11.11	6.80
Automotive electric	11.18	10.80	10.40	12.93	8.88	7.42	4.59	8.77	6.49	11.11
Electric lamps[a]	8.29	7.11	5.18	7.55	4.47	4.93	6.95	6.06	5.47	5.71
Communications[j]	5.75	9.38	7.78	11.60	6.42	6.34	5.12	5.56	4.52	5.36
Miscellaneous electric	8.61	8.14	7.68	9.51	5.85	5.24	5.91	4.16	3.05	5.00

NOTES: [a] Data unreliable because of year-to-year differences in classification of large companies.

[c] Adjusted for variability of assets due to shifts of large companies between industries.

* 1952 minor industry data not available. Major industry data appear below:

[d] 1952 = 8,358,000.
[e] 1952 = 9,157,139.
[f] 1952 = 8,250,000.
[g] 1952 = 9,038,684.
[h] 1952 = 7.36 per cent.
[i] 1952 = 6.85 per cent.

[j] Changes in classification procedures since 1953 have shifted some communications firms out of manufacturing. From 1954 on, percentage changes in the remaining firms have been linked to the 1953 assets figures to obtain estimated assets on the earlier basis. Assets for firms currently classified in the industry are as follows:

	1954	*1955*	*1956*	*1957*
Total assets, excluding other investments	2,588,624	2,836,433	2,982,467	3,174,587
Corporate assets, excluding other investments	2,568,326	2,816,716	2,964,384	3,158,165

TABLE A-54

TRANSPORTATION EQUIPMENT, EXCEPT VEHICLES, 1947–57

(assets in thousands of dollars)

	1947	1948	1949	1950	1951*	1953*	1954	1955	1956	1957
TOTAL ASSETS, EXCLUDING OTHER INVESTMENTS										
Total transportation (1947 prices)	3,095,000	3,024,000	2,858,000	3,016,000	4,305,000[d]	6,049,000	6,346,000	6,412,000	7,414,000	7,566,000
Total transportation (book values)	2,815,426	2,891,523	2,737,898	3,043,184	4,739,713[e]	6,374,967	6,334,356	6,728,028	8,326,329	8,531,042
Aircraft[a]	1,240,404	1,255,052	1,345,560	1,562,259	2,931,992	4,496,766	4,603,311	4,761,814	6,200,603	6,724,829
Ship and boat[a]	606,970	622,738	422,183	447,111	598,440	674,572	775,453	756,670	838,120	699,668
Railroad	918,782	965,374	925,377	981,610	1,153,292	1,153,313	1,085,148	1,170,688	1,231,138	1,038,223
Motorcycles and bicycles	28,935[c]	32,877[c]	32,725	44,436	46,515	41,730	46,700	50,527[c]	53,781[c]	56,290
Miscellaneous transportation[a]	9,633	8,889	9,258	6,185	9,846	13,186	5,359	12,909	9,271	7,969
CORPORATE ASSETS, EXCLUDING OTHER INVESTMENTS										
Total transportation (1947 prices)	3,044,000	2,979,000	2,820,000	2,979,000	4,257,000[f]	5,991,000	6,289,000	6,356,000	7,350,000	7,503,000
Total transportation (book values)	2,768,642	2,848,481	2,701,641	3,006,020	4,686,537[g]	6,313,481	6,277,070	6,669,007	8,255,006	8,459,727
Aircraft[a]	1,229,781	1,244,455	1,334,437	1,549,144	2,907,070	4,456,668	4,560,652	4,722,944	6,156,950	6,685,053
Ship and boat[a]	577,073	594,317	404,416	429,106	575,404	650,220	747,902	730,764	810,514	677,533
Railroad	914,093	961,355	922,319	979,016	1,150,969	1,152,288	1,084,758	1,169,460	1,229,000	1,035,706
Motorcycles and bicycles	28,616[c]	32,541[c]	32,417	44,035	46,113	41,390	46,325	50,160[c]	53,431[c]	55,967
Miscellaneous transportation	8,120	7,430	7,693	5,082	8,009	10,478	4,197	10,409	7,703	6,830

(continued)

TABLE A-54 (concluded)

	1947	1948	1949	1950	1951*	1953*	1954	1955	1956	1957
RATE OF RETURN ON CORPORATE ASSETS (per cent)										
Total transportation (1947 prices)	–1.18	5.23	4.61	7.06	4.63[h]	4.67	5.96	6.16	5.56	5.96
Total transportation (book values)	–2.09	4.77	4.13	6.63	4.10[i]	4.71	6.62	6.56	5.62	6.08
Aircraft[a]	–9.88	4.05	4.69	8.51	3.54	4.91	7.51	7.62	5.88	6.15
Ship and boat[a]	1.96	4.72	1.06	3.32	4.37	2.77	3.58	4.34	4.25	5.88
Railroad	5.18	5.69	5.02	5.21	5.49	5.06	4.24	3.86	5.23	5.93
Motorcycles and bicycles	12.10	5.32	–3.92	4.62	1.08	4.36	2.00	3.28	4.70	3.73
Miscellaneous transportation[a]	6.76	5.15	–5.28	5.73	5.89	2.72	–12.22	3.99	4.66	–0.64

NOTES: [a] Data unreliable because of year-to-year differences in classification of large companies.

[c] Adjusted for variability of assets due to shifts of large companies between industries.

* 1952 minor industry data not available. Major industry data appear below:

[d] 1952 = 5,530,000.
[e] 1952 = 5,791,012.
[f] 1952 = 5,472,000.
[g] 1952 = 5,730,657.
[h] 1952 = 4.25 per cent.
[i] 1952 = 4.16 per cent.

TABLE A-55

MOTOR VEHICLES, 1947–57

(assets in thousands of dollars)

	1947	1948	1949	1950	1951*	1953*	1954	1955	1956	1957
TOTAL ASSETS, EXCLUDING OTHER INVESTMENTS										
Total vehicles (1947 prices)	7,083,000	7,455,000	8,051,000	9,815,000	9,815,000[d]	11,008,000	10,509,000	12,365,000	11,691,000	11,501,000
Total vehicles (book values)	6,192,890	7,039,485	7,690,641	9,904,812	10,526,674[e]	12,101,673	11,626,859	14,393,912	13,967,781	14,252,848
Vehicles, bodies, etc.	5,046,050	5,833,416	6,444,602	8,380,307	8,715,570	10,269,175	10,024,595	12,567,998	12,180,270	12,429,042
Parts and accessories	1,191,988	1,248,919	1,287,141	1,570,822	1,875,339	1,902,997	1,645,769	1,870,303	1,830,738	1,869,743
CORPORATE ASSETS, EXCLUDING OTHER INVESTMENTS										
Total vehicles (1947 prices)	6,988,000	7,360,000	7,955,000	9,700,000	9,703,000[f]	10,885,000	10,391,000	12,247,000	11,598,000	11,429,000
Total vehicles (book values)	6,109,480	6,949,976	7,598,743	9,789,215	10,406,803[g]	11,966,731	11,496,383	14,256,056	13,856,926	14,163,195
Vehicles, bodies, etc.	5,012,742	5,798,645	6,410,122	8,338,535	8,675,205	10,227,175	9,985,532	12,506,840	12,109,309	12,344,728
Parts and accessories	1,096,731	1,151,294	1,189,289	1,450,579	1,731,109	1,751,835	1,511,021	1,748,862	1,744,042	1,815,320
RATE OF RETURN ON CORPORATE ASSETS (per cent)										
Total vehicles (1947 prices)	11.68	13.80	15.20	16.05	9.56[h]	8.09	8.37	14.16	9.17	10.13
Total vehicles (book values)	12.05	13.98	15.66	16.08	9.09[i]	7.66	7.82	13.67	7.91	8.51
Vehicles, bodies, etc.	12.04	14.05	16.74	16.61	9.07	7.74	8.09	14.19	7.94	8.59
Parts and accessories	12.11	13.61	9.86	13.03	9.20	7.12	6.06	9.98	7.71	7.97

NOTES: * 1952 minor industry data not available. Major industry data appear below:

[d] 1952 = 10,657,000.

[e] 1952 = 11,545,550.

[f] 1952 = 10,537,000.

[g] 1952 = 11,415,429.

[h] 1952 = 8.35 per cent.

[i] 1952 = 8.00 per cent.

TABLE A-56

PROFESSIONAL AND SCIENTIFIC INSTRUMENTS, 1947–57
(assets in thousands of dollars)

	1947	1948	1949	1950	1951*	1953*	1954	1955	1956	1957
TOTAL ASSETS, EXCLUDING OTHER INVESTMENTS										
Total instruments (1947 prices)	1,386,000	1,378,000	1,458,000	1,865,000	2,089,000[d]	2,361,000	2,334,000	2,742,000	2,930,000	3,080,000
Total instruments (book values)	1,175,659	1,298,753	1,367,333	1,832,920	2,238,046[e]	2,680,311	2,633,488	3,143,860	3,540,505	3,757,153
Instruments	1,004,843	1,105,404	1,180,744	1,621,571	1,995,767	2,377,051	2,351,114	2,894,130	3,298,162	3,531,247
Clocks and watches	164,519	187,263	181,236	205,565	237,572	297,901	278,346	250,128	247,397	236,569
CORPORATE ASSETS, EXCLUDING OTHER INVESTMENTS										
Total instruments (1947 prices)	1,336,000	1,333,000	1,416,000	1,816,000	2,039,000[f]	2,313,000	2,290,000	2,687,000	2,867,000	3,010,000
Total instruments (book values)	1,132,911	1,256,600	1,328,022	1,784,606	2,184,213[g]	2,625,835	2,583,850	3,080,645	3,464,867	3,672,179
Instruments	971,599	1,072,609	1,149,552	1,582,060	1,951,090	2,331,342	2,308,749	2,834,048	3,220,673	3,438,678
Clocks and watches	161,426	184,064	178,438	202,589	234,353	294,280	275,094	247,086	244,270	233,466
RATE OF RETURN ON CORPORATE ASSETS (per cent)										
Total instruments (1947 prices)	9.06	9.79	7.66	8.83	8.00[h]	7.14	8.33	8.26	8.51	7.63
Total instruments (book values)	9.42	9.58	7.38	8.67	7.31[i]	6.44	7.76	7.73	7.42	6.53
Instruments	9.15	9.64	7.86	8.76	7.52	6.52	8.31	8.02	7.74	7.23
Clocks and watches	11.01	9.25	4.32	8.00	5.58	5.82	3.20	4.40	3.18	−3.75

NOTES: * 1952 minor industry data not available. Major industry data appear below:

[d] 1952 = 2,291,000.
[e] 1952 = 2,498,914.
[f] 1952 = 2,240,000.
[g] 1952 = 2,443,521.
[h] 1952 = 7.24 per cent.
[i] 1952 = 6.66 per cent.

TABLE A-57

RESIDUAL MANUFACTURES, 1947–57

(assets in thousands of dollars)

	1947	1948	1949	1950	1951*	1953*	1954	1955	1956	1957
TOTAL ASSETS, EXCLUDING OTHER INVESTMENTS										
Total residual (1947 prices)	3,205,000	3,035,000	2,933,000	3,015,000	3,054,000[d]	3,081,000	3,041,000	3,439,000	3,524,000	3,553,000
Total residual (book values)	2,852,134	2,829,882	2,751,495	2,987,788	3,256,300[e]	3,333,689	3,384,315	3,988,196	4,211,474	4,410,799
Jewelry except costume	306,859	285,062	279,113	300,704	326,336	324,774	309,249	329,988	354,914	353,358
Costume jewelry	27,188	29,064	38,885	62,681	58,961	79,891	82,001	85,835	93,342	92,740
Fabricated plastics	158,126	175,775	199,351	247,704	283,800	352,796	396,420	458,753	490,782	528,478
Manufacturing, n.e.c.	2,382,591	2,378,339	2,284,452	2,443,208	2,678,246	2,703,465	2,741,599	3,249,225	3,347,570	3,503,169
CORPORATE ASSETS, EXCLUDING OTHER INVESTMENTS										
Total residual (1947 prices)	2,893,000	2,766,000	2,698,000	2,788,000	2,840,000[f]	2,888,000	2,859,000	3,222,000	3,290,000	3,305,000
Total residual (book values)	2,574,713	2,579,068	2,530,692	2,763,220	3,027,713[g]	3,125,346	3,182,196	3,736,190	3,931,364	4,102,878
Jewelry except costume	278,405	259,607	255,225	275,156	298,848	297,208	282,500	299,390	319,826	316,283
Costume jewelry	23,382	24,942	33,348	53,457	50,036	66,915	68,067	72,157	79,481	80,001
Fabricated plastics	150,203	166,563	188,589	233,536	266,744	329,180	368,174	428,869	461,852	500,642
Manufacturing, n.e.c.	2,122,253	2,127,904	2,053,732	2,198,213	2,411,946	2,432,616	2,461,779	2,935,834	3,068,293	3,205,388
RATE OF RETURN ON CORPORATE ASSETS (per cent)										
Total residual (1947 prices)	8.05	7.88	5.91	9.07	7.11[h]	4.99	4.95	5.98	6.21	5.63
Total residual (book values)	7.90	7.53	5.36	8.69	6.32[i]	4.25	4.07	5.10	5.06	4.26
Jewelry except costume	11.07	9.16	4.90	7.82	5.18	3.60	3.55	4.10	3.63	3.09
Costume jewelry	3.78	4.19	2.92	4.82	2.99	2.18	2.25	−0.62	−1.11	1.02
Fabricated plastics	4.24	4.48	5.31	9.78	5.90	3.72	3.40	4.15	3.67	2.41
Manufacturing, n.e.c.	7.79	7.61	5.46	8.79	6.58	4.46	4.29	5.48	5.59	4.74

NOTES: * 1952 minor industry data not available. Major industry data appear below:

[d] 1952 = 2,998,000.
[e] 1952 = 3,240,236.
[f] 1952 = 2,799,000.
[g] 1952 = 3,025,358.
[h] 1952 = 5.73 per cent.
[i] 1952 = 4.93 per cent.

TABLE A-38

ORDNANCE, 1947–57

	1947	1948	1949	1950	1951	1952	1953	1954	1955	1956	1957
CORPORATE ASSETS, EXCLUDING OTHER INVESTMENTS (thousands of dollars)											
Total ordnance (1947 prices)	223,000	222,000	191,000	231,000	246,000	284,000	324,000	216,000	164,000	171,000	240,000
Total ordnance (book values)	197,878	211,673	181,047	220,644	258,276	303,146	350,658	240,855	189,886	196,095	284,902
RATE OF RETURN ON CORPORATE ASSETS (per cent)											
Total ordnance (1947 prices)	7.17	9.01	5.24	10.39	8.54	8.10	8.33	7.87	9.28	8.08	5.82
Total ordnance (book values)	7.47	8.94	5.12	10.89	8.00	7.82	7.92	6.89	8.50	7.40	4.97

NOTE: Noncorporate sector negligible. Ordnance industries excluded from analysis.

TABLE A-59

TOTAL MANUFACTURING, 1947–57
(assets in millions of dollars)

	1947	1948	1949	1950	1951	1952	1953	1954	1955	1956	1957
TOTAL ASSETS, EXCLUDING OTHER INVESTMENTS											
Total manufacturing (1947 prices)	126,498	131,118	132,060	142,056	151,878	157,327	160,345	161,229	171,445	175,710	175,999
Total manufacturing (book values)	106,580	116,106	118,088	135,142	153,948	162,853	169,695	173,111	190,670	203,107	209,892
CORPORATE ASSETS, EXCLUDING OTHER INVESTMENTS											
Total manufacturing (1947 prices)	121,302	126,061	127,241	137,023	146,883	152,162	155,103	155,974	165,961	170,200	170,777
Total manufacturing (book values)	102,143	111,619	113,731	130,314	148,856	157,472	164,062	167,426	184,519	196,690	203,620
RATE OF RETURN ON CORPORATE ASSETS (per cent)											
Total manufacturing (1947 prices)	9.85	10.05	7.92	9.99	7.78	6.46	6.54	6.26	7.97	7.71	7.40
Total manufacturing (book values)	10.38	10.43	7.93	9.97	7.34	5.96	6.05	5.68	7.47	6.85	6.29

APPENDIX B

Construction of the All-Manufactures Corporate Capital and Rate of Return Series for 1926–58

THE data on capital and rates of return in all manufacturing industries for the period from 1926 to 1958 are presented in Table B-1.

TABLE B-1

CORPORATE ASSETS, EXCLUDING OTHER INVESTMENTS, AND RATES OF RETURN, 1926–58

Year	*Corporate Assets* (millions of dollars)		*Rate of Return* (per cent)	
	Book Values	1947 Prices	Book Values	1947 Prices
1926	58,478	—	6.66	—
1927	58,604	—	5.75	—
1928	60,524	—	6.93	—
1929	63,720	—	7.36	—
1930	60,571	—	2.67	—
1931	56,160	—	−0.54	—
1932	49,563	—	−2.50	—
1933	48,651	—	1.17	—
1934	45,099	—	2.57	—
1935	44,796	—	4.12	—
1936	47,382	—	6.23	—
1937	48,046	—	6.22	—
1938	46,957	90,548	2.62	2.63
1939	49,035	92,582	6.00	5.77
1940	52,964	97,955	7.12	6.95
1941	63,395	109,198	8.56	8.36
1942	77,374	123,880	7.30	6.95
1943	86,461	130,445	7.30	6.80
1944	86,471	126,734	6.59	6.20
1945	81,677	116,002	5.43	5.26
1946	88,371	116,048	8.13	7.65
1947	101,951	120,809	10.34	9.84
1948	111,619	126,061	10.43	10.05
1949	113,731	127,241	7.93	7.92
1950	130,314	137,023	9.97	9.99
1951	148,856	146,883	7.34	7.78
1952	157,472	152,162	5.96	6.46
1953	164,062	155,103	6.05	6.54
1954	167,426	155,974	5.68	6.26
1955	184,519	165,961	7.47	7.97
1956	196,690	170,200	6.85	7.71
1957[a]	203,620	170,777	6.29	7.40
1957[b]	206,827	173,571	6.29	7.40
1958	212,909	171,784	4.92	6.26

[a] 1957 data on 1956 basis, employed in Chart 1.
[b] 1957 data on 1958 basis. See note d to Table E-1 for details.

The data for computing adjusted net profit after taxes and assets less investments in other companies were obtained primarily from *Statistics of Income, Corporation Income Tax Returns*, for 1926 to 1958. The basic method followed for 1926 to 1937 was the same as that employed for the later part of the period[1] (see Appendix A), but the less detailed reporting procedures of the Internal Revenue Service in the early years made necessary a series of estimates.

1. *Petroleum Refining Depletion*, 1926–37

To obtain a figure for depletion in the petroleum refining industry for 1937 and prior years, the 1938–39 average ratio of depletion in the petroleum refining (three-digit) industry to depletion in the chemicals and allied products(two-digit) industry was applied to the depletion figure given by IRS for the chemicals and allied products industry for 1926 to 1937; four-fifths of the resultant estimate of petroleum refining depletion was then excluded as a deduction from adjusted net income as in later years.

2. *Dividends Received from Foreign Corporations*, 1926–36

For 1929–36, dividends received from foreign corporations were estimated from the average of the 1937–38 ratios of foreign dividends received by manufacturing corporations to those received by all corporations. This average ratio was applied to the foreign dividends received, 1929–36, by all corporations (reported in the 1954 Supplement to *Survey of Current Business*, p. 214). The average ratios for 1929 and 1930 of this estimate of foreign dividends received by manufacturing corporations to total compiled receipts of manufacturing corporations was then applied to the IRS total compiled receipts figures for 1926–28 to obtain rough estimates of dividends received from foreign corporations in those years.

3. *Assets Less Other Investments*, 1926–30

Before 1931, IRS did not publish total compiled receipts figures for corporations submitting balance sheets, which would have enabled us to expand their assets figures to an "all returns" basis. Hence, the average ratio for 1931 and 1932 of total compiled receipts of all manufacturing corporations to receipts of corporations submitting balance sheets was used to adjust the assets data for 1926–30 to a basis roughly comparable to that of later years.

[1] The basic method was modified in only one minor respect: addition to adjusted net income of 5 per cent of dividends received, as an adjustment for the corporate tax on 15 per cent of dividends, was not employed before 1936, when the tax on the 15 per cent was introduced.

In addition, investments in other companies could not be segregated from miscellaneous assets (the latter including patents, good will, trade marks, etc.) before 1929. As we define assets to exclude investments in other companies, the average relationship for 1929 and 1930 was used to estimate the proportion of other investments in miscellaneous assets for 1926–28.

4. *Per Cent Change in Assets*, 1933–34

Although the asset series given in Table B-1 breaks in 1934, the IRS reports for 1933 and 1934 provide data enabling us to compute a 1933–34 per cent change in assets figure for manufacturing firms that did not file consolidated returns in 1933, and hence were not affected by the reclassification of firms that changed from consolidated to nonconsolidated reporting in 1934. The increase for this group, 0.5 per cent, is based on 1933 assets less other investments amounting to $22,760 million—slightly less than half the 1933 assets for all manufacturing corporations. From 1934 to 1941, consolidated returns were not permitted. Since 1942 consolidated returns have again been allowed, if 95 per cent of the stock of a subsidiary was owned (through 1953) or 80 per cent (since 1953).

APPENDIX C

The Concentration Ratios

THE concentration ratios for the various industries employed in the text are based upon concentration ratios calculated for finer industrial subdivisions. Before presenting the ratios calculated for the three-digit industries, therefore, a few notes on the problem of combining industries are presented.

1. *Combining Concentration Ratios*

PRODUCT RATIOS

If one defines a product very narrowly—for example, as soap with brand name X—the concentration ratio is always 100, because 100 per cent of the output is produced by the four largest firms (and for that matter, the one). The finest level of product classification so far calculated by the Bureau of the Census is the so-called five-digit level.[1] An example is the soap and glycerin product class, tabulated below.

Census Code	*Product*	*1954 Value of Shipments* ($000's)	*Concentration Ratio*
28411	Soaps, except specialty, packaged	309,401	76
28412	Soaps, except specialty, bulk	49,021	35
28413	Specialty soaps	42,949	52
28410	Soap and glycerin, not specified by kind	3,660	—
28414	Glycerin	75,810	71
2841	Soap and glycerin	480,841	63

Whether these five-digit classes are too narrow or too broad to catch the main forces of competition (good substitution from the viewpoint of buyers, or ability to shift among products from the viewpoint of producers) is in general an unanswered question. In our example, bulk and packaged soap do not seem sufficiently different to be noncompetitive, whereas soap and glycerin seem relatively uncompetitive from the viewpoint of buyers. The extent to which firms can shift their production from one product to another is unknown.

[1] All the relevant Census material is reprinted in *Concentration in American Industry*, report of the Subcommittee on Antitrust and Monopoly, 85th Cong., 1st sess., 1957.

The four-digit product class (soap and glycerin in our example) is the sum of a group of five-digit classes, but the concentration ratio for the product class bears no simple relationship to the five-digit ratios, as a rule. One can make definite statements only in extreme cases.

1. If no leading firm for a product produces other products in the product class, the class concentration ratio will be equal to the ratio for that product for which the four leading firms have the largest aggregate value of shipments, multiplied by the percentage of the product-class value constituted by the value of the product.[2]

   Example: Industry 2334, dresses, dozen price

Product	*Value of Shipments* ($000's)	*Concentration Ratio*
23341	296,789	14
23342	56,602	20
23340	14,340	—
2334	367,731	11

   If the leading firms of 23341 do not make the other products, their concentration ratio for the product class will be 296,789 to 367,731 times 14, or 11 per cent, which it is.
2. If the same four firms are leaders for each product, the product-class index is the weighted average of the product concentration ratios, the weights being the values of shipments of the products (see equation 5 at the end of this section).
3. As a result, if the weighted average of the product ratios is in excess of the product-class ratio, we may infer that the same four firms are not leaders on all product lines.[3]

   Example: Industry 2274, hard-surface floor coverings

Product	*1954 Value of Shipments* ($000's)	*Concentration Ratio*
22741	89,559	94
22742	70,120	79
2274	159,679	84

[2] The full condition is that the fourth largest firm manufacturing the product shall exceed in size any other firm making the other products in the product class.

[3] Actually, minor discrepancies arise, because the industry ratio takes account of miscellaneous receipts (e.g., from services) that are excluded from the calculation of the *S* ratios.

The weighted average is .561 × 94 + .439 × 79 = 87, so the four leaders of linoleum (22741) are not identical with the four leaders of asphalt felt base (22742).

INDUSTRY RATIOS

The Census industry class is the collection of plants whose primary product is in the given product class. The aggregate value of shipments of the hard-surface floor covering industry in 1954 was $181,582,000, or $21,903,000 more than the value of shipments of the product class. The excess arises because 15 per cent of the value of shipments of these plants was in other product lines, whereas only 3 per cent of the hard-surface floor covering product shipments were made by plants assigned to other industries.[4] The Census denotes the former of these ratios the primary product specialization ratio, and it is defined as

$$S = \frac{\text{Value of shipments of designated product classes}}{\text{Value of all shipments}},$$

in each case the shipments being from plants assigned to the industry. Normally, the Census requires that S be 75 per cent or higher. The second ratio is denoted the coverage ratio, and is defined as

$$C = \frac{\text{Value of shipments of product class by plants in industry}}{\text{Value of shipments of product class by all plants}}.$$

This ratio is also usually in excess of 75 per cent, but sometimes falls as low as 18 (lubricants, n.e.c., industry 2992).

An endless variety of relationships may hold between the industry concentration ratio (R_i) and the product concentration ratio (R_p), depending upon the particular structure of the four leading firms. The following are illustrative:

1. Obviously $R_i = R_p$ if $C = S = 1$.

2. If the leading firms make only the primary product,

$$\frac{R_i}{R_p} = \frac{S}{C}$$

(see equation (1) below)

Example: Industry 2284, hatters' fur

Here $R_i = 63$, $R_p = 66$, $S = 0.95$, $C = 1$.

$$\frac{63}{66} = 0.95.$$

[4] That is, 0.85 times $181,582 = $154,345, and 0.97 times $159,679 = $154,889. The difference is due to rounding.

3. If there are no leading producers outside the industry, and the leading firms within the industry produce the same share of secondary as of primary products (or secondary products are zero),

$$\frac{R_i}{R_p} = \frac{1}{C}$$

(see equations (2) and (3) below).

Approximate example: Industry 2443, cigar boxes

Here $R_i = 68,\ R_p = 65,\ S = 0.97,\ C = 0.94,$

$$\frac{R_i}{R_p} = \frac{68}{65} = 105; \quad \frac{1}{0.94} = 106.$$

In fact the R_p is generally smaller than R_i; in 1954 the comparative ratios were:[5]

	Number of Industries	
R_i exceeds R_p by:		
10 or more per cent	27	
5 to 9 per cent	77	
2 to 4 per cent	105	
1 per cent	65	
		274
R_i equals R_p		70
R_i is less than R_p by:		
1 per cent	26	
2 to 4 per cent	26	
5 to 9 per cent	7	
10 or more per cent	7	
		66

COMBINED INDUSTRY RATIOS

Since concentration ratios are reported at the four-digit level of industries, and we use three-digit industries in our analysis, we average the concentration ratios of the shipments at the four-digit level with value added as weights. This final step will lead to an overestimate of the correct concentration whenever the four-digit industries are highly competitive with one another,[6] but no correction can be made for this.

[5] *Concentration in American Industry*, Tables 35, 61, with correction of industry 2131.

[6] Unless the four largest firms are identical in the various competitive four-digit industries. A minimum estimate can be made of the concentration ratios in the fifty-eight three-digit industries which contain three or more four-digit industries. The minimum estimate is made by assuming that the four firms with the largest average size

Our characterization of industries as national, regional, or local is based on the National Resources Committee report, *The Structure of the American Economy*, Part I, Appendix 8.[7]

Algebraic Note on Concentration Ratios

Let V_0 be the value of output of the primary product by the four largest firms, W_0 be the value of output of the secondary products by the four largest firms, V be industry output of primary product, V^1 be total output of primary product inside and outside the industry, $V = CV^1$, where C is the coverage ratio, $W =$ industry output of secondary products, $\frac{V}{V+W} = S$ where S is the specialization ratio.

Then

$$R_i = \frac{V_0 + W_0}{V + W} = \text{industry concentration ratio,}$$

$$R_p = \frac{V_0}{V^1} = \frac{CV_0}{V} = \text{product concentration ratio,}$$

$$\frac{R_i}{R_p} = \frac{V_0 + W_0}{V + W} \cdot \frac{V}{CV_0}.$$

(1) Let $W_0 = 0$, then

$$\frac{R_i}{R_p} = \frac{V_0}{V + W} \cdot \frac{V}{CV_0} = \frac{V}{(V + W)C} = \frac{S}{C}.$$

(1.1) Let also $W = 0$

$$\frac{R_i}{R_p} = \frac{1}{C}.$$

(2) Let $W_0 = W$

$$\frac{R_i}{R_p} = \frac{V_0 + W_0}{V + W_0} \cdot \frac{V}{CV_0} = \frac{V + W_0}{CV_0} \cdot S = \frac{S}{C}\left(1 + \frac{W_0}{V_0}\right).$$

(3) Let the leaders have the same share of W, i.e.,

$$\frac{V_0}{V} = \frac{W_0}{W}$$

$$\frac{R_i}{R_p} = \frac{V_0 + W_0}{V + W} \cdot \frac{V}{CV_0} = \frac{V_0}{V} \cdot \frac{V}{CV_0} = \frac{1}{C}.$$

(the firms whose concentration ratio times the industry value added is the greatest of any four-digit industries) have no products in other four-digit industries. The rank correlation between the weighted average and the minimum estimates was .84 in 1954, which suggests that the ranking for all industries would be very close on the two bases.

[7] The following changes and additions were made: periodicals, national: breweries, wines, logging camps, petroleum refining, blast furnaces, regional.

(4) If $C = 1$, or we ignore output of the products outside the industry, and $W_0 = 0$,

$$R_i = \frac{V_0}{V + W} = \frac{V_0}{V} \cdot \frac{V}{V + W} = Sr_i,$$

where r_i is the concentration ratio in the primary product, provided each of the four largest producers of V exceed the largest firm producing W.

(5) If $C = 1$, or we ignore outputs of the products outside the industry, and the leading firms in V are the leading firms in W, with $r_i = \frac{V_0}{V}$, $r_j = \frac{W_0}{W}$, then

$$\begin{aligned} R_i &= \frac{V_0 + W_0}{V + W} \\ &= \frac{V_0}{V} \cdot \frac{V}{V + W} + \frac{W_0}{W} \cdot \frac{W}{V + W} \\ &= Sr_i + (1 - S)\, r_j. \end{aligned}$$

2. *The Industry Concentration Ratios*

The weighted average concentration ratios for 1935, 1947, and 1954 are presented in Table C-1 and C-2. The classification of industries, by degree of concentration, is based on the unweighted average of the ratios in 1935 and 1947 for the 1938–47 analyses, and the unweighted average of the ratios in 1947 and 1954 for the 1947–56 analyses. The criteria are: unconcentrated industries, national markets, ratios below 50 per cent; regional markets, ratios below 20 per cent; concentrated industries, national markets, ratios above 60 per cent. All other industries (including those with very different concentration ratios in the two years) are called ambiguous, and are not labeled in the tables.

TABLE C-1

CONCENTRATION RATIOS FOR MANUFACTURING INDUSTRIES, 1935 AND 1947

Industry (three-digit)	*Per Cent of Shipments Contributed by Four Largest Firms* 1935	1947	*Average*	*Classi-fication*
Bakery products	18.2	27.1	22.6	
Confectionary	38.8	32.4	35.6	U
Canning, preserving	23.1	28.9	26.0	U
Meats	52.5	38.6	45.6	U
Grain-mill products	27.8	24.9	26.4	U
Cereal preparations	68.1	74.9	71.5	C
Dairy products	29.8	38.8	34.3	
Sugar	66.0	66.5	66.2	C
Miscellaneous foods	44.0	43.5	43.8	
Brewery products	13.4	23.1	18.2	
Distilled liquors	47.3	74.6	61.0	
Wines, brandy	29.4	26.4	27.9	
Nonalcoholic beverages	8.7	10.4	9.6	
Tobacco manufactures	74.6	76.4	75.5	C
Cotton, broad woven	8.4	14.9	11.6	U
Wool, broad woven	24.2	28.6	26.4	U
Silk and synthetic fabrics	16.5	30.2	23.4	U
Knit goods	5.3	15.8	10.6	U
Hats	23.7	52.9	38.3	U
Floor coverings, woven	60.5	56.4	58.4	
Dyeing and finishing, except wool	13.9	13.7	13.8	U
Miscellaneous textiles	33.5	38.8	36.2	
Men's clothing	6.3	13.9	10.1	U
Women's clothing	1.4	7.4	4.4	U
Fur goods	2.6	2.6	2.6	
Millinery	1.4	7.0	4.2	U
Miscellaneous apparel, accessories	20.7	25.5	23.1	
Leather tanning, finishing	22.5	26.5	24.5	U
Leather footwear	26.6	28.0	27.3	U
Miscellaneous leather goods	18.1	18.5	18.3	U
Logging	4.7	7.8	6.2	U
Sawmills, planing mills	4.6	10.6	7.6	U
Wooden containers	17.9	31.3	24.6	
Furniture	8.7	20.0	14.4	U
Partitions and fixtures	5.6	20.0	12.8	U
Miscellaneous furniture, fixtures	30.4	26.1	28.2	
Pulp, paper, and products	17.6	19.1	18.4	U
Miscellaneous paper goods	20.3	23.4	21.8	U
Newspapers	20.3	20.9	20.6	
Periodicals	20.3	34.3	27.3	U
Books	5.7	20.9	13.3	U
Commercial printing	6.5	10.0	8.2	
Miscellaneous printing	16.7	22.8	19.8	
Industrial chemicals	44.4	53.3	48.8	U
Paints and varnishes	32.3	33.5	32.9	U
Soaps, detergents	73.5	79.0	76.2	C
Drugs, toilet preparations	24.3	37.0	30.6	U
Oils	46.2	47.4	46.8	U
Fertilizers	25.9	30.1	28.0	

(continued)

TABLE C-1 (concluded)

Industry (three-digit)	*Per Cent of Shipments Contributed by Four Largest Firms* 1935	1947	*Average*	*Classi-fication*
Rayon	74.3	78.4	76.4	C
Plastics	N.A.	59.0	59.0	
Miscellaneous chemicals	30.6	27.5	29.0	
Petroleum refining	38.2	37.3	37.8	
Miscellaneous petroleum and coal products	46.9	48.3	47.6	
Tires and tubes	80.9	76.6	78.8	C
Miscellaneous rubber goods	29.6	40.2	34.9	
Pottery and porcelain	19.7	43.3	31.5	U
Concrete products	32.0	30.8	31.4	
Cut stone products	9.5	8.3	8.9	U
Structural clay	19.3	27.7	23.5	
Glass and products	45.8	61.0	53.4	
Cement	29.9	29.5	29.7	
Miscellaneous stone products	49.8	50.7	50.2	
Blast furnaces, rolling mills	50.5	47.5	49.0	
Structural steel	26.3	23.7	25.0	
Tin cans	80.8	77.8	79.3	C
Hand tools, cutlery	37.1	32.0	34.6	U
Heating apparatus	37.9	18.5	28.2	
Miscellaneous iron and steel goods	25.7	24.7	25.2	U
Nonferrous basic metals	N.A.	64.4	64.4	C
Miscellaneous nonferrous metals	40.6	30.7	35.6	
Electric generating, transmission machinery	N.A.	51.9	51.9	
Automotive electric equipment	N.A.	66.0	66.0	C
Communications equipment	N.A.	52.2	52.2	
Electric appliances	N.A.	42.8	42.8	U
Miscellaneous electric goods	N.A.	72.4	72.4	C
Engines and turbines	30.7	49.5	40.1	U
Agricultural machinery	72.4	49.8	61.1	
Special industry machinery	11.0	21.3	16.2	U
General industry machinery	12.1	34.9	23.5	U
Metalworking machinery	16.2	15.1	15.6	U
Construction and mining machinery	18.2	22.1	20.2	U
Office and store machines	31.2	63.4	47.3	
Household and service industry machines	48.4	42.7	45.6	U
Miscellaneous machinery	7.1	19.8	13.4	
Motor vehicles and equipment	N.A.	72.1	72.1	C
Parts and accessories	N.A.	28.3	28.3	U
Railroad equipment	73.8	67.8	70.8	C
Aircraft and parts	53.9	57.7	55.8	
Ship and boat building	44.8	41.1	43.0	U
Motor cycles and bicycles	60.6	42.3	51.4	
Miscellaneous transportation equipment	45.8	37.2	41.5	
Clocks, watches, and parts	39.9	40.7	40.3	U
Jewelry, except costume	34.2	35.2	34.7	U
Matches	70.3	82.7	76.5	C
Miscellaneous manufactures	N.A.	35.1	35.1	

NOTE: Classification is: C or concentrated, if four largest firms ship over 60 per cent of the product in the national market; U or unconcentrated, if under 50 per cent in the national market, or under 20 per cent in a regional market; ambiguous (not labeled), if outside both categories.

TABLE C-2

CONCENTRATION RATIOS FOR MANUFACTURING INDUSTRIES, 1947 AND 1954

Industry (three-digit)	*Per Cent of Shipments Contributed by Four Largest Firms* 1947	1954	*Average*	*Classi-fication*
Nonalcoholic beverages	10.4	10.0	10.2	
Brewery products	23.1	27.9	25.5	
Wines, brandy	26.4	38.0	32.2	
Distilled liquors	74.6	64.0	69.3	C
Meats	38.6	32.7	35.6	U
Dairy products	38.8	37.6	38.2	
Canning, preserving	28.9	32.3	30.6	U
Grain-mill products	24.9	32.7	28.8	U
Bakery products	27.1	30.5	28.8	
Sugar	66.5	65.0	65.8	C
Confectionery	32.4	36.4	34.4	U
Cereal preparations	74.9	88.0	81.4	C
Miscellaneous foods	43.5	43.6	43.6	
Cigars	40.6	44.0	42.3	U
Other tobacco manufactures	86.7	79.4	83.0	C
Yarn and thread	25.2	33.0	29.1	U
Wool, broad woven	28.1	27.0	27.6	U
Cotton, broad woven	13.1	18.0	15.6	U
Cotton, narrow fabrics	17.0	13.0	15.0	U
Knit goods	15.8	17.3	16.6	U
Dyeing and finishing	15.0	24.9	20.0	U
Carpets, yarn	56.4	55.7	56.0	
Hats	52.9	54.2	53.6	
Miscellaneous textiles	33.7	32.6	33.2	U
Men's clothing	13.9	14.3	14.1	U
Women's clothing	7.4	9.0	8.2	U
Millinery	7.0	7.0	7.0	U
Fur goods	2.6	4.0	3.3	
Miscellaneous apparel	25.5	23.4	24.4	
Wooden containers	31.3	24.7	28.0	
Miscellaneous lumber	9.9	10.3	10.1	U
Furniture, wood and metal	20.0	19.5	19.8	U
Partitions and fixtures	20.0	18.0	19.0	U
Miscellaneous furniture	33.3	33.2	33.2	U
Pulp, paper, and products	19.1	23.8	21.4	U
Miscellaneous paper goods	23.4	25.9	24.6	U
Newspapers	20.9	18.0	19.4	
Periodicals	34.3	29.0	31.6	U
Books	20.5	21.0	20.8	U
Commercial printing	10.0	9.4	9.7	
Miscellaneous printing	22.7	22.9	22.8	
Drugs and medicines	35.0	30.5	32.8	U
Soaps, detergents	65.1	65.1	65.1	C
Paints and varnishes	33.5	36.4	35.0	U
Perfumes	23.8	25.0	24.4	U
Fertilizers	30.1	30.9	30.5	
Oils	43.2	43.8	43.5	U
Industrial and miscellaneous chemicals	54.4	55.1	54.8	
Petroleum refining	37.3	33.0	35.2	
Miscellaneous petroleum and coal products	46.6	46.9	46.8	
Tires and tubes	76.6	79.0	77.8	C
Miscellaneous rubber goods	40.2	33.4	36.8	
Leather tanning, finishing	26.5	18.0	22.2	U

(continued)

TABLE C-2 (concluded)

Industry (three-digit)	*Per Cent of Shipments Contributed by Four Largest Firms* 1947	1954	*Average*	*Classification*
Leather footwear	27.8	29.5	28.6	U
Miscellaneous leather goods	21.3	24.3	22.8	U
Glass and products	61.0	68.9	65.0	C
Cement	29.5	31.0	30.2	
Structural clay products	27.7	28.8	28.2	
Pottery and porcelain	43.3	46.0	44.6	U
Concrete	30.8	37.0	33.9	
Cut stone	8.3	12.0	10.2	U
Miscellaneous stone products	50.7	48.4	49.6	
Blast furnaces	48.4	56.0	52.2	
Iron and steel foundries	19.8	27.1	23.4	U
Smelting, nonferrous metals	69.2	72.2	70.7	C
Nonferrous foundries	25.7	22.0	23.8	U
Miscellaneous primary metals	36.4	34.2	35.3	
Tin cans	77.8	80.0	78.9	C
Hand tools	32.0	38.5	35.2	U
Heating apparatus	16.8	19.7	18.2	U
Fabricated structural metal goods	21.4	20.9	21.2	
Metal stamping	18.8	14.6	16.7	U
Lighting fixtures	18.1	20.0	19.0	U
Fabricated wire	21.3	18.6	20.0	U
Miscellaneous fabricated metals	29.4	26.2	27.8	U
Engines and turbines	49.5	65.3	57.4	
Agricultural machinery	49.8	55.2	52.5	
Construction and mining machinery	22.1	24.7	23.4	U
Metalworking machinery	15.1	17.0	16.0	U
Special industry machinery	21.3	24.6	23.0	U
General industry machinery	39.7	35.7	37.7	U
Office and store machines	62.6	64.8	63.7	C
Household and service industry machines	44.6	44.8	44.7	U
Miscellaneous machinery	17.8	13.6	15.7	
Electric generating, transmission machinery	52.9	49.5	51.2	
Electric appliances	35.8	50.0	42.9	U
Insulated wire and cable	40.7	48.0	44.4	U
Automotive electric equipment	66.0	62.0	64.0	C
Electric lamps	91.8	93.0	92.4	C
Communications equipment	52.2	41.3	46.8	U
Miscellaneous electric goods	63.0	59.5	61.2	C
Aircraft and parts	57.7	45.2	51.4	
Ship and boat building	41.1	40.6	40.8	U
Railroad equipment	67.8	76.6	72.2	C
Motorcycles and bicycles	42.3	50.0	46.2	U
Miscellaneous transportation equipment	37.2	38.0	37.6	
Motor vehicles, bodies	72.1	88.1	80.1	C
Parts and accessories	28.3	33.3	30.8	U
Scientific instruments	46.3	47.8	47.0	U
Clocks and watches	40.7	43.6	42.2	U
Jewelry, except costume	35.2	35.2	35.2	U
Costume jewelry	23.8	14.0	18.9	U
Fabricated plastics	22.2	8.0	15.1	U
Manufacturing, n.e.c.	30.3	28.6	29.4	

NOTE: Classification is: C or concentrated, if four largest firms ship over 60 per cent of the product in the national market; U or unconcentrated, if under 50 per cent in the national market, or under 20 per cent in a regional market; ambiguous (not labeled), if outside both categories.

APPENDIX D

The Employee and Annual Earnings Data

TABLES D-1 and D-2 are based on 4-digit data for numbers of employees and annual wage and salary payments, from *Census of Manufactures for 1939, 1947,*[1] and *1954*, which have been combined to correspond to three-digit Internal Revenue Service industry definitions; average annual earnings are simply ratios of wage and salary payments to numbers of employees for the resultant three-digit industries. However, discrepancies between Census and IRS industry coverage which are the result of the Census establishment-basis industry classification, in contrast to IRS classification at the company level, cannot be readily eliminated; hence the ratio of IRS total compiled receipts (including an estimate for the noncorporate sector) to Census value of products shipped was taken as a measure of this discrepancy, and only those industries for which this ratio fell between 2 to 3 and 3 to 2 are included in the labor and capital analysis[2] (Chapter 5) and in Tables D-1 and D-2.

In addition, the IRS-Census receipts ratios discussed above were used to adjust the capital per worker (i.e., ratios of IRS total assets to Census employees) data employed in Chapter 5.

TABLE D-1

EMPLOYMENT AND EARNINGS IN MANUFACTURING INDUSTRIES, 1939 AND 1947

	Employees			*Average Annual Earnings*		
	1939 (thousands)	1947 (thousands)	Per Cent Change 1939–47	1939	1947	Per Cent Change 1939–47
Bakery products	283.5	279.4	−1.46	$1,315	$2,739	108.29
Confectionery	73.6	91.7	24.55	1,108	2,340	111.19
Canning and preserving	151.4	201.6	33.16	779	2,076	166.50
Grain-mill products	64.5	101.9	58.10	1,329	2,757	107.45
Dairy products	86.4	92.7	7.25	1,273	2,431	90.97
Sugar	34.4	35.4	2.84	1,206	2,577	113.68
Nonalcoholic beverages	55.0	79.4	44.37	1,397	2,447	75.16
Cotton fabrics	428.8	479.3	11.79	773	2,104	172.19
Woolen and worsted fabrics	160.9	180.1	11.90	1,073	2,538	136.53
Silk and synthetic fabrics	127.0	127.0	a	858	2,312	a
Knit goods	256.1	230.5	−9.99	966	2,137	121.22

(continued)

[1] 1947 Census data have been combined alternately to fit IRS industry definitions for 1939 (Table D-1) and 1954 (Table D-2).

[2] To facilitate year-to-year comparisons, the analysis in Chapter 5 is usually limited to those industries in Table D-1 for which the receipts ratio in 1947 was within 25 per cent of that for 1939 and those industries in Table D-2 for which the 1954 receipts ratio was within 25 per cent of the 1947 ratio (i.e., those for which percentage changes are shown in the tables).

TABLE D-1 (concluded)

	Employees			*Average Annual Earnings*		
	1939 (thousands)	1947	Per Cent Change 1939–47	1939	1947	Per Cent Change 1939–47
Hats	26.7	21.4	a	1,175	2,574	a
Dyeing and finishing	b	78.0	a	b	2,807	a
Men's clothing	348.0	403.8	16.04	911	2,133	134.14
Women's clothing	331.3	456.1	37.68	1,074	2,511	133.80
Millinery	29.3	20.9	−28.60	1,254	2,847	127.03
Leather tanning and finishing	51.6	53.2	3.13	1,343	2,942	119.06
Footwear, except rubber	257.8	262.4	1.77	953	2,152	125.81
Logging camps	311.7	397.3	27.44	899	1,973	119.47
Sawmills and planing mills	86.8	118.0	a	1,156	2,518	a
Wooden containers	49.7	53.8	8.15	857	2,017	135.35
Furniture	192.3	268.0	39.39	1,133	2,497	120.39
Partitions, fixtures	17.8	27.7	a	1,460	3,202	a
Pulp, paper, and products	b	198.4	a	b	3,071	a
Newspapers	207.4	234.4	12.99	1,843	3,174	72.22
Periodicals	52.6	68.8	30.85	1,962	3,422	74.41
Books	34.4	62.9	a	1,792	2,833	a
Commercial printing	182.6	245.7	a	1,657	3,219	a
Paints and varnishes	46.2	67.8	46.86	1,812	3,316	83.00
Industrial chemicals	118.2	201.1	70.13	1,690	3,201	89.41
Soaps	b	27.7	a	b	3,385	a
Drugs and toilet preparations	57.4	112.4	95.76	1,537	2,811	82.89
Oils	26.6	30.8	15.90	993	2,525	154.28
Plastics	10.1	b	a	1,678	b	a
Fertilizers	24.1	31.9	32.61	973	2,242	130.42
Tires and tubes	67.2	b	a	1,819	b	a
Pottery, porcelain	37.1	58.0	56.37	1,265	2,534	100.32
Concrete products	35.2	70.2	99.11	1,261	2,416	91.59
Structural clay products	64.0	69.3	8.25	1,085	2,442	125.07
Glass and products	91.5	138.9	a	1,370	2,671	a
Cement	24.0	35.7	48.80	1,510	2,766	83.18
Structural steel	55.2	100.8	a	1,566	3,127	a
Tin cans	38.0	46.9	23.35	1,311	2,716	107.17
Hand tools, hardware	89.5	153.1	a	1,344	2,807	a
Heating apparatus	149.6	280.1	87.26	1,420	2,967	108.94
Electric generating, transmission machinery	146.9	339.5	131.14	1,621	2,918	80.01
Automotive electric equipment	21.0	49.0	133.59	1,552	2,864	84.54
Agricultural machinery	74.2	171.4	131.17	$1,532	$2,885	88.31
Special industry machinery	105.2	216.0	105.31	1,638	3,175	93.83
General industry machinery	187.1	307.3	64.22	1,602	3,025	88.83
Construction and mining machinery	46.9	113.9	a	1,663	3,121	a
Railroad equipment	b	91.1	a	b	3,112	a
Clocks and watches	24.4	40.2	a	1,305	2,745	a
Jewelry, except costume	33.5	54.8	63.67	1,452	3,054	110.33

NOTE: Industries shown are those for which IRS-Census receipts ratios fall between 2 to 3 and 3 to 2 in either 1939, 1947, or both.

[a] Percentage changes are shown only for those industries (37) for which IRS-Census receipts ratios fall between 2 to 3 and 3 to 2 in *both* 1939 and 1947, and for which 1939 and 1947 ratios differ by no more than 25 per cent.

[b] Data for employees and average annual earnings are not shown where IRS-Census receipts ratio falls outside the 2 to 3–3 to 2 range, or where data are not available for calculation of this ratio.

TABLE D-2

EMPLOYMENT AND EARNINGS IN MANUFACTURING INDUSTRIES, 1947 AND 1954

	Employees			*Average Annual Earnings*		
	1947 (thousands)	1954 (thousands)	Per Cent Change 1947–54	1947	1954	Per Cent Change 1947–54
Nonalcoholic beverages	79.4	91.6	15.39	$2,447	$3,492	42.71
Brewery products	85.1	83.9	−1.30	3,550	5,184	46.03
Meat products	274.4	311.4	13.45	2,849	3,965	39.17
Dairy products	92.7	a	b	2,431	a	b
Canning and preserving	201.6	199.2	−1.19	2,076	2,876	38.54
Grain-mill products	101.9	98.4	−3.46	2,757	3,901	41.49
Bakery products	279.4	291.1	4.20	2,739	3,863	41.04
Sugar	35.4	30.2	−14.84	2,577	3,906	51.57
Confectionery	91.7	80.4	−12.31	2,340	3,171	35.51
Cereal preparations	11.3	11.5	2.29	2,722	4,422	62.45
Cigars	47.1	38.5	−18.22	1,622	2,319	42.97
Other tobacco products	64.7	56.4	−12.90	2,001	3,024	51.12
Yarn and thread	a	135.9	b	a	2,529	b
Broad-woven woolens	a	62.5	b	a	3,430	b
Broad-woven cotton, synthetics	357.4	296.2	−17.12	2,139	2,644	23.61
Narrow fabrics	27.7	25.7	−7.18	2,309	3,079	33.35
Knit goods	230.5	a	b	2,137	a	b
Dyeing and finishing textiles	83.8	a	b	2,807	a	b
Carpets, yarn	57.2	a	b	2,760	a	b
Hats	21.4	13.0	−39.39	2,574	3,149	22.34
Men's clothing	403.8	407.3	0.86	2,133	2,507	17.53
Women's clothing	456.1	553.7	21.39	2,511	2,758	9.84
Millinery	20.9	20.2	−3.15	2,847	3,252	14.23
Wooden containers	53.8	39.7	−26.12	2,017	2,628	30.29
Partitions, fixtures	27.7	33.1	19.72	3,202	4,301	34.32
Pulp, paper, and products	198.4	216.3	9.02	3,071	4,508	46.79
Newspapers	a	281.8	b	a	4,481	b
Periodicals	a	62.4	b	a	5,009	b
Books	a	57.4	b	a	4,272	b
Commercial printing	a	278.0	b	a	4,552	b
Drugs	81.8	92.1	12.54	2,896	4,632	59.94
Soaps	45.0	46.2	2.80	3,331	4,747	42.51
Paints	67.8	70.0	3.19	3,316	4,630	39.63
Toilet preparations	26.0	24.8	−4.67	2,520	3,818	51.51
Fertilizers	31.9	31.8	−0.52	2,242	3,511	56.60
Oils	43.4	40.0	−7.98	2,701	3,821	41.47
Industrial and miscellaneous chemicals	336.4	434.6	29.19	3,105	4,782	54.01
Leather tanning and finishing	53.2	43.5	−18.30	2,942	3,868	31.48
Footwear except rubber	240.3	230.3	−4.19	2,151	2,690	25.06
Glass and products	138.9	137.5	b	2,671	4,179	b
Cement	35.7	39.8	11.52	2,766	4,216	52.42
Structural clay products	69.3	72.8	5.11	2,442	3,669	50.25
Pottery	58.0	50.9	−12.19	2,534	3,408	34.49
Concrete products	70.2	89.6	27.69	2,416	3,797	57.16
Cut stone products	a	21.6	b	a	3,626	b
Iron and steel foundries	267.3	212.4	−20.55	2,968	4,218	42.12
Smelting nonferrous metals	150.0	159.4	b	2,984	4,560	b

(continued)

TABLE D-2 (concluded)

	Employees			*Average Annual Earnings*		
	1947 (thousands)	1954	Per Cent Change 1947–54	1947	1954	Per Cent Change 1947–54
Nonferrous foundries	65.3	73.5	12.47	$3,045	$4,462	46.54
Tin cans	46.9	55.2	17.77	2,716	4,438	63.40
Hand tools, hardware	153.1	143.7	−6.72	2,807	4,176	48.77
Heating apparatus, except electric	150.9	a	b	2,910	a	b
Fabricated structural metals	212.4	284.1	33.78	3,113	4,508	44.81
Metal stamping	183.0	183.8	0.47	2,849	4,229	48.44
Lighting fixtures	a	45.1	b	a	4,036	b
Fabricated wire products	60.6	62.6	3.27	2,824	4,061	43.80
Agricultural machinery	171.4	139.1	−18.85	2,885	4,328	50.02
Construction and mining machinery	113.9	109.4	−3.94	3,121	4,658	49.25
Metalworking machinery	214.5	262.7	22.46	3,397	5,317	56.52
Special industry machinery	216.0	165.7	−23.26	3,175	4,552	43.37
General industrial machinery	235.2	245.7	4.45	3,115	4,597	47.58
Office and store machines	97.8	a	b	3,100	a	b
Electric generating machinery	321.4	340.0	5.80	2,928	4,394	50.07
Electric appliances	44.4	48.6	9.49	2,816	4,154	47.51
Insulated wire	21.3	a	b	2,727	a	b
Automotive electric equipment	43.9	46.3	5.53	2,855	4,321	51.35
Communications equipment	303.4	a	b	2,793	a	b
Railroad equipment	91.1	51.6	b	3,112	4,722	b
Motorcycles and bicycles	a	7.1	b	a	3,974	b
Scientific instruments	a	243.1	b	a	4,448	b
Clocks and watches	40.2	29.5	b	2,745	4,040	b
Jewelry except costume	54.8	47.9	−12.58	3,054	3,814	24.89
Costume jewelry	a	27.7	b	a	2,848	b
Fabricated plastics	a	92.0	b	a	3,000	b

NOTE: Industries shown are those for which IRS-Census receipts ratios fall between 2 to 3 and 3 to 2 in either 1947, 1954, or both.

[a] Data for employees and average annual earnings not shown where IRS-Census receipts ratios fall outside the 2 to 3–3 to 2 range, or where data not available for calculation of this ratio.

[b] Percentage changes shown only for those industries (49) for which IRS-Census receipts ratios fall between 2 to 3 and 3 to 2 in *both* 1947 and 1954, and for which 1947 and 1954 ratios differ by no more than 25 per cent.

APPENDIX E

Capital and Rates of Return in 1957 and 1958, on the New Industrial Classification

ALTHOUGH the 1958 data became available too late to be included in our study, others may wish to continue the basic series. Unfortunately, the extensive revision of the industrial classification introduced in *Statistics of Income* in 1958 was not accompanied by transition tables of the type available to link 1947 and 1948, so an intricate and indirect procedure is necessary to preserve continuity of even 62 three-digit 1957 industries.[1]

The general procedure for constructing 1957 asset data comparable to 1958 is as follows:

1. The *Census of Manufactures* for 1958 provides a classification of value added, by industries, on the old (1954) and new industry (1958) classes (Appendix C).
2. The old-basis four-digit value-added data were first converted to *corporate* value added, by using the 1958 ratios of corporate to total value added (new basis), to estimate corporate value added of each component industry of the 1957 (three-digit) industry classes. In some cases (roughly 30 four-digit industries), lack of information compelled use of earlier noncorporate ratios.
3. The estimated old-basis corporate value added was then summed, and compared with new-basis corporate value-added information available in Final Report MC58(1)–3 of *Census of Manufactures, 1958.*
4. The ratios of these new-basis value-added figures to old-basis figures were in turn used to convert the 1957 corporate assets to the new industry basis.
5. Rates of return for 1957, new basis, are weighted averages of the rates of return of the constituent old-basis industries, the weights being corporate assets contributed to the new-basis industry.

The concepts and procedures for 1957 and 1958 are those described in Appendix A.

This sketch of the procedure does not begin to convey a notion of the variety of problems encountered, and expedients adopted. The main departures are as follows:

1. Where 20 per cent or more of a 1957-basis industry or a 1958-basis industry was reclassified elsewhere on the alternative basis, the value-added data seem too weak a bridge to carry the load. Combinations of three-digit industries were made where possible (13 combinations involving 30 industries) in the belief that a smaller number of reliable links was preferable to a larger number of unreliable links.
2. In 29 additional industries, combinations were not feasible and no reliable comparison was possible. The total number of linked three-digit industries therefore falls to 62, slightly over half the original

[1] This appendix was prepared by Claire Friedland.

number (108). Except for the ordnance industry, which has been combined with fabricated metals, two-digit industries were preserved.

3. The noncorporate value-added ratios for 1958 are taken directly from the 1958 census. The value-added ratios could not be converted into an asset ratio by value-added/assets in corporations with less than $250,000, as in previous years, because the $100,000 to $250,000 assets class has been eliminated in *Statistics of Income.* The receipts and assets in each three-digit $100,000 to $250,000 class were therefore estimated from the corresponding two-digit information, which is still reported.

TABLE E-1

CORPORATE ASSETS, RATES OF RETURN, AND NONCORPORATE SHARES, 1957 AND 1958, BY 1958 STANDARD INDUSTRIAL CLASSIFICATION

Industry	*Corporate Assets Excluding Other Investments (millions of dollars)* 1957	1958	*Ratio of Non-corporate to Corporate Assets* 1958	*Rate of Return on Corporate Assets (per cent)* 1957	1958
Total beverages (1947 prices)	3,498	3,434.6	—	6.84	7.01
Total beverages (book values)	4,247	4,593.3	.0042	5.69	5.31
Bottled soft drinks	a	1,185.5	.1001	a	6.63
Malt	1,621	1,578.9	.0013	5.47	5.54
Wine and distilled liquors (total)	1,468	1,828.9	.0010	5.03	4.25
Wine	b	185.1	.0911	b	4.26
Distilled liquors	b	1,643.8	.0005	b	4.25
Total food and kindred products (1947 prices)	12,510	12,538.9	—	6.29	7.12
Total food and kindred products (book values)	14,933	15,628.9	.0928	5.13	5.71
Meat	2,319	2,464.2	.1032	2.95	2.91
Dairy	a	2,797.1	.1975	a	5.53
Canning	2,339	2,563.2	.0768	3.95	5.72
Grain mill and cereal	2,190	2,366.1	.0765	6.43	6.76
Bakery	1,379	1,443.5	.0636	7.12	6.60
Sugar	988	1,025.2	.0031	5.60	4.31
Confectionery	709	731.4	.0494	8.15	7.75
Vegetable oil mills	a	703.5	.0602	a	4.11
Miscellaneous foods	a	1,534.7	.0468	a	8.61
Total tobacco (1947 prices)	2,323	2,064.4	—	8.37	10.53
Total tobacco (book values)	3,016	3,066.8	.0040	8.01	9.04
Total textile mill products (1947 prices)	6,879	6,513.0	—	4.69	4.58

(continued)

TABLE E-1 (continued)

Industry	*Corporate Assets Exluding Other Investments (millions of dollars)* 1957	1958	*Ratio of Non-corporate to Corporate Assets* 1958	*Rate of Return on Corporate Assets (per cent)* 1957	1958
Total textile mill products (book values)	8,110	7,875.7	.0203	3.42	3.37
Yarn and thread	1,260	1,335.6	.0054	3.35	2.92
Broad cotton	1,985	1,809.0	.0020	4.10	3.48
Broad wool	584	500.6	.0228	1.75	2.34
Narrow woven	176	181.1	.0311	4.22	4.78
Knit goods	968	1,052.9	.0656	3.29	3.66
Dyeing and finishing	324	314.2	.0196	−0.62	1.28
Floor coverings	[a]	457.5	.0169	[a]	4.60
Broad synthetic and miscellaneous (total)	2,414	2,224.8	.0233	4.00	3.56
Broad synthetic	[b]	674.1	.0090	[b]	3.32
Miscellaneous textile products	[b]	1,550.7	.0295	[b]	3.68
Total apparel, and products made from fabrics (1947 prices)	2,641	2,819.8	—	3.95	3.87
Total apparel, and products made from fabrics (book values)	3,249	3,831.1	.1527	3.17	2.95
Men's clothing	1,268	1,434.9	.0750	3.97	2.74
Women's clothing	1,104	1,419.1	.1989	2.83	2.99
Hats, millinery, furs, etc. (total)	877	977.1	.2123	2.30	3.19
Hats, millinery, and furs	[b]	345.6	.1891	[b]	2.89
Miscellaneous apparel	[b]	631.5	.2250	[b]	3.36
Total basic lumber (1947 prices)	3,828	3,777.8	—	4.49	5.92
Total basic lumber (book values)	4,401	4,583.5	.1486	3.27	4.77
Logging camp products	[b]	2,670.0	.2057	[b]	4.86
Millwork products	[b]	1,401.0	.0809	[b]	5.20
Containers and miscellaneous lumber	[b]	512.5	.1393	[b]	3.07
Total furniture and finished lumber (1947 prices)	1,579	1,610.9	—	6.37	4.83
Total furniture and finished lumber (book values)	1,936	2,081.5	.0818	5.36	3.60
Household	[b]	1,384.6	.0813	[b]	3.09
Office and miscellaneous	[b]	696.9	.0822	[b]	4.61
Total paper and allied products (1947 prices)	7,120	7,178.2	—	7.61	6.88
Total paper and allied products (book values)	8,381	8,723.0	.0065	6.54	5.58

(continued)

TABLE E-1 (continued)

Industry	*Corporate Assets Excluding Other Investments (millions of dollars)* 1957	1958	*Ratio of Non-corporate to Corporate Assets* 1958	*Rate of Return on Corporate Assets (per cent)* 1957	1958
Pulp, paper, and paperboard (total)	5,764	5,744.1	n.a.	6.51	5.49
Pulp	b	588.8	n.a.	b	3.65
Paper and paperboard	b	5,155.3	.0016	b	5.70
Containers and miscellaneous (total)	2,617	2,978.9	.0155	6.62	5.74
Containers	b	1,351.4	.0164	b	4.60
Miscellaneous paper	b	1,627.5	.0147	b	6.70
Total printing and publishing (1947 prices)	4,993	5,142.1	—	8.26	7.08
Total printing and publishing (book values)	6,280	6,655.8	.0746	6.95	5.71
Newspapers	2,322	2,470.2	.0054	7.73	7.24
Periodicals	702	792.3	.0267	5.90	1.41
Books	776	825.5	.0330	6.33	5.23
Greeting cards and commercial	2,082	2,035.2	.1284	6.70	5.90
Miscellaneous printing	a	532.6	.1234	a	5.05
Total chemicals and allied products (1947 prices)	14,646	14,940.6	—	9.14	8.43
Total chemicals and allied products (book values)	17,671	18,381.9	.0061	7.69	6.83
Drugs	1,940	2,043.0	.0074	12.51	10.97
Soaps	1,055	1,071.6	.0198	8.10	8.79
Perfume and cosmetics	328	390.2	.0077	9.87	9.78
Agricultural chemicals	a	823.7	.0510	a	3.25
Industrial chemicals (total)	13,406	14,053.4	.0074	7.41	6.21
Industrial	b	3,142.5	.0006	b	5.15
Gum and wood chemicals	b	1,270.9	.0217	b	6.28
Miscellaneous chemicals	b	4,747.5	.0089	b	5.90
Plastics materials	b	3,445.7	.0007	b	7.38
Paints	b	1,446.7	.0201	b	6.65
Total petroleum refining and related products (1947 prices)	26,053	26,320.9	—	7.70	6.41
Total petroleum refining and related products (book values)	30,109	31,455.3	.0060	6.44	5.00
Petroleum refining	29,638	30,892.7	.0012	6.46	5.01
Paving materials and miscellaneous	a	562.6	.0275	a	4.47
Total rubber and miscellaneous plastics products (1947 prices)	3,170	3,119.3	—	6.10	6.82

(continued)

TABLE E-1 (continued)

Industry	Corporate Assets Excluding Other Investments (millions of dollars) 1957	1958	Ratio of Non-corporate to Corporate Assets 1958	Rate of Return on Corporate Assets (per cent) 1957	1958
Total rubber and miscellaneous plastics products (book values)	3,951	4,218.6	.0132	4.76	4.69
Tires and tubes	2,760	2,739.0	.0008	5.48	5.37
Miscellaneous rubber	671	802.2	.0080	6.66	4.10
Plastics products	520	677.4	.0474	2.41	2.68
Total leather and products (1947 prices)	1,177	1,151.6	—	6.18	5.31
Total leather and products (book values)	1,490	1,538.0	.0340	5.24	4.23
Footwear, except rubber	970	954.7	.0121	6.05	4.93
Other leather	520	583.3	.0848	3.93	3.07
Total stone, clay, and glass products (1947 prices)	6,125	6,146.9	—	7.89	7.14
Total stone, clay, and glass products (book values)	7,440	7,769.3	.0342	6.37	5.29
Glass	1,512	1,584.7	.0097	9.65	8.00
Cement	1,451	1,600.9	n.a.	5.07	4.98
Structural clay	756	756.8	.0249	4.92	3.40
Pottery	254	234.6	.0554	3.37	1.55
Concrete	[a]	1,950.9	.1061	[a]	6.32
Cut stone and miscellaneous	1,516	1,641.4	.0295	4.77	3.04
Total primary metal products (1947 prices)	19,264	19,383.1	—	6.93	5.08
Total primary metal products (book values)	22,058	23,544.9	.0040	6.33	4.01
Blast furnaces	[a]	14,355.9	n.a.	[a]	5.00
Iron and steel foundries	1,228	1,196.2	.0176	6.69	2.61
Smelting nonferrous metals	[a]	6,877.6	.0013	[a]	2.39
Nonferrous foundries	283	294.8	.0717	2.82	3.16
Miscellaneous primary metals	[a]	820.4	.0267	[a]	2.63
Total fabricated metal products, and ordnance (1947 prices)	8,891	8,496.4	—	6.69	5.70
Total fabricated metal products, and ordnance (book values)	10,579	10,444.3	.0434	5.70	4.53
Metal cans	1,318	1,420.6	.0014	5.56	6.31
Hand tools	909	1,021.1	.0308	6.60	5.87
Heating apparatus	[a]	1,442.5	.0180	[a]	3.64
Fabricated structural	2,697	2,584.2	.0561	6.74	4.36

(continued)

TABLE E-1 (continued)

Industry	*Corporate Assets Excluding Other Investments (millions of dollars)* 1957	1958	*Ratio of Non-corporate to Corporate Assets* 1958	*Rate of Return on Corporate Assets (per cent)* 1957	1958
Metal stamping, coating, and engraving (total)	1,163	1,114.5	.0829	4.92	3.62
Metal stamping	b	874.2	.0358	b	3.76
Coating and engraving	b	240.3	.2544	b	3.11
Screw machine products	a	768.7	.0568	a	1.99
Fabricated wire and miscellaneous fabricated	a	1,816.2	.0340	a	4.76
Ordnance	242	276.5	.0020	4.97	6.05
Total machinery, except electrical and transportation (1947 prices)	13,791	13,805.4	—	7.53	5.90
Total machinery, except electrical and transportation (book values)	17,066	17,034.1	.0352	6.22	4.51
Engines and turbines	492	511.5	.0007	8.12	7.63
Agricultural	a	3,157.1	.0194	a	3.95
Construction	a	2,669.6	.0101	a	4.85
Metalworking	2,665[c]	2,294.6	.0656	6.64	1.56
Special industry	1,805	1,697.3	.0261	4.80	2.95
General industry	a	2,091.6	.0264	a	5.30
Office and store	2,126	2,133.5	.0031	6.72	8.32
Service industry	a	821.5	.0162	a	5.46
Miscellaneous machinery	a	1,657.4	.2372	a	3.40
Total electrical machinery and equipment (1947 prices)	9,637	9,311.5	—	7.57	6.67
Total electrical machinery and equipment (book values)	11,328	11,697.8	.0077	6.79	5.50
Electrical transmission, industrial, and lighting and wiring (total)	4,669	4,442.6	.0088	8.79	7.40
Electrical transmission	b	3,184.4	.0060	b	8.19
Electrical industrial	b	655.7	.0060	b	5.86
Lighting and wiring equipment	b	602.5	.0265	b	4.91
Household appliances	a	1,448.6	.0040	a	3.90
Radio and television, communications equipment, and electronic components (total)	3,084	3,591.4	.0042	5.36	4.66
Radio and television sets	b	1,861.3	.0027	b	4.34
Communications equipment	b	1,086.0	.0015	b	4.60
Electronic components	b	644.1	.0130	b	5.70
Miscellaneous electrical machinery	2,085	2,215.2	.0121	8.10	4.12

(continued)

TABLE E-1 (concluded)

Industry	*Corporate Assets Excluding Other Investments (millions of dollars)* 1957	1958	*Ratio of Non-corporate to Corporate Assets* 1958	*Rate of Return on Corporate Assets (per cent)* 1957	1958
Total transportation equipment (1947 prices)	8,015	7,299.1	—	5.96	4.70
Total transportation equipment (book values)	9,038	8,495.7	.0090	6.07	4.47
Aircraft and parts (total)	7,124	6,610.8	.0060	6.08	5.09
Aircraft, except parts	[b]	4,482.3	n.a.	[b]	4.48
Aircraft parts	[b]	2,128.5	n.a.	[b]	6.36
Ship and boat	678	731.2	.0306	5.88	1.20
Railroad	1,044	961.1	.0027	5.93	2.94
Motorcycles, bicycles, and miscellaneous transportation	[a]	192.6	.0480	[a]	3.66
Total motor vehicles (1947 prices)	11,382	10,414.7	—	10.13	5.14
Total motor vehicles (book values)	14,102	13,299.6	.0041	8.49	3.07
Vehicles, bodies, etc.	[b]	11,522.0	n.a.	[b]	2.76
Parts and accessories	[b]	1,777.6	n.a.	[b]	5.06
Total professional and scientific instruments (1947 prices)	3,063	3,106.4	—	7.63	7.16
Total professional and scientific instruments (book values)	3,736	3,869.5	.0257	6.53	6.01
Engineering, optical, and photographic (total)	3,503	3,659.5	.0255	7.23	6.39
Engineering and scientific	[b]	1,962.2	.0130	[b]	4.78
Optical and surgical	[b]	633.5	.0948	[b]	5.43
Photographic	[b]	1,063.8	.0073	[b]	9.92
Clocks and watches	234	210.0	.0099	−3.75	−0.54
Total residual manufacturing (1947 prices)	2,986	3,208.4	—	5.63	5.21
Total residual manufacturing (book values)	3,706	4,118.1	.0788	4.21	3.94
Jewelry, except costume	321	339.3	.1249	3.09	3.37
Costume jewelry	80	82.4	.1404	1.02	2.26
Toys, sporting goods, and products n.e.c. (total)	3,306	3,696.4	.0714	4.66	4.04
Toys and sporting goods	[b]	523.6	.0636	[b]	4.31
Products, n.e.c.	[b]	3,172.8	.0727	[b]	3.99
TOTAL MANUFACTURING					
Total manufacturing (1947 prices)	173,571[d]	171,784	—	7.40	6.26
Total manufacturing (book values)	206,827[d]	212,909	.0305	6.29	4.92

[a] Included in major industry total, but minor industry data considered unreliable due to extensive reclassification.

[b] Not available separately on a basis comparable with 1958.

[c] Adjusted for variability of assets due to shifts of large companies between industries.

[d] Inclusion of industries formerly classified as nonmanufacturing is responsible for a 0.9 per cent increase over the 1957 figure in Table A-59. An additional 0.7 per cent increase results from our estimating technique.

INDEX